International Political Economy Series

General Editor: Timothy M. Shaw, Professor and Director, Institute of International Relations, The University of the West Indies, Trinidad & Tobago

Titles include:

Hans Abrahamsson
UNDERSTANDING WORLD ORDER AND STRUCTURAL CHANGE
Poverty, Conflict and the Global Arena

Morten Bøås, Marianne H. Marchand and Timothy Shaw (*editors*)
THE POLITICAL ECONOMY OF REGIONS AND REGIONALISM

Sandra Braman (*editor*)
THE EMERGENT GLOBAL INFORMATION POLICY REGIME

James Busumtwi-Sam and Laurent Dobuzinskis
TURBULENCE AND NEW DIRECTION IN GLOBAL POLITICAL ECONOMY

Elizabeth De Boer-Ashworth
THE GLOBAL POLITICAL ECONOMY AND POST-1989 CHANGE
The Place of the Central European Transition

Bill Dunn
GLOBAL RESTRUCTURING AND THE POWER OF LABOUR

Myron J. Frankman
WORLD DEMOCRATIC FEDERALISM
Peace and Justice Indivisible

Helen A. Garten
US FINANCIAL REGULATION AND THE LEVEL PLAYING FIELD

Barry K. Gills (*editor*)
GLOBALIZATION AND THE POLITICS OF RESISTANCE

Richard Grant and John Rennie Short (*editors*)
GLOBALIZATION AND THE MARGINS

Graham Harrison (*editor*)
GLOBAL ENCOUNTERS
International Political Economy, Development and Globalization

Patrick Hayden and Chamsy el-Ojeili (*editors*)
CONFRONTING GLOBALIZATION
Humanity, Justice and the Renewal of Politics

Axel Hülsemeyer (*editor*)
GLOBALIZATION IN THE TWENTY–FIRST CENTURY
Convergence or Divergence?

Helge Hveem and Kristen Nordhaug (*editors*)
PUBLIC POLICY IN THE AGE OF GLOBALIZATION
Responses to Environmental and Economic Crises

Takashi Inoguchi
GLOBAL CHANGE
A Japanese Perspective

Jomo K.S. and Shyamala Nagaraj (*editors*)
GLOBALIZATION VERSUS DEVELOPMENT

Dominic Kelly and Wyn Grant (*editors*)
THE POLITICS OF INTERNATIONAL TRADE IN THE 21st CENTURY
Actors, Issues and Regional Dynamics

Craig N. Murphy (*editor*)
EGALITARIAN POLITICS IN THE AGE OF GLOBALIZATION

George Myconos
THE GLOBALIZATION OF ORGANIZED LABOUR 1945–2004

John Nauright and Kimberly S. Schimmel (*editors*)
THE POLITICAL ECONOMY OF SPORT

Morten Ougaard
THE GLOBALIZATION OF POLITICS
Power, Social Forces and Governance

Jørgen Dige Pedersen
GLOBALIZATION, DEVELOPMENT AND THE STATE
The Performance of India and Brazil Since 1990

Markus Perkmann and Ngai-Ling Sum
GLOBALIZATION, REGIONALIZATION AND CROSS–BORDER REGIONS

Marc Schelhase
GLOBALIZATION, REGIONALIZATION AND BUSINESS
Conflict, Convergence and Influence

Leonard Seabrooke
US POWER IN INTERNATIONAL FINANCE
The Victory of Dividends

Timothy J. Sinclair and Kenneth P. Thomas (*editors*)
STRUCTURE AND AGENCY IN INTERNATIONAL CAPITAL MOBILITY

Fredrik Söderbaum and Timothy M. Shaw (*editors*)
THEORIES OF NEW REGIONALISM

Susanne Soederberg, Georg Menz and Philip G. Cerny (*editors*)
INTERNALIZING GLOBALIZATION
The Rise of Neoliberalism and the Decline of National Varieties of Capitalism

Ritu Vij (*editor*)
GLOBALIZATION AND WELFARE
A Critical Reader

Matthew Watson
THE POLITICAL ECONOMY OF INTERNATIONAL CAPITAL MOBILITY

International Political Economy Series

Series Standing Order ISBN 978–0–333–71708–0 hardcover
Series Standing Order ISBN 978–0–333–71110–1 paperback
(*outside North America only*)

You can receive future titles in this series as they are published by placing a standing order. Please contact your bookseller or, in case of difficulty, write to us at the address below with your name and address, the title of the series and one of the ISBNs quoted above.

Customer Services Department, Macmillan Distribution Ltd, Houndmills, Basingstoke, Hampshire RG21 6XS, England

---

Globalization, Regionalization and Business

Conflict, Convergence and Influence

Marc Schelhase
King's College London, UK

First published 2008 by
PALGRAVE MACMILLAN

Palgrave Macmillan in the UK is an imprint of Macmillan Publishers Limited,
registered in England, company number 785998, of Houndmills, Basingstoke,
Hampshire RG21 6XS.

Palgrave Macmillan in the US is a division of St Martin's Press LLC,
175 Fifth Avenue, New York, NY 10010.

Palgrave Macmillan is the global academic imprint of the above companies
and has companies and representatives throughout the world.

Palgrave® and Macmillan® are registered trademarks in the United States,
the United Kingdom, Europe and other countries.

ISBN-13: 978–0–230–57329–1   hardback
ISBN-10: 0–230–57329–0   hardback

This book is printed on paper suitable for recycling and made from fully
managed and sustained forest sources. Logging, pulping and manufacturing
processes are expected to conform to the environmental regulations of the
country of origin.

A catalogue record for this book is available from the British Library.

Library of Congress Cataloging-in-Publication Data

Schelhase, Marc, 1975–
    Globalization, regionalization, and business : conflict, convergence,
and influence / Marc Schelhase.
        p. cm.—(International political economy series)
    Includes bibliographical references and index.
        ISBN 978–0–230–57329–1 (alk. paper)
        1. Argentina – Economic integration. 2. Brazil – Economic integration.
    3. Business and politics – Argentina. 4. Business and politics – Brazil.
    5. Regionalism – Argentina. 6. Regionalism – Brazil. 7. MERCOSUR
    (Organization) 8. Globalization. I. Title.

HC173.S37 2008
338.8'8881—dc22   2008027561

10 9 8 7 6 5 4 3 2 1
17 16 15 14 13 12 11 10 09 08

Printed and bound in Great Britain by
CPI Antony Rowe, Chippenham and Eastbourne

In memory of Jane Greenaway
It was a privilege to have known her

Disclaimer

The analysis, opinions and conclusions expressed or implied in this book are those of the author and do not necessarily represent the views of the JSCSC, the UK MOD or any other government agency.

Contents

Acknowledgements

To start with, I would like to thank Wyn Grant, Richard Higgott and Nicola Phillips for their help and support throughout the project. Wyn in particular has helped enormously with detailed comments and advice, for which I will always be indebted to him. I would also like to thank Jill Steans and Matthew Paterson, who first taught me political economy.

I would also like to thank all the interviewees for their help and support with my research. In particular, I am very grateful to Guilherme Duque Estrada de Moraes, Andrés López, Sandra Rios and Rodolfo Rúa Boiero for the time they spared to read draft chapters.

I am also very grateful to Tim Shaw, the editor, Philippa Grand and Alexandra Webster from Palgrave Macmillan, who strongly supported this project and helped me through the various stages of the publication process, from writing to reviewing and the final editing process.

Financial support from the Economic and Social Research Council (ESRC) of the United Kingdom (Award No. R42200034368) and the Centre for the Study of Globalization and Regionalization (CSGR) at the University of Warwick, UK, is also gratefully acknowledged.

I am also grateful to my mother, Brigitte Schelhase-Bergen, who taught me to always follow my interests.

Finally, I would like to thank my wife Fabienne for all her love and support during the almost four years of research and writing that went into this project. Without her, it would not have been completed.

Abbreviations

ABIQUIM	Associação Brasileira da Indústria Química
ACE	Acordo de Complementação Econômico
ADEFA	Asociación de Fábricas de Automotores
AEA	Asociación Empresaria Argentina
AEB	Associação de Comércio Exterior do Brasil
AHK	*Auslandshandelskammer* – German Chamber of Commerce Abroad
AMCHAM	American Chamber of Commerce
ANFAVEA	Associação Nacional dos Fabricantes de Veículos Automotores
BBC	Brazilian Business Coalition
BDI	Bundesverband der Deutschen Industrie
BNDES	Brazilian Development Bank
BNHI	Business Network for Hemispheric Integration
CAC (a)	Cámara Argentina de Comercio
CAC (b)	Cámara Argentina de la Construcción
CAI	Consejo Argentino de la Industria
CAN	Comunidad Andina
CBI	Confederation of British Industry
CEA	Consejo Empresario Argentino
CEAL	*Consejo Empresario de América Latina* – Congress of Latin American Businessmen
CEFIC	European Chemical Industry Council
CEO	Chief Executive Officer
CET	Common External Tariff
CGE	Confederación General Económica Argentina
CGI	Confederación General de la Industria
CICYP	Consejo Interamericano de Comercio y Producción
CIM	Consejo Industrial de Mercosur
CIQUIM	Council of the Chemical Industry of the Mercosur
CIQyP	Cámara de la Industria Química y Petroquímica
CIU	Cámara de Industrias del Uruguay
CMC	Common Market Council
CMG	Common Market Group

CNA	Confederação da Agricultura e Pecuária do Brasil
CNC	Confederação Nacional de Comércio
CNI	Confederação National da Indústria
CNIF	National Confederation of Financial Institutions
CP	Comparative Politics
CPE	Comparative Political Economy
CRA	Confederaciones Rurales Argentinas
CSN	Comunidad Sudamericana de Naciones
ECJ	European Court of Justice
ECLAC/CEPAL	Economic Commission for Latin America and the Caribbean
ERT	European Round Table of Industrialists
EU	European Union
FCES	*Foro Consultivo Economico y Social* – Advisory Forum on Economic and Social Matters
FDI	Foreign Direct Investment
FEMA	*Foro Empresarial de las Americas* – Americas Business Forum
FIESP	Federação das Indústrias do Estado de São Paulo
FTA	Free Trade Agreement
FTAA	Free Trade Areas of the Americas
GDP	Gross Domestic Product
ICCA	International Council of Chemical Associations
IEDI	Instituto Estudos para o Desenvoliemento Industrial
IEL	Instituto Euvaldo Lodi
IPE	International Political Economy
IR	International Relations
ISIs	Import Substituting Industries
M&A	Mergers and Acquisitions
MEBF	Mercosur-EU Business Forum
Mercosur	Mercado Común del Sur
MP	Member of Parliament
NAFTA	North American Free Trade Agreement
PICAB	Programa de Integración y Cooperación Argentina – Brasil
PTA	Preferrential Trade Agreement
PNBE	Pensamento Nacional de Bases Empresariais
R&D	Research and Development
RTAs	Regional Trading Agreements

SACU	Southern African Customs Union
SEA	Single European Act
SENAI	Serviço Nacional de Aprendizagem Industrial
SESI	Serviço Social da Indústria
SMEs	Small and Medium-sized Enterprises
SMI	Small and Medium-sized Industries
SRA	Sociedad Rural Argentina
TABD	Trans-Atlantic Business Dialogue
TEU	Treaty on European Union
TNCs	Trans-National Corporations
UIA	Unión Industrial de Argentina
UIP	Unión Industrial de Paraguay
UNASUR	Unión de Naciones de Suramérica
UNCTAD	United Nations Conference of Trade and Development
UNICE	Union of Industrial Employers' Confederation of Europe
WTO	World Trade Organization

1
Organized Business Interests in the Mercosur: Setting the Scene

1.1 Conceptual framework of the book

The idea to study the evolution and the role of organized business in the Mercado Común del Sur (Mercosur) came as a result of my initial interest in the study of processes of regionalisation and regionalism in Latin America and East Asia. The focus on Latin America and in particular the Mercosur, as one of the most advanced forms of regional cooperation and integration outside the European Union (EU) emerged as a result of the limited amount of literature that exists not only in English but also in Spanish and Portuguese on the subject, in comparison to the large amount of work that has been done on business and business interests in the context of East Asian regionalisation and regionalism.

The starting point for the book is therefore the observation that organized business as both a subject and more recently an agent of change has been underestimated and understudied in the context of regional integration in the Southern Cone of Latin America.[1] The term organized business interests in the context of this book therefore refers to both business associations and less formalized forms of interest representation, which are centred on relatively few companies, for example.[2]

Despite studies referring to Western Europe and North America that analyse the role played by organized business interests in the evolution of the EU or the North American Free Trade Agreement

(NAFTA), studies on the Mercosur have focused primarily on certain industrial sectors (the automobile industry in particular) or have analysed how high levels of Foreign Direct Investment (FDI) and widespread privatisation have changed the structures of production and the economic frameworks of countries such as Brazil and Argentina.

What is neglected by these studies, however, are the fundamental changes that have affected organized business interests on all levels as a result of the changing economic and political landscape of Latin America. The emergence of new forms of interest representation on the national level, the transformation of old structures or even their increasing lack of influence, combined with the emergence of new forms of regional interest representation, underline the importance and the relevance of studying the transformation of organized business in the Mercosur.

The geographical focus of the book will be on Argentina and Brazil as by far the two most important economies in the Mercosur and also because the main actors within the business community come from those two countries. A focus on those two countries will therefore also contribute to the overall clarity of the arguments made in the book.

Historically, the Mercosur is also the continuation of the so-called *Acta de Buenos Aires*, an agreement reached as part of the initial cooperation and integration accord between Argentina and Brazil signed in 1986, the *Programa de Integración y Cooperación Argentina – Brasil* (PICAB). The *Acta de Buenos Aires*, primarily aimed at overcoming the deep political divisions between Argentina and Brazil after decades of hostility, was signed in 1990 and is also known as the *Acordo de Complementação Econômica 14* (ACE-14).[3] Later, this formed the nucleus for the trade liberalisation measures contained in the Treaty of Asunción, Mercosur's founding agreement.[4]

Over and above that it was also necessary to restrict the geographical scope of the book to maintain the feasibility of the project, both in terms of financial resources and the time available to conduct the research; hence the book focuses primarily on Argentina and Brazil as the economically and politically most important countries in the Mercosur.

1.2   Theoretical framework of the book and central hypothesis

The initial starting point for the research presented in this book was the hypothesis that business interest representation in the Southern

Cone has been increasingly regionalized in the wake of the launch of the Mercosur in the early 1990s. As such, the author expected to see a growth in the number and importance of these organisations, and a diminishing influence of the domestic level of interest representation under conditions of internationalisation and globalisation from the mid-1990s onwards. Moreover, the author also expected to see an emphasis placed by these newly formed organisations and structures on strengthening the institutional framework of the Mercosur, to create a systematic framework of rules and norms aimed at improving the effectiveness of the Mercosur as a common market.

Consequently, the most adequate way to study these processes of transformation would be within the framework of International Political Economy (IPE), centred on theories of region-building and region formation (regionalisation and regionalism), and using the extensive literature on globalisation as a reference to demonstrate the linkages between the regional and the global level of governance.[5] Within this IPE framework, an empirical investigation would then be carried out to test the hypothesis and the theoretical framework, which emphasizes the growing importance of the regional level of interest representation, and to generate relevant and interesting insights into organized business interests in the Mercosur.

After studying secondary literature on the subject, familiarizing himself with the structure of organized business in the Mercosur member countries, and after gathering information on the various interest associations working on the regional level within the Mercosur framework, the author came to the conclusion that the existing IPE-centred theoretical framework could not adequately conceptualize a very important level of analysis for the study of organized business interests in the Southern Cone – the domestic level.

The domestic level is important due to two central observations. First, the state is still an important actor in the context of the Mercosur. Although this is also the case in relation to the EU, for example, the qualitative difference lies in the lack of meaningful institutional structures within Mercosur. Administered by a very small Secretariat in Uruguay's capital Montevideo, without a policy-making capacity of its own, the structure of the organisation does not lend itself to supra-national lobbying. As a consequence, regional business associations are forced to primarily use domestic channels of access to the policy-making process within the Mercosur member states.

Second, business does not even come close to having a united approach to regionalisation, regionalism and trans-regional processes of change, for example the – now stalled – Free Trade Area of the Americas (FTAA) talks, where a regional forum for interest representation on an *ad hoc* basis does exist with the *Foro Empresarial de las Americas* (FEMA). Moreover, changes on the domestic level as a result of the internationalisation of the Mercosur economies through trade liberalisation and privatisation from the mid-1980s onwards have been accompanied by changes resulting from the regionalisation of the economies of the newly founded Mercosur member states.

This transformation of the domestic and regional economic environment under conditions of internationalisation and later on globalisation resulted in important changes concerning interest representation on the domestic level, which in turn resulted in new conflicts as well as convergence of business interests on the domestic and the regional level.

The initial hypothesis that business interest representation has become increasingly regionalized resulting in a diminishing influence of interest representation on the domestic level had to be redefined, namely, while business interests have developed significantly on the regional level, the domestic level maintains its importance, as mentioned above.

The theoretical framework was therefore modified to accommodate the analysis of domestic interest group formation and activism. Comparative Political Economy (CPE), centred on theories of interest group formation, lobbying activities in relation to the policy-making process as well as the 'varieties of capitalism' debate, was integrated into the theoretical framework.[6,7] The latter is important, because as we will see in the subsequent chapters, interest group structures and avenues of access for organized business in both Argentina and Brazil are very different; hence, an emphasis on 'varieties of capitalism' is very relevant. Thus, CPE theories are important in theoretically complementing the empirical analysis of how interest groups on the domestic level of the Mercosur member states have evolved, how they have or have not adapted over time to changes in their economic and political environment and how above all, these interests are then connected to the regional level of interest representation. The regional level, subsequently, provides both a theoretical and empirical interface in which CPE and IPE connect.

1.3 Methodology

After redefining the theoretical framework of the book to include both CPE and IPE, the author conducted extensive field research in Argentina and Uruguay in March and April of 2002; in Spain in August of 2002; and in Brazil in August and September of 2002. These interviews were followed-up by email exchanges with various interviewees to expand on key themes or to enquire about new and emerging topics in subsequent years. The overall cut-off point for primary data collection is late 2004.

As mentioned at the beginning of this chapter, the main empirical contribution of the book is the study of organized business in the Mercosur, as the majority of studies so far have focused primarily on the role of governments in the regional integration process or have centred on country- or industry-specific case studies. As such, the business community generally welcomed and was very interested in the research conducted, as there are very few studies of organized business on the national and regional level in the Mercosur.

In relation to the fieldwork in Argentina, it is also important to mention the practical difficulties the author had encountered in the country at the time of the fieldwork – March/April 2002. The focus of the book is on the role of organized business in the Mercosur; hence, the original plan for the fieldwork included only a limited number of interviews with government officials. However, the economic and political crisis that engulfed Argentina since the currency devaluation in December 2001 resulted in the fact that government representatives and some representatives of business associations were not available for interviews.

Consequently, the level of the state was left out of the primary research programme of the book, as it would not have been possible to adequately conceptualize the point of view of governments towards organized business without including a comprehensive set of interviews with government representatives.

This first part of the fieldwork reaffirmed the need for, as well as substantiated the viability of my CPE- and IPE-based theoretical framework, which includes both theories of domestic interest formation and theories taking into account internationalisation, regionalisation and globalisation.

The second half of the fieldwork, this time in Brazil, was organized differently from the one in Argentina in the sense that the contacts, which had been established in Argentina, were used again to access leading business representatives and academics. Altogether seven interviews with eight interviewees were conducted.

As mentioned earlier in relation to the fieldwork in Argentina, the state level and hence interviews with government representatives was excluded from the primary research programme in Brazil, too, to present a coherent research design and to not include another level of analysis – the state – in Brazil but not in Argentina.

1.4   Structure of the book

The book is divided into seven chapters including the introduction and conclusion.

Chapter 2 will provide the theoretical framework needed to study the evolution and the role played by organized business interests within the theoretical structures of CPE and IPE. Consequently, this chapter will clearly position the overall argument of the book within the wider theoretical body of both CPE and IPE, and will demonstrate that only by connecting the theoretical tools of CPE and IPE, one can adequately account for the changing nature of business interest representation on the national and regional level in the Mercosur.

Chapter 3 starts the empirical analysis of the changes that have taken place regarding the organisation of business interests in the Mercosur on the national and regional level. It details and analyses the various actors and organisations, their evolution and relationship with each other and points to the emerging trends and continuing changes in relation to organized business interests in the Mercosur.

Chapter 4 will focus on the conflict between and the convergence of business associations on the national and regional level with particular reference to the complexity of and the shifts in the articulation of organized business interests, based on changes in business leadership, trade liberalisation and regional integration. Both chapters will support the hypothesis made previously, which is the increasing relevance of organized business interests in the evolution of the Mercosur.

Chapter 5 will add to the analysis presented so far by two examples of the growing importance of organized business in relation to the evolution of the Mercosur. Focusing on the evolution of the chemical industry in the Mercosur and the Mercosur-EU Business Forum (MEBF) as examples of how organized business can successfully shape policy outcomes through their technical expertise and knowledge, the chapter supports the hypothesis of the book.

Chapter 6 will then focus on integrating the empirical research presented in Chapters 3 and 4 with the theoretical insights of Chapter 2. By doing so, the chapter will present an empirical analysis of business interests in the Mercosur embedded into the theoretical debate of connecting CPE and IPE. This chapter will therefore firmly link the theoretical framework employed in this book with the empirical evidence gathered to support it.

1.5   Summary of the argument

It is important to point out that although CPE and IPE start out from different theoretical assumptions, the emerging regionalisation of organized business interests in the context of the Mercosur, for example, shows that CPE increasingly has to address the regional dimension more comprehensively than it may have done in the past. Therefore, IPE, too, has to take into account the regional level as a level of analysis, which cannot simply be seen as either a building block or an obstacle towards globalisation.

Consequently, the regional arena is a level of analysis where, from an empirical and theoretical point of view, CPE, coming from below, and IPE, coming from above, are potentially complementary tools of analysis. In this regard, the regional level emerges as a level of analysis at which both theoretical traditions have to engage with each other to provide adequate theoretical and empirical explanations for emerging trends, such as the regionalisation of organized business interests and its links with the national and global level of analysis. The empirical evidence that will be provided in the following chapters will underline the need to connect both CPE and IPE theories to provide a rigorous theoretical framework capable of explaining and analysing these trends and transformation and confirming the central argument of the book, the growing significance of organized business interests in the evolution of the Mercosur.

2
Studying Organized Business Interests in the Mercosur: A Theoretical Framework for Analysis

Introduction

The main purpose of this chapter is to provide a comprehensive theoretical framework for the analysis of the role played by organized business interests in the evolution of the Mercosur.

From the empirical research conducted for this book, it has become clear that the theoretical analysis of, and critical reflection on, the current literature has to cover the domestic as well as the regional level of interest representation and articulation. Two distinct theoretical perspectives will be used as the two pillars which form the basis for the theoretical framework of the book.

First, it is important to reflect comprehensively on the existing literature covering the 'varieties of capitalism' debate and the role of organized business interests, which exists in Comparative Political Economy (CPE). Second, it will be important to include a comprehensive survey of the relevant literature on regionalization, regionalism and globalization, to bring into the analysis the analytical tools of International Political Economy (IPE).[1]

By doing so, this chapter will, first, form the theoretical framework for connecting both approaches, CPE and IPE, to explain the role of organized business interests in the evolution of the Mercosur. Second, the chapter will show that to reflect on the role played by regional organized interests in processes of region-building, one has to use theories of CPE and IPE as lenses, which highlight different characteristics of the regional integration process. The theoretical framework of the book therefore builds on a growing body of literature in IPE that seeks to utilize the tools of both CPE and IPE to provide new insights.[2] As Dickins highlights, 'forward-looking IPE scholars of all types are calling for the integration of comparative and international political economy to create *global* political economy, new (international) political economy or, simply, political economy'.[3]

In this context, the book looks specifically at organized business, and, more specifically, at the interplay between the domestic and the regional organized business interests and the evolving lines of cooperation and conflict between both levels. Moreover, the book argues for the need for new forms of regional governance and regional interest articulation and demonstrates that these new structures are already actively pursued or studied by the relevant business actors.[4]

These new forms of regional governance are supported by processes of globalization, which highlight the tensions between established domestic economic interests and changing regional realities, which then in turn result in new divisions of interest on the domestic level. Especially from the mid-1990s onwards, an increasingly clear distinction emerged between, on the one hand, business interests aimed at protecting national industries and slowing down, if not avoiding it altogether, domestic economic and social reforms, and, on the other hand, business interests, which were strongly in favour of building regional and export-oriented economic structures within the Mercosur. Thus, the structural shifts taking place in the regional economy as a result of globalization were accompanied on the national level by an increasing rift between traditional modes of interest articulation focusing on mostly protectionist policies, and those interests, which started to actively engage with building structures of regionalization.

One other important phenomenon has emerged as a result of these new and conflicting national and regional processes. The state is (still) the referent object in the context of the political economy of Latin America, and, in many ways, plays an important role in this part of the world. Increasingly, however, the state and with it its capacity to build a regional space (regionalism) has lost some of its driving force to processes of regionalization and business-driven initiatives. One reason for this is that regional trading entities, such as the Mercosur, are primarily built to enhance trade, to create growth and to instil a certain degree of dynamism into a given region. Thus, it should come as no surprise that regional economic actors, having realized the economic potential of regional investment areas, then start to pressure governments, especially when they have the impression that processes of regionalism are not implemented fast enough to complement regionalization.[5] This is the case for the Mercosur, where the problems in relation to a strengthening of the Mercosur institutions from the mid-1990s onwards have seen an increasing pressure on the national and regional level by organized business interests to overcome these problems. The same is the case for the national level, where economic actors have increasingly started to leave national peak associations that have failed to support region-centred policies or these associations have become more and more paralysed by the fact that there is a widening rift between companies with a regional and global outlook and those with a focus on national markets and continuing protectionism.[6]

As a result, the book proposes that the theoretical discussion and the empirical analysis of organized business interests in the Mercosur not just connects elements of CPE and IPE; rather it aims to show that processes of regionalization are increasingly important in the Southern Cone region and, especially since the mid-1990s, are increasingly significant in keeping the Mercosur as a viable economic model for regional development on the agenda.[7]

Despite the political turmoil in Argentina in 2001 and 2002 and the political uncertainty in Brazil in the run-up to the election of President Luiz Inácio 'Lula' da Silva in 2002, regional organized business has contributed to keeping the Mercosur process on track, especially in areas directly relevant to its core interests, that is, the MEBF and the Free Trade Area of the Americas (FTAA) negotiations, supported by a new permanent arbitration tribunal and new powers for the Mercosur Secretariat to create and monitor technical norms.[8] Thus, the main aim of this chapter and the book as a whole is to add a fresh approach to the current literature, focusing on the increasingly important role of organized business in the Mercosur region as a driving force for regionalization and regionalism.

At the beginning, however, the chapter will start out with some definitions of the central terms used in this book.

2.1   Key definitions

The study of organized business interests in the context of the Mercosur is first and foremost characterized by various sets of very different actors. This makes it necessary, first, to define the term 'region' in the context of this book.

Although Mercosur is, for the purpose of this research, considered to be a regional organization, one could easily refer to it as a subregional organization, if Latin America or even the Americas are considered a 'region'.[9] All this is linked with questions of identity, religion, culture and history, which underline the social construction of the term 'region'.[10] Therefore, it is important to point to the fluctuations in the extent of 'regioness', as Hettne and Söderbaum argue. For them, 'mostly when we speak of regions we actually mean regions in the making. There are no "natural" or "given" regions, but these are created and recreated in the process of global transformation'.[11] Thus, the Oxford English Dictionary probably more usefully defines the term 'region' as 'an area of the world made up of neighbouring countries that, from an international point of view, are considered socially, economically, or politically, interdependent'.[12] This definition is the most functional for the purpose of this book, because it accommodates the varying extent of 'regioness' while at the same time laying down some minimum requirements for defining a number of states as a region.

Second, it is important to look at the term 'organised business interests'. First, this can be understood in the context of business associations, which are more or less formalized in their structure and interest representation. Following Grant, for example, the term 'business' means 'a company, public corporation, partnership or individual [of all kinds] which sells goods and/or services with the intention of generating a surplus from its trading activities for its owners'.[13] The *Oxford English Dictionary* defines the term 'association', among others, as 'a body of persons who have combined to execute a common purpose or advance a common cause; the whole organization which they form to effect their purpose; a society'. In addition, society is defined by the *Oxford English Dictionary* as 'a number of persons associated together by some common interest or purpose'. Taken together, these definitions describe a 'business association' as a voluntary organization set up by individual members to promote their interests *vis à vis* other groups in society as well as state actors.

Over and above that, with reference to the definition of the term 'region' given above, regional business associations, as understood in the context of this book, are Mercosur-wide associations comprised of various national business associations, which aim to promote their policies on a regional scale.

Second, the more broader term 'regional organised business interests' refers to the fact that members of these regional business associations may also be Trans-National Corporations (TNCs) as well as individual companies from the four member states of the Mercosur, whose links which each other are less formalized than those of 'regional business associations'.[14] These may also only be set up for a limited period of time. One example for this would be the MEBF, which might or might not continue to exist after the conclusion of a Mercosur-EU Free Trade Agreement (FTA).

Consequently, a broad definition of regional organized business interests allows accommodating the very diverse and currently emerging set of regional business interest representation, which is being formed as a direct result of the evolution of the Mercosur and the ongoing integration of the Mercosur economies into the world economy.

2.2   Theorizing business interests

As one of the chapters of this book will look at the importance of the national level as a means to lobby for interests on the regional level, it is important to start this literature review with an overview of the more recent debates in CPE. Particularly relevant to this book is the discussion of the role of interest groups on the national level and how this is related to lobbying on the regional level. In Section 2.3, the chapter will focus on EU integration theories as an important body of literature in relation to regional level of governance. From there, the chapter will turn towards an analysis of the literature with regard to lobbying on the regional level, thereby moving in Section 2.4 of the chapter towards a theoretical discussion of regionalization and regionalism, thus adding IPE theory to the CPE framework.

2.2.1 Theories of CPE

When looking at the link between the interest articulation of organized business on the national and the regional level, it is important to start with the discussion of the central role of the nation state within theories of CPE.

The primary focus of CPE is the comparative study of national economies and how these economies develop different responses to economic, social and political changes; if responses vary from country to country or if there is a degree of conversion; if some institutions respond better to change than others and provide superior levels of performance; and, finally, how the nature of and the responses to the economic environment are different for the various actors in a national economy.[15] Historically, therefore CPE is identified with the 'models of capitalism' debate, which centres on three distinct models of capitalist development within the international political economy. These models are ' "the Anglo-American (neo)liberal" model, the state-led "developmental" model characteristic of the Japanese and other Asian economies, and the European "welfare" or "Rhineland" model'.[16]

Consequently, an extensive debate emerged within CPE about the way in which the different models of capitalism and their specific national institutional settings would adapt in the light of the increasing internationalization of the IPE and which model would be best suited to adapt and survive.

Katzenstein for example notes in *Between Power and Plenty* with reference to advanced industrial states,

> The loss of control deplored in the foreign ministries of all advanced industrial states is rooted not only abroad but at home. Lack of action, or inappropriate action, taken in domestic politics often leads to serious consequences in the international political economy. In itself, a global approach to meeting global needs appears to be an inefficient and ineffective way of trying to cope with the problems of the international political economy. The management and analysis of interdependence must start at home.[17]

This focus on the domestic factors as the primary reason for variations in economic performance among advanced industrial states was accompanied by the late 1970s and early 1980s by a revival of the study of corporatism. This so-called neo-corporatism focused on institutional variations within states to explain differences in economic growth and development with a particular emphasis on corporatist forms of governance.

Schmitter, whose article in 1974 to some extent started the revival of corporatism, defines corporatism as,

> a system of interest representation on which the constituent units are organised into a limited number of singular, compulsory, non-competitive, hierarchically ordered and functionally differentiated categories, recognised or licensed (if not created) by the state and granted a deliberate representational monopoly within their respective categories in exchange for observing certain controls on their selection of leaders and articulation of demands and supports.[18]

What is important to note in this respect is the distinction between societal corporatism and state corporatism made by Schmitter. Whereas a country such as Brazil is historically characterized as state corporatism, countries such as Germany or Sweden are examples for societal corporatism.[19]

By the mid-1980s, the neo-corporatist debate had been broadened, and Katzenstein's *Small States in World Markets* was the most prominent attempt to include factors located in the international political economy into the analysis of variations of policy responses on the level of the nation state, this time in relation to small states in Western Europe.[20] Of particular interest in this regard is the emphasis by Katzenstein on the formulation of political strategy under conditions of economic internationalization rather than economic performance. As he explains,

> two kinds of crises, recurrent capitalist instability and intermittent systemic war, created corporatism as an institutional innovation in response to both. [This demonstrates]...that this institutional innovation includes but goes beyond the stabilisation of capitalism through the incorporation of labour, thus creating a broader and more enduring type of politics.[21]

Another interesting aspect of the neo-corporatist debate is also the emergence of the concept of 'private interest governments with devolved responsibilities – of agencies of "regulated self-regulation" of social groups with special interests which are made subservient to general interests by appropriately designed institutions'.[22] By employing the concept of private interest governments, Streeck and Schmitter aim to overcome the well-established *state and markets* paradigm. They argue, 'for all its powerful influence on the public mind, the widely accepted antimony of *state vs. market/community* appears to be insufficiently complex for both analytical and practical purposes'.[23]

What is important to note in this regard is that by 1997, Crouch and Streeck edited a volume, which was aimed explicitly at bringing together CPE approaches with their emphasis on national models of capitalism with IPE accounts of a possible convergence of national economies in an era of globalization. *Political Economy of Modern Capitalism* nevertheless still aims at finding viable institutional alternatives beyond national economies that will help to 'tame' the global political economy to preserve a European-style welfare state. As Crouch and Streeck point out,

> the all-important question today, we believe, is how to recapture public governance of the private economy at some international level, after the national one has become obsolete.... National social institutions and national democratic politics can support internationally viable, egalitarian high-wage economies only in a conducive international context, and it is only within such a context that they can continue to generate and maintain capitalist diversity and its beneficial consequences for economic performance.[24]

Consequently, CPE literature is still rooted in a preference for the national level of analysis. As Coates explains, '*to stay on the terrain of the national is therefore to stay on the terrain of labour and the state, and to stay close to what will be our central concerns*.... Namely the viability of nationally based commercial concerns'.[25]

Another very interesting approach to the model of capitalism literature is the theoretical concept advanced by Hall and Sockice in *Varieties of Capitalism*. It is interesting, because rather than relying on the previously mentioned well-known three models of capitalist development, Hall and Soskice start off by introducing the distinction between liberal market economies and coordinated market economies.[26] Central to their approach is the focus on the firm as the primary actor in modern economies. Consequently, liberal market economies are characterized by markets based on the competitive nature of the economy, whereas in coordinated market economies 'firms depend more heavily on non-market relationships to coordinate their endeavours with other actors and to construct their core competencies'.[27] This approach is subsequently expanded by the authors to take into account the institutional settings in which firms in liberal and coordinated market economies operate. This gives rise to the concept of comparative institutional advantage, 'the basic idea [of which] is that the institutional structure of a particular political economy provides firms with advantages for engaging in specific types of activities there'.[28] By doing so, Hall and Soskice argue that, the concept of 'varieties of capitalism' is here to stay and reject the notion that under conditions of internationalization and globalization, national economies will somehow converge around a single established model.[29]

In the context of this book, the national level is an important contact point for organized business, namely to influence policy making on the regional level or on issues related to the regional level. The reason for this is the nature of organized business interests or, to be more precise, its membership structure. Regional business associations, for example, consist of national business associations, but they may also have major national companies, or TNCs, or a mix of all three as their main members. All these groups have their own means of influencing public policy making, in addition to their membership in the relevant regional business associations and structures and the lobbying activities related to this. Furthermore, some national business associations are dominated by powerful sub-national business associations, making the emerging structures and overlapping interests even more complex.[30] In turn, these sub-national interests may even have no interest at all in regional structures or the regionalization of business representation, as they are fundamentally opposed to the regional integration process *per se*.[31]

As explained before with reference to corporatism and neo-corporatism, the role of organized interests or pressure groups is a widely studied subject in CPE.[32] Interest groups are central in pluralist, corporatist and semi-corporatist societies as a means to influence policy making and agenda setting within their respective national settings while at the same time taking responsibility for implementing the policies agreed on. Some of the central and more recent debates concerning interest groups will be introduced and discussed later in the chapterto point to the diverse and sometimes overlapping range of strategies and avenues used by the various actors involved in influencing and gaining access to policy-making communities. As previously remarked, the main focus of the literature is on the EU.[33] However, the next part of this chapter will not only summarize the main theoretical arguments in the literature; rather, it will also point towards the main problems and advantages that become evident if one applies these theories to the study of organized business in the Mercosur.

If one looks at the role played by organized business in the context of a regional organization such as the Mercosur, the question of effectiveness is important in assessing that role.

To start with, it is important to establish why business would be interested in forming organized structures in the first place. Following Olson, it is important to state that 'the widespread view...that [large] groups tend to further their interests is...unjustified, at least when it is based...on the (sometimes implicit) assumption that groups act in their self-interest because individuals do'.[34] Consequently, business as a large group

> will *not* act to advance their common group objectives unless there is coercion to force them to do so, or unless some separate incentive, distinct from the achievement of the common or group interest, is offered to the members of the group individually on the condition that they help bear the costs...involved in the achievement of the group objectives.[35]

By contrast, smaller groups tend to be more willing to advance their common group interest, simply because their interests are much more narrowly defined and members are therefore often more committed to pursuing their interests.[36] As Chapter 5 will demonstrate, with reference to the chemical industry in the Mercosur and the MEBF, highly organized and relatively small business associations and organizations are often highly influential and effective simply because of their limited size and a high degree of interest group coherence.

Very often, some interest groups are also offered privileged access to the policy-making process. In the literature which focuses on interest articulation and lobbying in the context of Western Europe, Grant for example introduces the distinction between insiders and outsiders and links this to the effectiveness of interest groups.[37] He argues, 'insider groups are regarded as legitimate by government and are consulted on a regular basis. Outsider groups either do not wish to become enmeshed in a consultative relationship with officials, or are unable to gain recognition'.[38] Page, however, disagrees. He points out,

> if government departments only consulted interest groups once or twice a year, then an argument based on the impossibility of hundreds of groups having access to decision-making would be quite plausible. However, government departments consult so frequently on such a wide range of issues, both broad issues affecting hundreds of groups and narrow issues affecting one or two, that it is quite possible to see how two-thirds can claim some degree of success in influencing government at some stage.[39]

He argues further, 'the evidence…suggests that to characterise a group as an insider or outsider in the process of policy-making is at best an oversimplification and at worst simply misleading'.[40]

Nevertheless, it could be argued that pressure groups rely to a certain extent on a mix of insider/outsider lobbying to achieve their objectives. As Page points out, 'groups can act in a concerted manner, so that some pursue outsider tactics of mobilising public support as part of a broader strategy which involves other groups pursuing insider approaches of calm, factual and reasoned argument, a "good cop/bad cop" strategy'.[41] This argument is also supported by Grant, who uses the example of Greenpeace to illustrate the effective use of the insider/outsider lobbying strategy.[42] Moreover, the insider/outsider problem highlights the role played by the state in, to some extent, influencing the role and shape of business associations. Following Grant,

> above all, an important point about the insider/outsider distinction is that it highlights the way, in which the state sets the rules of the game of group activity. Access and consultation flow from the adoption of a pattern of behaviour which is acceptable to government, particularly to civil servants.[43]

Richardson argues along similar lines by pointing out, 'in Britain, by the mid-1980s, the balance of power has shifted decidedly in favour of government in terms of setting the agenda and initiating policy change'.[44] He goes even further by extending this argument to the European level when he argues,

> it does seem that the kinds of [economic] pressures which helped the British governments to tackle the many reform deficits ... eventually spread to the rest of Western Europe. In many Western European states, a gradual shift in policy style also seems apparent, although usually in ways more subtle than Mrs Thatcher's hand bagging approach.[45]

Fishman, by contrast, foresees a new corporatism for Britain as a result of EU directives concerning workers councils and workers participation, thus resulting in a strengthening of trade unions generally.[46] One could argue, however, that this strengthening of the role of organized labour represents just a shift towards a much more balanced relationship between trade unions on the one hand and organized business on the other hand, especially after the excesses of the Thatcher years.

Christiansen and Rommetvedt, however, argue interestingly enough that corporatism is much more a reflection of a clear-cut distinction between privileged insiders than the much more open, culture of lobbying in Britain or the United States, for example. They point out, 'corporatism as an institution exactly specifies which organisations enjoy privileged access to decision-making arenas, whereas the rules for access are much more open and ambiguous under lobbyism'.[47] Munk Christiansen and Rommetvedt as well as Blom-Hansen agree with Richardson, however, that a gradual shift in business-state relations in Western Europe has indeed taken place over the past two decades. Scandinavia in particular has witnessed a fundamental change from a culture of corporatism towards a society in which interest groups and lobbying activities play a much greater role than before.[48]

It is debatable, however, if this is a result of a general strengthening of the role of the state *vis à vis* organized interests, or if it is more the result of the emerging global pressures to reform entrenched

corporatist or semi-corporatist societal relations, first and foremost
in Western Europe. As Sandholtz and Zysman point out,

> the real trigger [for the economic and structural changes within
> the EU, such as the Single European Act (SEA) and the Maastricht
> treaty] has been a real shift in the distribution of economic power
> resources…. What is just as important is that European elites
> perceive that the changes in the international setting require that
> they rethink their roles and interests in the world.[49]

Coen argues along similar lines. However, he points out, in contrast to the previous argument made by Richardson, that in the late
1970s and early 1980s regional organized business was indeed ahead
of national governments in terms of cooperation on a European
level, and it was also ahead of the development of the EU, in terms of
the limited regulatory competence of the EU at that specific moment
in time.[50] As Coen states,

> The agenda-setting strength of the firm in this period was most
> visibly demonstrated by the European Round Table of Industrialists
> (ERT) single market initiatives. Fortuitously for business interests,
> the Commission was receptive to those market-led initiatives….
> However, this window of opportunity for big business political
> autonomy was to be short-lived.[51]

2.2.2 The Latin American experience

Where does this take us with respect to Latin America and why is the
previous theorizing about 'varieties of capitalism' approaches and the
extent of and the changing roles for organized business in Europe
relevant to the study of business interests in the Mercosur countries?

To start with, there are some apparent similarities between the
European and the Latin American experience. In the early years of
economic cooperation and integration among the countries of the
Southern Cone, the role played by and given to business interests in
influencing national policy regarding regionalization and regionalism was very limited. This was largely due to the nature of the
political systems in many Latin American countries. This is especially true for Brazil, Argentina and Chile in the 1970s and early

1980s, where successive military governments were either brought to power with the support of the relevant business communities or tried to suppress attempts to influence policy outcomes. This policy environment changed from the mid-1980s onwards with the wave of democratization that swept over most of Southern Latin America, starting with Argentina and Brazil. These policy changes on the national level were accompanied by a general tendency to open up the previously closed markets of the Southern hemisphere and to lock-in neo-liberal reform strategies, mentioned above. As a result of these processes of liberalization, interest representation in the form of business associations and the support of these business groups for the liberalization efforts was important in implementing these reforms successfully. As Silva and Durand argue,

> Latin American business elites responded to these challenges with a new political activism…. They took forceful public positions on economic change, mobilised public opinion on their behalf, took direct action, and even declared their support for democracy. This was indeed a reversal from behavioural patterns in which Latin American business elites generally negotiated policy behind closed doors and had an elective affinity for military governments.[52]

Thus, the main driving force for closer economic cooperation and integration since the early 1980s in Latin America were the newly elected democratic governments, who regarded an institutionalized form of cooperation in the form of the Mercosur as extremely important. As Skidmore and Smith argue, 'in a sense, Mercosur would provide civilian democrats throughout the sub-region with a regular opportunity for consultation and mutual support, thus offsetting the long-established conclaves for representatives of the armed forces'.[53] Hirst argues along similar lines. She points out, 'loyalties [between Argentina and Brazil, the central actors in the Mercosur] arose out of convergent perceptions about the need to associate democratic consolidation with economic stability and became the main source of Mercosur's political identity'.[54] Domestic economic considerations were in so far important, as they provided an impetus for change in connection with regional and global economic pressures. As Hirst argues elsewhere with reference to the internal dynamics,

> at the internal level, it is considered that a catalytic effect [for regional co-operation and integration] has been exerted by the economic reform process begun ... [since 1990] in ... [Argentina and Brazil], which has led to a profound redefinition of the rules governing the productive sectors, with regard to their relations with both the State and the international market.[55]

The regionalization of domestic markets in the Southern Cone has also forced sectors of the economy previously resistant to tariff reductions and trade liberalization measures to soften their stance.[56] Moreover, the global spread of Regional Trading Agreements (RTAs) has also contributed to consistent pressure in Latin America to respond to this changing socio-political environment.[57]

Nevertheless, at least smaller interest groups and interest coalitions have had some effect on the ongoing processes of economic liberalization within the Latin American region. As Schamis points out, 'the evidence ... demonstrates that collusion between political and economic power and the formation of small distributional coalitions have been the driving forces behind the policy reform process in Latin America'.[58] Thus, domestic interest groups supported the unfolding economic and political change after some initial hesitation.

Consequently, the launch of the Mercosur in 1991 was widely seen as an attempt to consolidate economic reform in the Southern Cone region and to reintegrate the region into the world economy.[59] As a result of this shift in economic strategy and policy outlook, the attention of national business associations shifted to the regional level to influence the agenda setting within these newly developing processes of regionalization and regionalism.[60]

Nevertheless, it is important to note that some industrial sectors, such as the chemical and petrochemical industry, were pursuing regional cooperation ahead of the politically driven regionalism in the Southern Cone. At first, their involvement was focused on maintaining influence over the process of integration and focused on controlling tariff levels and trade liberalization matters. From the mid-1990s onwards, this involvement of business increased in importance for driving the process of integration itself by negotiating among sectoral peak associations of the Mercosur member states, before submitting the agreed tariffs and measures to the national governments for approval. By doing so, the Council of the Chemical Industry of the Mercosur (CIQUIM) was able to push through 80 per cent of all its policy initiatives, thus avoiding the problems and pitfalls of bargaining with governments on the national level.[61]

Moreover, at the beginning of the integration process in the context of Latin America and specifically the Mercosur, the overlap between business and government interest was very significant, thus making the assessment of the effectiveness of lobbying discussed in the previous subchapter difficult to assess. The importance of informal ties between public and private sector, with a resulting lack of transparency, makes it difficult to distinguish between government-driven and business-driven initiatives. Thus, in the context of Latin America, it is important to take into account that a seemingly clear-cut assessment of state *vis à vis* business actors is not that easy to make. Thus, business involvement is generally overlooked or at least downplayed in most of the current literature.[62]

In addition to the informal, there was also a degree of formal input into the Mercosur process by business and other civil society groups. The institutional structure of the Mercosur, however, made it difficult for these groups to become directly involved in the decision-making process of the organization initially. As Alimonda argues,

> [the public criticism of the Mercosur] pointed to the lack of consultation with regard to the Treaty of Asunción and the integration procedures; the consequent absence of debate and exchange of information, and the limited mechanisms foreseen for interest groups' participation and representation; the emphasis on commercial mechanisms as the framework of the process, and the limited time allowed for the formation of the common market.[63]

Therefore the two decision-making bodies of the Mercosur, the Common Market Council (CMC) and the Common Market Group (CMG), are essentially intergovernmental and are more modelled along the lines of the EU Council of Ministers. The Commission on Trade, which implements and monitors the common trade policy, is also organized along intergovernmental structures. Only the Joint

Parliamentary Commission, consisting of Members of Parliament (MPs) of the Mercosur member states, provides some form of supranational forum to influence the development of the Mercosur in general and the policy-making processes in particular.[64] Although a strengthening of the supranational structures of the Mercosur is envisaged, the attempts to implement these proposals are blocked on a regular basis by the Mercosur's biggest member state, Brazil.[65,66] Due to its importance for the Mercosur, Brazil's partners have limited room to manoeuvre and, quite often, have to accept Brazilian policy priorities for the Mercosur.[67] As *The Economist* points out, 'Brazil, jealous of its sovereignty, has claimed to see in [the institutional strengthening and expansion of Mercosur bodies] an expensive, Brussels-style bureaucracy'.[68] As a consequence, it has become clear that the national level is still the most important point of access for influencing policy making within the Mercosur, hence the relevance of CPE theories in the context of this book.

However, to account for the growing linkages between the national and the regional level and the increasing influence of decisions made within the context of the Mercosur on national and sub-national policies, the Protocol of *Ouro Preto*, which came into effect on 1 January 1995, established the Advisory Forum on Economic and Social Matters (FCES) within the institutional structure of the Mercosur.[69] This forum is drawn from the four member states of the organization and represents employers associations, unions and consumer groups. As a consequence, a wide range of civil society groups are involved in it. Despite the fact that the Forum is currently only advisory, there are plans to make consultation with the Forum mandatory, namely for those decisions within the Mercosur framework affecting important social issues, similar to the early consultation procedures with regard to the European Parliament. This will be referred to again in Chapter 3.

Generally, most interviewees described the FCES as highly ineffective and dominated by ideological infighting between employers' associations and trade unions. One interviewee went so far as to describe it as 'a big freezer', although he requested anonymity for this remark.

As a result of these institutional changes, caused to a large extent by the civil society engagement with the regional project, and despite the shortcomings of the institutional framework of the Mercosur in terms of influencing policy outcome, regional business associations and other forms of business representation on the level of the Mercosur have emerged since the mid-1990s. The reasons for these are mainly threefold.

First, in terms of Foreign Direct Investment (FDI), Mercosur is increasingly seen as a single investment area.[70] Especially in relation to the automobile sector, the Mercosur-wide market is more and more in the process of becoming integrated. As Leipziger, Frischtak, Kharas and Normand point out,

> both assemblers and auto part producers are also directing their investments with a view of the common market, and setting up complementary production lines, in order to reap the considerable economies of scale (and product differentiation) which characterises the industry.[71]

At the same time, TNCs are increasingly present in the Mercosur and have an interest in a regional representation in addition to lobbying on the national level.[72] Moreover, this has also resulted in the founding of the previously mentioned MEBF in 1998, which was set up by Brazilian and German companies with a strong interest in the EU and Mercosur markets to promote a Mercosur-EU FTA (also known as an association agreement). This support from regional organized business interests was vital for the EU Commission to study the feasibility of the proposal and to launch formal negotiations with the Mercosur. Since then, the high degree of business involvement on both sides, the Mercosur and the EU, was essential in keeping the project on track, especially in the light of the current economic crisis in the Southern Cone region and the resulting lack of politically driven regionalism.[73]

Second, the 1990s have seen a rise of intra-Mercosur trade and investment, and increasingly Brazilian companies investing in Argentina and *vice versa*. This has resulted in an increasing interest in cross-border links and has also contributed to the emergence of regional business associations at Mercosur level, although the process was not always without friction, especially in the automobile sector.[74] As Cason argues,

> Brazil's political and economic weight in the process [of economic integration] gives it the power to drive the agenda. But the

increasing inter penetration of the main economies in the region, Argentina and Brazil, is another major factor. The potential costs of reversing the integration process rise daily.[75]

Third, during the trade talks aimed at concluding the FTAA, the Mercosur managed to develop a common position towards the United States. These trade talks and the fact that the Mercosur, despite internal conflicts, has maintained its common negotiating position, support the case for interest representation on a regional level. Add to this the ongoing and fairly promising talks with the EU concerning a Free Trade Area (FTA) between the Mercosur and the EU, and a picture emerges, which makes regional business associations a conclusive rationale.[76]

Moreover, the definition of a common regional interest in relation to organized business, which is emerging in respect of the Mercosur, is also taking place in the context of the FTAA negotiations. Here, the *Foro Empresarial de las Americas* [Business Forum of the Americas] is developing and putting forward clear positions on the FTAA negotiation process with regard to market access, agriculture, investments, services, public procurement, intellectual property rights, competition policy, state aid, anti-dumping measures, dispute settlement and electronic commerce. In addition to that, the *Foros* are held at the same time as the annual Ministerial Meeting of the Americas, so there is a close exchange between national politicians meeting on a regional level and regional organized business.[77] These meetings have gained in importance in the past few years.

2.3   Beyond cooperation: A functional explanation of regionalization and regionalism

To explain the role of regional business associations and the link between the national level and the regional level of governance in the Mercosur, there is merit in introducing a set of theories developed to understand and to interpret the development and the nature of the EU. Of course, these theories are by definition EU-centred theories; they are important, however, for highlighting the role of national and regional business associations as part of the process of regionalization and regionalism. Over and above that, one cannot analyse the emerging processes of region-building and the emergence of a regional civil society in the context of the Mercosur without taking into account theories developed in the context of the EU.

Although they may have limited potential to predict the future development of the Mercosur as an evolving regional project, it would be a mistake to suggest that the decisions made on the institutional and legal structure of the Mercosur are made in a political or theoretical vacuum. Many of the early problems of the regional project in Latin America are similar to the challenges posed by processes of European integration in the 1950s and early 1960s. The emergence of cross-border linkages and regional cooperation with regard to business associations only emerged in Western Europe because of the growing importance of EU institutions from the late 1960s onwards.

Thus, to provide a truly comprehensive framework for analysing regional business associations in the context of CPE and IPE, one has to reflect on the potential of these theories of European integration for an, albeit limited, applicability to Latin America. Moreover, as previously remarked, theories are essentially lenses, which highlight different aspects, and often only a combination of a set of lenses gives a full picture.

At first glance, it is not necessarily obvious why theories of EU integration should be included or at least reflected on in a study of business interests in the Mercosur and the role these organized interests are playing in the context of processes of regional integration in the Southern Cone region. However, it is important to note that the EU started essentially as a politically driven project to overcome the divisions and conflicts of the Second World War, mainly between France and Germany. Only later on business interests became involved in the process. Especially from the mid- to late 1990s onwards, they became a driving force for further harmonization and integration in the EU.[78] This happened at a time, when several EU member states started to resist pressure for further integration and the balance of power in the EU tilted slightly towards more intergovernmental policy initiatives, rather than more integrationist ones. Thus, looking at theories of European integration and, more specifically, at the role business interests play in these theories, can yield interesting insights for studying these interests in the context of the Mercosur.

Indeed, very early on in the evolution of the EU, business associations were considered important and, in many ways, vital to the success of the European project. The general assumption was that interest groups would become an important link between the national and the supranational or regional level of governance in the EU.[79] As Streeck and Schmitter argue, '[interest articulation and lobbying on a regional level] was to bring about the socialisation of powerful forces in European civil society into a world view compatible with that of European bureaucrats'.[80] They argue further, 'when [regional lobbyists] returned to their national capitals, they...would again become a lobby; this time not of their interest group *vis à vis* Brussels, but of Brussels *vis à vis* their national leaders, including their governments'.[81] This 'fostering [of] a transnational system of organised interest representation' would, in turn, strengthen the regional level as an arena for policy formulation and articulation.[82]

In this respect, it is important to note that the increasing speed of European integration resulted in the formulation of the theory of neo-functionalism, which was developed in the 1950s and 1960s by Haas and later redefined by Lindberg.[83] Haas draws on Mitrany's theory of functional integration, which argues that cooperation on technical and administrative tasks of government would over time result in the emergence of international and supranational cooperation and, later on, integration.[84] For Haas, however, neo-functionalism had a clearly defined end point, a federalist system of government for Europe.[85] Important is also Haas' understanding of the process of political integration. For him,

> [p]olitical integration is the process whereby political actors in several distinct natural settings are persuaded to shift their loyalties, expectations and political activities towards a new centre, whose institutions possess or demand jurisdiction over the pre-existing national state.[86]

Thus, Hass focuses not only on governments but also on national interest groups.[87]

Important for an understanding of neo-functionalism is also the notion of 'spill over', which leads to a blurring of the separation of 'low' and 'high' politics. As Hurrell argues,

> [by neo-functionalists] supranational institutions were seen as the most effective means of solving common problems, beginning

with technical and non-controversial issues, but 'spilling over' into the realm of high politics and leading to a redefinition of group identity around the regional unit.[88]

Over and above that, the argument could also be considered a constructivist one by arguing, 'Europeanisation requires the discursive construction of the idea of a European economic space and of discernible "European" economic agents'.[89] This is also an argument, which Jelin develops in respect of the emerging processes of cooperation and integration in the Mercosur. She argues,

> the establishment of Mercosur at a regional level is an ongoing process through which various actors and forces will have to redefine their identities and scenarios in terms of space and territory. Social movements, actors, the meaning of action, participation and commitment, including 'identity', are not static phenomena that are fixed and that crystallise once and for all.[90]

Thus, as remarked earlier, organized business is increasingly becoming involved in and, in many ways, is increasingly important to keep the Mercosur project on track. This is because the identities of various actors and with it their perceived interests have shifted in the light of regional and global processes. The changes taking place on the regional level are replicated on the national level, with an increasing split between, on the one hand, business interests centred around regional and global markets and, on the other hand, economic interests centred around national markets. Chapters 3 and 4 will discuss and analyse these changes.

Despite attempts by Lindberg to redefine functionalism as a process of integration without an end point, neo-functionalism subsequently lost much of its influence from the 1970s onwards until the early 1980s, due to limited progress of the EU towards further integration.[91] This so-called 'Eurosclerosis' resulted in increasing scepticism towards neo-functionalism and the idea of a functional spillover. For example, Hoffmann argued,

> there are co-operative arrangements [such as the EU] with a varying degree of autonomy, power, and legitimacy, but there has been no transfer of allegiance toward their institutions, and their authority remains limited, conditional, dependent, and reversible.[92]

Consequently, intergovernmentalism as a theoretical approach focuses on the interstate agreements which are a necessary precondition for integration, and therefore for 'spill over' to occur.[93] Finally, Moravcsik developed intergovernmentalism into liberal intergovernmentalism by including in his analysis not only the role of states in the integration process but also of domestic interest groups, thereby discounting lobbying on the supranational level.[94]

Without a doubt, the development of the Mercosur region into a single economic space is something which is still very much in the making. Nevertheless, as previously remarked, TNCs and increasingly also domestic companies understand the Mercosur as an investment region. It is important to note, however, that the Mercosur has not yet developed into what Marks calls 'multilevel' governance. 'Multilevel' governance describes a system of governance where states are not the only important actors, because a level of supranational governance has emerged, which is the focus, not only of national actors but also of regional and local actors.[95] As Phillips points out,

> as such, the South American case currently conforms far more closely with the arguments of the 'inter-governmentalist' camp in the literature on EU regionalism than the neo-functionalist emphasis on supra-nationalism or the 'decisional reallocation' of multilevel governance approaches.[96]

Nevertheless, it is important to note the assumption that the state continues to be the central actor in the context of the Mercosur has increasingly lost some of its explanatory power. As mentioned before, the high degree of overlap between private and public interests in the Mercosur member states and the increasing importance of organized business on a national and on a regional level for keeping the Mercosur project on track highlights the fact that intergovernmentalist and liberal intergovernmentalist theories are not sufficient to describe the interplay between national, regional and global dynamics. Rather one has to add to intergovernmentalist theories the various processes of regional and interregional business interest representation, which are designed to coordinate policies which are then pursued primarily on the national level due to lack of common Mercosur institutions.

In this respect, it is important to state that the role played by regional business interests in the formulation and realization of the EU has been increasingly studied in recent years, as previously remarked. The role of the ERT of Industrialists , for example, is widely credited with bringing about, or at least with the provision of vital impetus for, the decision to launch the SEA in 1986 and to embark on the Single Market Programme, culminating in the Treaty on European Union (TEU), commonly known as the Maastricht treaty, and its successor, the Treaty of Amsterdam.

In this instance, it is important to mention that Greenwood is much more sceptical regarding the role of the ERT. He argues that the ERT has lost influence in recent years and its role has been overstated in most of the current literature due to successful self-marketing by the ERT members.[97]

The ERT consists of about forty to forty-five Chief Executive Officers (CEO) of large European companies, and membership is by invitation only. Also the ERT is often very vocal in its demands for structural, regulatory and social reforms in Western Europe. This is in turn often quoted by EU governments for justifying specific policy measures, such as the liberalization of EU employment markets.[98] In addition to the ERT there are other organizations such as the Union of Industrial Employers' Confederations of Europe (UNICE) or its national counterparts, for example the Confederation of British Industry (CBI), which participate actively through the various committees and consultation fora that are part of the supranational level of governance in the EU.[99]

Thus, institutionalized and non-institutionalized representation complement each other, although the ERT is often perceived as more influential and has a more focused approach with regard to specific issues, such as labour market flexibility, and does not lobby on behalf of specific companies or industrial sectors.[100,101]

In addition to the already mentioned concepts of intergovernmentalism and liberal intergovernmentalism, the neo-functionalist concept of 'spill over' could also be applied in the context of the Mercosur. Out of a nascent arbitration system a much, more developed system of dispute settlement has already grown over time. The recently signed *Protocolo de Olivos* established a *Tribunal Permanente de Revisión* (Permanent Review Tribunal) for Mercosur trade disputes, thus replacing the previous ad-hoc tribunals.[102]

This in turn reflects the growing importance of legal certainty in the context of a common market, the development of a common legal tradition and the imposition of legal limits on individual member states, thus strengthening the collectivity at the expense of any given Mercosur member state.[103] In this respect, it is also important to remark, that the first ad-hoc arbitration tribunal referred frequently to EU law and the legal doctrines established by the European Court of Justice (ECJ).[104] As Ventura points out,

> in order to interpret and enforce ... [the judicial order referred to in the Treaty of Asunción, Mercosur's founding treaty] the tribunal turned ... to the European Community law doctrine, despite the profound differences between the European and the Mercosur models.[105]

Thus, there is an even more direct link between the evolution of Mercosur and the European experience.

In addition, the previously mentioned creation of the FCES was heavily influenced by the growing criticism of civil society groups on the lack of formal input into Mercosur's decision-making. This underlines the idea of a 'spill over' because of the increasing importance of the regional level for national and sub-national actors. Thus, theories of EU integration can provide useful tools adaptable to the context of the Mercosur, for analysing the role played by organized business interests in processes of regionalization and regionalism in the Southern Cone.

2.4   Theorizing the role of regional business associations with reference to regionalization, regionalism and globalization

To assess and theorize the role of regional business associations in the evolution of the Mercosur, one has to integrate the IPE dimension into the theoretical tools of CPE reflected on previously in this chapter. This is necessary, because the theoretical tools provided by IPE add two important areas to the theoretical structure of this book.

First, there is the theoretical discussion regarding what drives these processes of regionalization and regionalism and in what way one can relate this to the role played by organized business within and as a result of these processes.

Second, the existence of globalization as a significant phenomenon has profoundly altered the international political economy since the early 1970s. In this respect, it is important to clarify what is meant by the term globalization in the context of this research and what the main consequences of globalization with reference to regional organized business in the context of Latin America in general and the Mercosur region in particular are. Thus, the role of regional business associations is closely linked to regionalization, regionalism and also to globalization and the way these three phenomena re-enforce each other.

This part of the chapter will introduce the IPE framework, namely the main theoretical debates concerning regionalization and regionalism, and it will also reflect on regional and global linkages. It will then locate regional business associations within this framework to show how CPE and the regionalization/regionalism/globalization debate connect with each other.

The current theoretical debate is often referred to as the 'new regionalism' approach in contrast to the 'old regionalism' discourse of the 1960s and 1970s. Before discussing this 'new regionalism' and the related theoretical debate, it is important to summarize briefly the main theoretical assumptions of the first wave of theorizing about regional cooperation and regional integration. Most importantly, the first wave of studying the emerging regional structures and organizations in the early 1960s centred around Balassa's theory of economic integration. For Balassa, 'economic integration ... can take several forms that represent varying degrees of integration. These are a free-trade area, a customs union, a common market, an economic union, and complete economic integration'.[106] Moreover, Allen, for example, argues in favour of an economic theory of integration, because he considers the issues surrounding economic cooperation and economic integration as too much dominated by political arguments. Consequently, he argues, 'there has developed a *mystique* concerning integration .... Much of the force behind the integration movement is political in character and political benefits may be considerable'.[107] Thus, despite the emphasis on an economic theory of integration, the 'old regionalism' is essentially concerned with an analysis of state-driven forms of integration.[108]

With the second wave of regional integration projects from the late 1980s onwards, the theoretical discussion shifted. The concept of regionalization was added to the theoretical conception of regionalism. This was a direct result of the newly emerging regional and subregional structures and a structural shift towards non-state actors in the wake of the globalization discourse. Consequently, the distinction between state-driven regionalism and market-driven regionalization became central to the theoretical debate and gave rise to the concept of 'new regionalism'.

For the concept of regionalization, the growth of intra-regional trade and investment is the primary reason for increasing regional cooperation.[109] Higgott, for example, understands regionalization and regionalism as closely linked, however he places greater emphasis on processes of regionalization. He points out, '*market driven* economic integration drives change. *State driven* institutional co-operation provides a framework – with varying degrees of success – for the management of change'.[110] Beeson and Jayasuriya also emphasize the importance of economic competition in a globalized world market as the driving force of processes of integration and only find it to be supported by institutional structures.[111] They bring the aspect of political rationality into the analysis by arguing that 'political rationalities ... are a reflection of the contingent political forces, institutional structures and discursive practices that inform policy-making and, ultimately, attitudes to international co-operation'.[112]

Consequently, the concept of regionalism underlines the political rational of regional integration processes. On the one hand, increasing economic interdependence within regions and across regions encourages states to cooperate and to establish new economic realities within their respective region. On the other hand, it is also important to remember that regionalization may foster regionalism, which could then be used as a buffer to withstand further pressure from an increasingly globalized world economy. As Brook argues, 'regionalism is seen then as providing a measure of security against the vagaries of the global economy and a strong base from which to compete within'.[113]

The Mercosur, for instance, could be understood in this context. Certainly, as mentioned earlier, at the beginning it was primarily seen as a means to enhance economic reform and to strengthen democracy. The previously mentioned MEBF, however, and the ongoing negotiations between the EU and the Mercosur with the aim of concluding a Mercosur-EU FTA underline the advantages that result from negotiating as a bloc rather than as an individual country. Also with regard to the current FTAA negotiations, the Mercosur has become an important vehicle for raising the voice and the profile of its members *vis à vis* Mercosur's global trading partners. In 2001, for example, Mercosur member states agreed to accept the US offer to launch talks aimed at concluding a FTA between the Mercosur and the US as part of the FTAA process under the so called 4 + 1 formula. This decision was called a 'fundamental landmark' by the Argentine foreign minister at the Annual Assembly of the Congress of Latin American Businessmen (CEAL).[114] As a consequence, Mattli argues,

> economic institutional theories have rightly been criticised as 'naive', for assuming that [economic] demand alone would miraculously generate institutional change. What they have overlooked are supply conditions. These are the conditions under which political leaders are willing and able to accommodate demands for functional integration at each step of the integration process.[115]

It is important to state, however, that increased regionalization does not necessarily result in reduced globalization.[116] As Zysman points out, 'if we look at trade relations, we can conclude that in economic terms, expanded regional trade has contributed to, rather than sub-tracting from, global trade'.[117] Moreover, for him, changes in the extent of regionalization are driven by nation states or are the result of interaction of nation states on the regional level. These processes may result in regional integration, for example in the form of institutional cooperation, which in turn shapes national policies. Consequently, 'national developments have ... driven changes in the global economy; even more than a so-called "globalisation" has driven national evolutions'.[118] In Zysman's understanding, therefore, regionalism drives regionalization.

Marchand, Bøås and Shaw by contrast argue,

> regionalisation processes constitute an important dimension of global restructuring ... but they have an explicit *spatial* articula-tion. Processes of regionalisation can be state-led, but do not

necessarily need to be. Within each regional project there will be more than one regional vision, and often more than one actor pursuing regionalisation.[119]

Thus, processes of regionalization are similar to what has been previously described as processes of regionalism. Furthermore, with reference to regionalization they argue further,

> the state is most often one of the regionalisation 'actors', but equally important actors can be identified within the two realms of the state-society-economy triangle: NGOs [Non-Governmental Organisations], media, companies, as well as a range of actors based in the second economy of the informal sector, are involved in processes of regionalisation.[120]

Therefore, Marchand, Bøås and Shaw explicitly allocate other actors such as regional business associations an increasingly important role in processes of shaping regional projects. Moreover, this role of non-state actors is also important in relation to their understanding of the term regionalism. For them, 'regionalism ... should be understood in a similar vein as globalism. Regionalism concerns ideas, identities and ideologies related to a regional project, but it is obviously not necessarily *state-led*, as states are not the only political actor around'.[121] Thus, overlapping and sometimes conflicting interests and visions of a regional project are central for a comprehensive understanding of these regional processes. They conclude, 'within each regional project (official or not), several competing regionalisation "actors" with different regional visions coexist, who sometimes co-operate and who, at other times, are in open conflict with each other'.[122]

Where does this leave us with respect to the Mercosur? Marchand, Bøås and Shaw's analysis is helpful in highlighting the changes and shifts that have taken place within the business community of the Mercosur as a result of processes of regionalization, regionalism and globalization. They also point out the many actors involved in these processes of region-building. For the purpose of this book, however, the distinction between regionalism as essentially describing forms of regional institutional governance, and regionalization as essentially being concerned with increased trade flows, cross-border linkages and forms of regional identity should be maintained. This is important to maintain the clarity of the argument and to guard against these terms becoming meaningless due to their complex nature.

What is important to note, however, is the assumption made in this book that processes of regionalism do not need to be state-driven. As the previous discussion of the MEBF or the CIQUIM has shown, forms of regional governance do not have to be directly linked to a regional organization in an institutional sense. They may result in increased levels of regionalization; however, they are essentially new or alternative forms of regional governance.

Of course, the opening-up of the markets in Latin America, the efforts to liberalize and modernize these markets and, finally, the launch of the Mercosur are all a direct result of global pressure and the perceived need to re-engage with the global trading system. As such, Mercosur member states have benefited from economic and trade growth, which is attributable to both regional cooperation and integration *and* globalization. As Floyd points out, 'trading blocs [such as the Mercosur]...are experiencing the effects of economic integration for the most part in terms of increased trade within the customs union as well as some impact of the globalisation process'.[123]

Consequently, Mercosur member states have been subjected to the increasing power of global capital as a result of the various processes of globalization. As Zysman points out,

> 'globalism' is only an emblem .... The suddenly pervasive intrusion of the notion of globalism is an effort by governments and companies to apply a label to a diverse package of changes that they do not understand and to devise strategies to adjust to a new economic world they cannot specify.[124]

As a consequence, the challenge of globalization is a challenge for both governments and business actors. It is this challenge that states try to overcome through enhanced regional cooperation and regional integration, for example, in the form of the Mercosur. As Grugel and de Almeida Medeiros argue,

> whereas NAFTA [the North American Free Trade Agreement] is about trade and investment, Mercosur...explicitly encompasses a double process of economic integration and political co-operation.

It builds on economic integration as a way to expand political autonomy…. Hence Mercosur challenges the dominant hub and spoke mode of region-building in the Americas.[125]

The success of these attempts, however, is subject to an intense debate concerning the very nature of globalization.

As a consequence, the next part of this chapter will give a brief overview over the various debates concerning the phenomenon 'globalisation' and how it is related to the general discussion of the role of the state and sub-national and transnational actors in a more and more regionalized and globalized world.

To start with, Ohmae presents the most extreme view of globalization in relation to regional cooperation. For him, the ability of the traditional nation-state to influence national, regional or global economies is more and more undermined by the emergence of what he calls 'region states', links between highly economically interdependent regions within different states, which share a common economic interest with each other rather than with the state they are situated in.[126] As Ohmae argues, 'in a borderless world, … [region states] are the natural economic zones. Though limited in geographical size, they are often huge in their economic influence.'[127] Thus, states, even if they try to cooperate on the regional level, will still be undermined by a sub-national level of governance, the 'region states'.[128]

Hirst and Thompson, by contrast, draw a more sceptical picture of globalization. They argue 'that the level of integration, interdependence, openness, or however one wishes to describe … [globalisation], of national economies in the present era is not unprecedented.'[129] Although Hirst and Thompson agree that the nature of the state is changing as a result of globalization, both authors also argue that the state is still important as one level within a multi-level system of governance, because the state is still central in distributing power to the supranational as well as to the regional and sub-regional level.[130] Hirst and Thompson add,

> politics is becoming more poly centric, with states as merely one level in a complex system of overlapping and often competing agencies of governance …. This … implies a world quite different from that of the rhetoric of 'globalisation', and one in which there is a distinct, significant and continuing place for the nation state.[131]

The previous aspect of Hirst and Thompson's argument of the state as a distributor of power contrasts with another more sceptical view of globalization presented by Weiss. She emphasizes the 'catalytic' nature of states, which means, 'contemporary states are constantly seeking power-sharing arrangements which will give them scope for remaining an *active centre*, hence "catalytic" states.'[132] From her point of view, joining regional organizations such as the Mercosur is a possibility for states to adapt to the changing and globalizing international environment, whilst maintaining a high degree of influence.[133]

Perraton, Goldblatt, Held and McGrew, by contrast, choose a path between the 'hyper-globalisation school', as they call it, and the more sceptical view of globalization represented by Hirst and Thompson as well as Weiss.[134] On the one hand, they agree that there is still a place for the state in a globalizing economy and accuse the supporters of the 'hyper-globalisation school' of ignoring the economic and structural differences between countries and regions 'that make international transactions profitable in the first place'.[135] On the other hand, following Perraton et al., sceptics of globalization under-estimate the structural shift of power from state or state institutions towards global markets and TNCs that has taken place as a result of globalization.[136] It is this shift in structural power, however, which poses the challenge to states and regional organizations in the form of globalization. The result of this power shift has been the increasing dominance of what Gill calls 'globalisation of liberalism'.[137] Emphasizing a Gramscian perspective, Gill argues elsewhere that a so-called 'transnational historic bloc of forces' emerged in the 1970s and 1980s as a result of, but also as a driving force of the globalization of production and capital.[138]

As a result, through regional cooperation and regional integration states try to maintain their position as providers of social welfare and security in the light of the 'globalisation of liberalism'. As Gill points out, 'the logic of neoliberalism is contradictory: it promotes global economic integration..., but also generates depletion of resources and the environment, as well as undermining the traditional tax base and the capacity [of states] to provide public goods.'[139] And, as Devetak and Higgott argue, 'globalisation has improved economic efficiency and it has provided enhanced individual liberty for many; but in its failure to ensure social justice on a global scale, it also inhibits liberty for many more.'[140] Gamble and Payne argue along similar lines when they point out,

> regionalisation, like globalisation, however, is normally uneven in its impact. Certain places and sites will be integrated while others are marginalised. Unless the regionalist project embraced by the core explicitly addresses the issue of inequality and uneven development, the process of deepening integration is also likely to be a process of increasing polarisation.[141]

This is also an issue, which has to be addressed by the Mercosur to overcome the traditionally entrenched domestic and economic structures, which favour only a few well-connected businessmen or a small economic elite.[142] Moreover, the uneven internal economic development of the Mercosur member states may even threaten the regional project as such, and issues of poverty and social inequality have to be addressed alongside the need to reform and restructure internal markets and to strengthen regional structures.[143] The challenges arising from the interplay of the processes of regionalization and globalization may then act as a catalyst for wide-ranging social and economic change. Organized business interests are increasingly playing a part in supporting processes of economic and social change. Of course, as noted earlier in this chapter, it is important to look at the membership structure of these organizations to determine the 'interest behind the interest'. In addition to TNCs with a strong interest in an integrated Mercosur-wide market, there is also a consistent rise in cross-country investment between companies in the Mercosur.[144] On the other hand, influential domestic business actors continue to see the Mercosur as a means to achieve some degree of protection from global market forces, although this position is in turn coming under pressure from other domestic business interests in favour of liberalization and market reform.[145]

What is also important to note is that if one looks at the Mercosur, actors have changed their focus away from protecting markets to engaging with other regional and global actors primarily under the influence of trade liberalization. Consequently, initially at least, Mercosur governments viewed the regional project as not only necessary for fostering democracy but also for strengthening the domestic economies, which was central in opening-up the national markets for competition. Wide-ranging liberalization programmes from the early 1990s onwards, primarily in Argentina but also in Brazil, have resulted in the opening-up of the respective economies and a significant reduction in the role of the state. The beneficiaries were sometimes local or regional conglomerates or well-connected individuals, but also TNCs, especially in sectors which required high levels of capital investment, for example infrastructure or oil and gas exploitation.[146] Individual companies, such as the Bridas Corporation, YPF (now Repsol YPF) and Arcor in Argentina, and Embraer in Brazil have managed to go beyond the domestic and regional markets by becoming companies with a global interest and a global market.[147]

From the late 1990s onwards, the regionalization and globalization of the Southern Cone economies has directly led to the increasing split between business interests focused on maintaining and protecting national markets and business interests actively engaged in forming regional or interregional forms of economic governance. The previously noted shift in interest representation on the national level, away from business associations supporting national solutions towards business associations engaged with regional and global structures, is a direct result of this.

Consequently, regional organized interests play an increasing role in influencing the direction and, to some extent, the agenda of the regionalist project itself, as states are under pressure from above (globalization) and below (sub-national actors) to respond to the economic *and* the social challenges posed by the need to fundamentally reform their institutions and their societies. As such, regionalism has to respond to these challenges by increasingly involving sub-national and cross-regional interests, for example in the form of regional business associations. Thus, it is important to note that, 'most [authors] see this phenomenon [regionalism] as co-operation among sovereign territorial entities, and do not appreciate the extent to which regional relations among states and other relevant actors are in a state of flux'.[148]

To locate the book in a particular line of argument and to provide a working definition of globalization in the context of the research presented here, it is first important to distinguish between internationalization and globalization. Whereas internationalization describes enhanced trade and interaction between states, globalization essentially is supraterritorial in nature.[149] This emphasis on supraterritoriality is necessary, because, as Scholte notes, 'pre-existent words like "internationalisation", "supranational" and "transnational" do not adequately capture the key *geographical* point at issue'.[150] Therefore, globalization is indeed 'happening' and it is the logical 'next step up' from internationalization. As Scholte argues further, 'within the domain of our planet, location distance and borders place no insurmountable constraints on supraterritorial relations. In this sense they are suitably called "global" phenomena.'[151] However, it is also important to remember that territoriality still remains important in the context of globalization. As Scholte points out, 'we should not replace territorialism with a globalist methodology that neglects territorial spaces.... To say that social geography can no longer be understood in terms of territoriality *alone* is not to say that territoriality has become irrelevant'.[152]

Second, globalization and the spread of neo-liberal economic ideas are of course closely related and enhance each other, but they are not inseparable. As Scholte points out, 'the two trends remain distinct. Liberalisation is a question of regulation, whereas globalisation (as relative deterritorialisation) is a question of geography'.[153]

In many ways, it is also important to state that globalization should be considered as neither a 'good' nor a 'bad' thing *per se*. Rather, globalization poses challenges to various actors within the realm of civil society, but it also opens up new avenues for cooperation and change, thus overcoming entrenched interests and structures. As a result of these continuing changes, the institutional environment in which sub-national, national, regional and supra-regional actors operate is constantly changing and contributing to the new and emerging fault lines on the national and regional level outlined above. This, in turn, supports new forms of regionalist governance that are discussed and advanced by various actors and that are the focus of this book.

2.5   Key theoretical concepts of the book

After the previous comprehensive discussion of both CPE and IPE approaches and their application to the study of organized business interests in the Mercosur, it is now important to summarize how these approaches will be applied throughout the book.

The theoretical toolkit – the key literature within CPE and IPE applied in this book – is guided by parsimony, internal coherence of the method, and relevance.[154] These essentially provide the controls to what Phillips has termed *'controlled eclecticism'*, which she argues 'offers a more constructive understanding of political economy' with the aim of 'finding a common ground between CPE and IPE ... rather than simply a bridge over the dividing (troubled?!) water'.[155,156] These controls are central to responding to the criticism eclecticism commonly faces. This becomes evident in its definition as ' "the principle or practice of taking one's views from a variety of philosophical and other sources" sometimes in ways "that make no strenuous effort to create intellectual harmony between discrete elements" '.[157] A synthesis, by contrast, is defined as 'a composition or combination of parts or elements so as to form a whole'.[158] Therefore, the controls are crucial to create a successful path through a synthesis of both CPE and IPE to political economy, overcoming the pitfalls faced by eclecticism.

As Söderbaum argues with reference to Southern Africa, 'it has become increasingly evident that there is an intriguing interaction between the "domestic" and the "international". This makes it more appropriate to speak of one broad "political economy", rather than two separate disciplines'.[159] In the case of this book, the common ground is the regional level of governance as the means of conceptualizing an internally coherent whole. This synthesis of CPE and IPE is guided by the key controls mentioned above: parsimony, internal coherence and relevance. A toolkit constructed in this way is necessary, as organized business in the Mercosur operates on three different levels, namely the domestic, regional and global.

To apply parsimony, internal coherence and relevance in this sense to the study of organized business in the Mercosur, means to apply specific literature to the relevant levels of governance, that is the national, regional and the global level. Consequently, the specific literature for the study of the national level within CPE is the 'varieties of capitalism' debate and the study of interest group strategies, issues of getting access and influencing policy. This is the first of two pillars on which the theoretical framework is based.

The second and equally important pillar is IPE theory with the key literature on regionalization, regionalism and globalization.

Here, regionalization and regionalism and the conditions under which these two processes evolve is important to understand the role played by organized business in the context of the Mercosur; the influences to which these interests are subjected to; and with whom and how they interact. Moreover, processes of globalization also play an important part in the shape and the extent of the new regional environment, while at the same effecting changes at the national level.

In many ways this connection between CPE and IPE, in which CPE with its emphasis on national economies and the 'varieties of capitalism' debate is an almost 'natural' complement to IPE. Susan Strange's critique of CPE as 'not to see the wood for the trees, to overlook the common problems while concentrating on the individual differences'[160] while defining IPE as 'the study ... that ... concerns the social, political and economic arrangements affecting the global systems of production, exchange and distribution, and the mix of values reflected therein'[161] provides an example for this. As Phillips argues, 'countries and regions – the "trees" – that comprise the global political economy *and are fundamentally constitutive of it* have generally been ignored, such that we are left in the main with a somewhat disembodied and decontextualised field of enquiry'.[162]

Thus, as this book will demonstrate theoretically and empirically, it makes little sense to only talk about *either* the 'wood' *or* the 'trees'. Rather, the regional level of governance is so much dependent on its links with national economies while at the same time being the interlocutor of national economies and global economic currents that only by successfully creating this synthesis between CPE and IPE with emphasis on parsimony, internal coherence and relevance can we adequately conceptualize it.

In this respect, it is important to reiterate the fact that the new regional focus of national and sub-national actors is a direct result of the changes taking place within the economic and social environment in which these actors operate. As Marchand, Bøås and Shaw argue,

> 'the debate has also widened. At least, it is beginning to acknowledge that regional interactions and organisations focus not only on states but on continuing linkages among a heterogeneous set of actors and realms, including states, economies/companies and societies/civil societies.[163]

2.6 Central questions that guide the research in this book

The book makes two tentative arguments, which will be evaluated according to their empirical and theoretical validity.

First, organized business has been a neglected area of study and it has been underestimated in the role it is playing in the regional integration process. In the wake of the active engagement of the business community from the mid-1990s onwards and enabled by an organizational strengthening and capacity-building on the side of business interest associations on the national and regional level, the influence of organized business in the integration process has been increasing.

Following on from there, the empirical evidence employed throughout the book will aim to describe and analyse the existing public policy processes in the Mercosur on the domestic level while at the same time highlighting the link between those processes and the ones developing on the regional and inter-regional level. In particular, the book will highlight how business associations have been changing on the domestic level *vis à vis* state actors to maintain or enhance their relevance to the policy-making process; how business associations push actively for change to create more formalized channels of access to their respective governments; and how business associations have been drawn into the policy-making process by state actors, both on the national and the regional/inter-regional level.

This will be discussed, for example, in Chapters 3 and 4 with reference to domestic interest representation in Argentina and Brazil. In Argentina and to a large extent also in Brazil, the wider business community initially failed to engage *positively* with the regional integration process, despite requests by the respective governments to do so. Consequently, it was only from the mid-1990s onwards in response to the emerging regional economic space that organized business started to engage effectively with the regional integration process. This happened not only in response to government requests but also as a result of pressure on business associations from within the business community to enable them to compete more effectively in the light of trade liberalization measures and increasing competition on the domestic market. This in turn resulted in significant changes to the landscape of organized business interest representation on the domestic level of the Mercosur in the sense that established interest associations either adapted to the changing economic and political environment to increase their influence in the policy-making process or lost influence.

In this respect the chemical industry in the Mercosur, which will be discussed in Chapter 5, is an example of how organized business cooperated on a regional level even before the politically driven regional integration process and has consequently achieved a high degree of influence in the policy-making process. The MEBF process, also discussed in Chapter 5, is another example of the business sector providing important momentum to sustain the trade negotiations between the Mercosur and the EU despite significant political upheavals. Both the example of the chemical industry and the MEBF also highlight the increasing relevance of the regional level of interest representation, despite the fact that the majority of lobbying activity still takes place on the domestic level due to the lack of a meaningful institutional structure in the Mercosur.

Second, the emerging regional dimension of business interest representation and its linkages with the domestic and global levels of governance cannot be adequately conceptualized by either CPE or IPE alone. Rather there is a need for a successful synthesis of the two using a set toolkit consisting of the 'varieties of capitalism' debate, interest group formation, regionalization, regionalism and globalization, which has been selected through parsimony, internal coherence of the method and relevance. A consequence of this synthesis will be the emergence of the regional level of governance as the arena where both approaches connect, namely CPE coming from below and IPE coming from above. This synthesis is essential for understanding the ongoing processes of change in this arena.

Conclusion

The focus of this book, a successful synthesis of the theoretical approaches of CPE and IPE, is of course located in the wider theoretical debate of bridging the gap between Comparative Politics (CP) and International Relations (IR) in general.[164]

Hix and Blondel, for example, argue that the study of closely knit regions in particular is more adequately done by using the tools of CP than the theoretical approaches of IR.[165] Others, such as Hurrell and Menon and also Jachtenfuchs, point to the need to connect both approaches to move the theoretical analysis and debate beyond a narrow CP versus IR discussion, by applying theoretical insights of both theoretical strands. This approach is often labelled as the 'new governance' approach.[166] As Hurrell and Menon point out, 'as in political science in general, the important arguments are between the proponents of ... [CP and IR], not between an abstracted discourse of "comparative politics" on the one hand and "international relations" on the other'.[167]

By connecting CPE and IPE using parsimony, internal coherence and relevance, to analyse and to reflect upon organized business within the Mercosur, the book is bridging the gap between CP and IR. By doing so, it aims to advance the theoretical debate and enhance the understanding of the role played by organized business in the evolution of regionalism in Latin America, pointing out the linkages and overlaps between interest representation on the national and regional level and the wider global economic space.

In conclusion, only a successful synthesis of CPE and IPE provides an adequate set of lenses to fully understand the evolving role of business associations within the context of the Mercosur.

By focusing on organized business as a driving force not only for regionalization, but also for regionalism, the book attempts to advance the empirical as well as the theoretical debate on the increasing role played by organized business in the evolution of the Mercosur.

3
Structures of Business Interest Articulation in the Mercosur: The National and the Regional Dimension

Introduction

Since the early 1990s, The Southern Cone region of Latin America has witnessed the implementation of a wide range of neo-liberal reforms. Previously closed markets with a strong emphasis on Import Substituting Industries (ISIs) were gradually opened up, beginning with Chile and Argentina and later followed by Brazil, amongst others. The opening-up of these markets was to a large extent driven by the strong *political* desire to reinsert the Southern Cone economies into the world economy; to bring spiralling inflation levels under control; and above all to achieve sustainable long-term development. This was precipitated by the increasing internationalization and, much later, regionalization and globalization of the Southern Cone markets.

As mentioned in the previous chapter, organized business interests were not very supportive of these new politically inspired processes of liberalizing the Southern Cone economies. Consequently, organized business initially did not engage at all in the drive to regionalize and globalize these markets. They also had very little input, at least from the outset, into the creation of the first 'new regionalism' organization in Latin America, the Mercosur. It is important to mention the one exception to this, namely the chemical industry, which from the mid-1980s onwards developed a forum for regional cooperation in terms of policies, tariffs and so on that predated the Mercosur and later became known as the CIQUIM.[1]

As a result of this lack of interest on the side of the business sector, organized business interests only started to develop a coordinated response to the new challenges of internationalization and, later on, regionalization and globalization from 1991/92 onwards, *after* the Mercosur came into force. In this respect it is important to remember that organized business in Argentina and Brazil was consulted on the liberalization and integration proposals contained in the so-called *Acta de Buenos Aires*, an agreement reached as part of the initial cooperation and integration accord between Argentina and Brazil signed in 1986, the *Programa de Integración y Cooperación Argentina – Brasil* (PICAB). The *Acta de Buenos Aires*, primarily aimed at overcoming the deep political divisions between Argentina and Brazil after decades of hostility, was signed in 1990 and is also known as the *Acordo de Complementação Econômica 14* (ACE-14).[2] This later formed the nucleus for the trade liberalization measures contained in the Treaty of Asunción, Mercosur's founding agreement.[3] As such, business interests, due to the often highly technical nature of sectoral negotiations in particular, were consulted and had considerable input into the initial integration process, although they had not initiated it and were not actively driving it forward.[4] This point is often neglected in the literature, and this results in a distorted picture of business involvement in the Mercosur process as a whole.[5]

Therefore, as this chapter will show, organized business interests in the Mercosur have undergone a fundamental transformation from the early 1990s onwards. This has happened on both the national and the regional level. On the one hand, a shift in interest articulation on the national level away from the traditional and entrenched lobbying structures towards either reformed or entirely new forms of interests articulation has taken place; on the other hand, new forms of lobbying on the regional and even the interregional level have been developed to reflect the new industrial and commercial realities of the Mercosur and to engage with the changing national and regional political structures.[6]

As a consequence, this chapter will be divided into two parts. The first one will look at the transformation that has taken place on the national level across the countries in the Mercosur. The second part of the chapter will then move to the regional level and analyse the emergence of new forms and the strengthening of existing forms of interest representation by various actors in the business community.

3.1   The national level of interest representation in the Mercosur: Transforming structures under conditions of regionalization and globalization

As mentioned in the Introduction, when the process of regional integration in the form of the Mercosur was launched in the early 1990s, organized business had more or less no interest in substantially pushing this government-driven project forward. It is from this initial lack of interest in regionalizing the Southern Cone economies on the side of the business community that the Mercosur is often referred to as a government-driven project and more of an example for state-driven regionalism. Initially, at least, this was clearly the case. The initial reluctance on the side of business to embrace new regional trading opportunities is largely explained by the fact that the pre-Mercosur economies were by and large trading with North America and Europe rather than with each other, to some extent also as a result of former colonial structures.[7] Only after the inauguration of the Mercosur, and to some extent since closer economic cooperation between Argentina and Brazil from the mid-1980s onwards, trade started to increase and patterns of trade started to shift. Indeed, the volume of intra-Mercosur trade increased significantly from 1991/92 onwards, and this is often quoted as the most obvious success of the regional integration scheme.[8]

As previously mentioned, it is central to this chapter to explain and analyse the change that has taken place because of the newly emerging regional and global realities from the perspective of organized business in the Mercosur. In the following part, the transformation that could be witnessed on the level of national interest representation towards embracing or averting structural change will be discussed. It is important to note that this analysis will focus mainly on Argentina and Brazil as the two most important economies in the Mercosur, supported by interviews from Uruguay.

3.1.1 Argentina

Up until the mid-1990s, interest representation on the national and non-sectoral level in Argentina and Brazil was dominated by established business associations. In the case of Argentina, the most important business federations were the Unión Industrial de Argentina (UIA), the Sociedad Rural Argentina (SRA) and the Cámara Argentina de la Construcción (CAC) (b). The Cámara Argentina de Comercio (CAC) (a), the Consejo Argentino de la Industria (CAI) and the Confederación General de la Industria (CGI) are less important.[9] In addition to these organizations, the Consejo Empresario Argentino (CEA), which lost influence from the mid-1990s due to internal conflicts, was an important supporter of the privatization process which started in 1991/92 under President Carlos Menem.[10] Nevertheless, the CEA is still considered important in the sense that it brings together various corporate interests on non-sectoral lines and continues to finance research into neo-liberal reform in Argentina.[11]

However, it is important to state that organized business associations in Argentina are historically highly dependant on voluntary contributions from their institutional and non-institutional members, as funding is not mandatory. This stands in sharp contrast to the compulsory employer and employee contributions to the so-called *obras sociales*, social security funds, which are controlled by the trade unions, thus giving them considerable influence. This contributed to a relatively high level of funding and hence professionalization of trade union staff. As a consequence, business associations in Argentina mainly focus on lobbying activities, rather than funding research projects and collecting professionally relevant information for their members.[12]

The UIA, has always been highly dependant on its members' support and has often been in conflict externally with the Argentine government, in particular under Peronist governments or internally, when conflicts emerged between UIA's protectionist and economically more liberal oriented members.[13] This is highlighted in an example given by Felix Peña, who in 1998/99 was the Under-Secretary of State for Foreign Trade in the Argentine government. He explained that when he requested a position paper from the UIA to assist the government in trade negotiations in the Common Market

Council (CMC) of the Mercosur, the paper presented did not list one common position. Rather, it would give two completely opposed opinions that existed within the UIA with regard to a certain issue, and basically left it to the government to decide which issue should be prioritized. From Peña's point of view, these position papers were of no help at all, and they highlight the problems of the UIA ' to produce the trade-off between the inter-sectoral caucus of the organisation'.[14]

This inherent weakness and lack of a distinct profile of the UIA as a result of these internal and external problems explain why the UIA was initially very hesitant in engaging with other business association in the Mercosur, that is the Confederação Nacional da Indústria (CNI) of Brazil or the Cámara de Industrias del Uruguay (CIU), and only after pressure from the Argentine government did the UIA participate in the Consejo Industrial de Mercosur (CIM).[15] This reluctance of the UIA to participate in the CIM might partially be explained by the worries of Argentine companies regarding Brazilian competition.[16] The CIM was designed to be a forum for the exchange of information across the business community of the Mercosur, and to help coordinate policies and develop common positions towards the Mercosur policies pursued by the member states.[17]

The involvement of the private sector in the Mercosur negotiations increased in 1993/94, when the preliminary talks in relation to the Protocol of *Ouro Preto*, signed in 1994, were conducted. Business involvement increased, because with the *Ouro Preto* agreement the Mercosur moved from being a Free Trade Area (FTA) towards becoming a customs union with a Common External Tariff (CET) by 2005. It is important to note, however, that the participation of organized business was largely to protect weaker and non-competitive industries, rather than proposing liberalization in certain areas.[18]

Another sector where business was closely involved in the Mercosur negotiations and the one sector always mentioned in the literature is the automobile industry. The reason for this is that one can show very effectively the structural change that has taken place as a result of the reinsertion of the Mercosur economies into the global political economy caused by the economic reforms of the early 1990s in the Southern Cone region. If one visited Argentina and Brazil in 1991, just before the convertibility plan linking the Argentine *Peso* to the *US Dollar* came into effect or the *Plano Real*, linking the Brazilian currency to the *US Dollar*, one could witness a very different automobile sector than today. In 1991, the automobile market in both countries was dominated by a handful of car manufacturers, namely Ford of America and Volkswagen of Germany cooperating together in what was then called Autolatina, GM of the US and some other smaller joint ventures with other car producers limited to a country-specific market. Models were either outdated or specifically designed to meet the (limited) expectations of the local market.

Due to high import tariffs, prices for locally produced cars were artificially high, innovation was limited due to the lack of competitive pressure and imported cars were prohibitively expensive. When the automobile sector and, more importantly, trade in cars was liberalized as a result of the Mercosur treaty coming into effect in 1991, the market conditions and with it the nature of Foreign Direct Investment (FDI) in this market started to change fundamentally.[19]

The combination of, on the one hand, domestic economic reform, successful attempts to bring inflation under control and increasing efforts to liberalize the markets of the Mercosur and, on the other hand, Trans-National Corporations (TNCs) using these reform strategies to break away from the entrenched structure of decades of ISI, transformed the automobile sector. Output increased fivefold over a period of six years from 1991/92 onwards, and with it an enormous increase of FDI, superseding all other sectors of the Mercosur economies.[20] As a result, the Mercosur was increasingly understood by TNCs as single investment area, with production being shifted form Argentina to Brazil and *vice versa* according to exchange rates and economic conditions.[21,22]

It is important to bring the role of TNCs into the discussion of the role of organized business interests in the Mercosur, because especially the automobile industry is one of the few sectors, which rely heavily on their own lobbying activities on the national, regional and global level. As such, they rely on their own sectoral organization, which in the case of Argentina is the Asociación de Fábricas de Automotores (ADEFA), and in the case of Brazil the Associação Nacional dos Fabricantes de Veículos Automotores (ANFAVEA). The membership list of both organizations includes all major automobile producers. This points to the increasing importance of the Mercosur market.[23] As previously mentioned, ADEFA and ANFAVEA have developed strong associational profiles outside their respective national peak associations. This is also reflected in the fact that few TNCs are directly involved with the relevant peak associations in the Mercosur member states. Rather, they prefer to either be represented through the American Chamber of Commerce (AMCHAM) or the German Chamber of Commerce (AHK) in the relevant countries, often due to the fact that the United States and Germany are traditionally the most important contributors of FDI to the region.[24,25] This was also confirmed by a BankBoston employee, who in an informal email suggested to contact these two chambers to gather information regarding business interests in the Mercosur members states. In general, individual companies are rarely willing to be openly associated with a certain policy position, if they are not part of a wider business interest group or association.

This points to an important aspect when assessing the role played by TNCs. Although the majority of companies is either represented by their various chambers of commerce or, as is the case in the automobile sector and also the chemical sector, through sectoral associations, the increasing presence and with it the emerging competition coinciding with the opening-up of the Mercosur economies, as mentioned before, has fundamentally altered the economic, and more specifically the industrial structure of the Mercosur economies. In Argentina and Brazil, TNCs have increasingly been agents of change, driven by the economic liberalization process that started in the 1990s.[26] As a consequence, they have forced domestic organized business to adapt to this change or to lose influence.

In relation to organized business, this means, first, a reorganization and a realignment of these interests to reflect the new economic realities. As previously mentioned, from the mid- to late-1990s onwards the UIA lost considerable influence as a result of the problems in overcoming sectoral divisions among its members, and also because some companies actually left the UIA, due to its increasingly protectionist positions on various issues including trade.[27] The rift within the UIA was mainly a result of the recession in Argentina in the late 1990s. At this point in time, a division among the main business sectors in Argentina begun to emerge. Until then, the so-called *Grupo de los Ochos* existed, which consisted of the UIA, the SRA, the CAC(a), two banking associations, which later merged, two chambers representing the construction industry, which later merged to form the CAC(b) and the Confederaciones Rurales Argentinas (CRA). In 1999, *Grupo de los Ochos* split, and the *Grupo Productivo* was formed by the UIA, the CRA and the CAC(b). The *Grupo Productivo* distanced itself from the two banking associations and advocated compensating Argentine companies for the economic consequence of the overvaluation of the *Peso*. In fact, many members within the UIA actively pressed for a devaluation of the *Peso* and an end of the convertibility regime.[28] Overall, the *Grupo Productivo* 'emerged as a mild critic of the 90s policies and favoured [a] stronger state involvement in the economy, opposing ... the more "liberal" approach of the SRA, the CAC[(a)] and the banking association'.[29]

As a result of the emerging rift within the UIA, alternative business associations such as the CEA, mentioned above, were formed to support the economic reform process. However, even within the CEA tensions emerged in the late 1990s when traditional Argentine industrial conglomerates such as Techint and Arcor also Perez Companc, which later in the wake of the Argentine currency crisis bought by Petrobras of Brazil, started to lobby for more protectionism in the light of foreign competition and the threat of foreign takeovers. Techint later on became the driving force behind the UIA.[30]

Second, the importance of sectoral business associations increased considerably as a result of the differences within the UIA. Not only the previously discussed automobile sector, which is not even part of the UIA, but also the chemical sector, represented by the Cámara de la Industria Química y Petroquímica (CIQyP), have been very active in creating small but highly professional and well-funded sectoral business associations supporting the needs of their particular industrial sector. Sectoral business associations have also been able to bring together the domestic parts of their respective sector and the TNCs active in this market segment. The agricultural sector, also highly competitive, has four sectoral associations, which are well resourced.[31]

Third, as a result of the collapse of the currency board and the deepening economic and financial crisis in Argentina in 2001/02, a new and potentially powerful business associations was formed, the Asociación Empresaria Argentina (AEA), combining 47 of Argentina's most powerful companies and conglomerates, representing roughly 40 per cent of the Argentine Gross Domestic Product (GDP).[32] This association is unique in the sense that it presents a clear shift from the traditional forms of organized business interest articulation, such as the UIA, towards new forms and alternative fora of interest

Table 3.1 Business interest associations in Argentina (selected)

	National Level	Federal State-level	Sectoral	Foreign
Corporatist		Confederación General Económica Argentina (CGE) (1952–55)		*Auslandshandelskammern* – German Chamber of Commerce Abroad (AHK)
Private	Unión Industrial de Argentina (UIA) Asociación Empresario Argentino (AEA) Cámara Argentina de Comercio (CAC)(a) *Consejo Empresario de America Latina* – Congress of Latin American Businessmen (CEAL) Sociedad Rural Argentina (SRA) Confederación General de la Industria (CGI) Consejo Empresario Argentino (CEA) Consejo Argentino de la Industria (CAI)	Confederaciones Rurales Argentinas (CRA) Confederación General Económica Argentina (CGE) (1958 –)	Cámara Argentina de la Construcción (CAC)(b) Cámara de la Industria Química y Petroquímica (CIQyP) Asociación de Fábricas de Automotores (ADEFA)	American Chamber of Commerce (AMCHAM)

articulation, which follow more a Round Table model. More importantly, the AEA represents two previously opposed groups of the Argentine commercial and industrial sectors. On the one hand, companies such as Techint, Clarín, Arcor and Loma Negra are members, all of which are considered 'national' industrial and commercial groups. On the other hand, companies such as Bridgestone/ Firestone Argentina, Repsol-YPF, Telefoníca and Volkswagen Argentina are also members, representing TNCs and foreign-owned Argentine companies. Thus, as previously mentioned, the AEA brings together in a meaningful way two important groups of the Argentine industrial and commercial sectors for the first time, thus potentially strengthening the role of organized business.

This change in the domestic interest representation of organized business in Argentina underlines the analysis developed so far as that under conditions of globalization and regionalization patterns of interest representation change fundamentally and ultimately move to support new forms of regional economic governance and restructuring.

3.1.2 Brazil

If one looks at organized business on the domestic level in Brazil, there are fundamental and, with regard to the focus of the research presented here, important differences in the way these business interests are represented and how influential they are. Thus, the following part of this chapter will focus on Brazil and how domestic organized business interests have developed over time, specifically during the 1990s since the inauguration of the Mercosur.

Generally, organized business in Brazil, primarily in the form of the CNI, has been much closer involved in the Mercosur trade negotiations than the UIA in Argentina. However, it is important to note that it was not until after the Mercosur came into force in 1991 that the business sector in Brazil developed a stronger interest in the emerging processes of regionalization and regionalism in the Southern Cone region. The reasons for this are primarily twofold. First, there was a widespread belief in business circles that the Mercosur and also its predecessor, the PICAB, were not particularly important for the Brazilian industry as such, and thus becoming involved in this government-driven process was not necessary. Second, there was generally a low level of expectations in the possibility that such a wide-ranging agreement could be concluded. The belief that either the Mercosur would not work or at least not be very effective in terms of opening-up the closed Southern Cone markets, combined with a disbelief in its actual formation led to the fact that Brazilian business interests engaged actively with the Mercosur process and its related negotiations from 1992/93 onwards. At this point especially the Brazilian industrial sector started to become involved in the negotiations. Yet there was the general perception in business circles that the momentum had been lost due to the initial lack of interest of organized business to become involved in the process.

From 1993, the CNI became involved in the CIM, together with the UIA, the CIU and the Unión Industrial de Paraguay (UIP). Especially the first two to three years, up until 1996, the CIM proved surprisingly effective in terms of negotiating common positions for the industrial sector across the Mercosur and in responding effectively to the unfolding process of trade negotiations. It is important to mention that the CNI, the UIA and the CIU were the main contributors to the CIM, as the UIP had problems in actively following the trade negotiations, mainly due to a lack of funding and, thus, limited resources.[33] Nevertheless, the CIM met about four times a year and, in its early years, managed to come up with common position papers and, more importantly, specific recommendations for the governments of the Mercosur member states.

To re-engage with the Mercosur process, the CNI started to gather information and to liaise with Brazilian government departments to obtain up-to-date information on the trade negotiations. It also started to collect opinions on issues important to various sectors of the Brazilian economy in relation to the ongoing trade negotiations, to develop a coherent and industry-wide response to the politically driven Mercosur process.

The initial starting point for these efforts was the 2nd *Foro Empresarial de las Americas* (FEMA – Americas Business Forum) in Cartagena in Columbia in 1996. Here, CNI was only represented on the invitation of the Brazilian government, and the business sector realized it lacked the coordination and the knowledge to conduct regional and international trade negotiations efficiently and effectively. In 1997, as the result of the third FEMA held in Belo Horizonte in Brazil, CNI initiated the Brazilian Business Coalition (BBC), to coordinate a common response and to develop common positions and recommendations across the various sectors of the Brazilian economy. The BBC brings together the CNI, the Confederação da Agricultura e Pecuária do Brasil (CNA), the Confederação Nacional do Comércio (CNC), the National Confederation of Financial Institutions (CNIF), the Associação de Comércio Exterior do Brasil (AEB) and the Brazilian Chapter of the *Consejo Empresario de América Latina* (CEAL).[34] The organization of the BBC is deliberately loose and flexible. It does not have formal headquarters nor a Secretariat, and its logistical, technical and professional support is provided almost entirely by the CNI, which also coordinates its meetings.

The BBC initially focused on the FTAA negotiations, but was later expanded to deal with the MEBF as part of the Mercosur-EU Free Trade Agreement, and also with the Mercosur in general. Thus, the BBC is central in discussing sector-wide issues related to trade and then engaging with the Brazilian government to lobby on behalf of the interests of its members.

In relation to this very developed network of organized business in Brazil in contrast to Argentina, it is important to mention that the system of funding organizations such as the CNI, the CNC, the CNT and the CNIF is fundamentally different to the funding arrangements in Argentina. Dating back to 1940s, the then Brazilian President Getulio Vargas created sectoral peak associations for employers and employees which were linked to compulsory funding, therefore introducing the still largely unchanged system of state corporatism in Brazil. Thus, companies and company employees have to be members of their relevant National Confederation or trade union, respectively. This in turn results in compulsory membership fees.[35] Therefore, business associations and trade unions have a relatively stable and comparatively high level of income, in contrast to the situation in Argentina where only the trade unions can generate such an income. This in turn results in a high level of professionalization, which is important for the CNI and others to provide not only a lobbying capacity but also more importantly, technical advice on related trade issues and to contribute effectively in the negotiations with the government in regional economic fora related to trade issues, as seen in the case of the FEMA or the MEBF.[36]

The same is the case for the sectoral organizations in Brazil, such as the Associação Brasileira da Indústria Química (ABIQUIM), for example, which has similar to the Cámara de la Industria Química y Petroquímica (CIQyP) in Argentina a wide range of members, including many TNCs and also important local producers.

When analysing the structure of interest representation on the domestic level in Brazil, it is important to look at the Federação das Indústrias do Estado de São Paulo (FIESP), the federation representing the industrial sector of the state of São Paulo, the industrial heart land of Brazil.[37] Until the early 1990s, FIESP was considered the most influential of all the industrial federations in Brazil. It was considerably more powerful than the CNI, despite being a member of it. The reason for this lies in the industrial structure of Brazil that has evolved since the start of heavy industrialization and the introduction of policies designed to support ISI in the 1940s and 1950s. From the 1950s through to the 1980s, the industrial landscape of Brazil was dominated by three pillars; the government, the national industry and the TNCs already active in the country, such as the previously mentioned Volkswagen, Daimler Chrysler (then still Mercedes Benz), Ford and others. Moreover, the majority of Brazilian industrial capacity is historically concentrated in São Paulo, Minas Gerais in the North and the state of Paraña in the South.

However, as a result of the opening-up of the Brazilian market and the process of liberalization that started in the late 1980s under President Collor de Mello, the Brazilian industrial structure and with it the nature of the Brazilian business associations have changed fundamentally. For example, FIESP has lost some of its influence as a result of these changes, although it still represents ca. 40 per cent of the Brazilian GDP.

Nevertheless, the problem and the main criticism from the point of view of FIESP in relation to the CNI is that FIESP has only got one vote as part of the 27 federal states which form the CNI and each have one industrial sector association, too. As a consequence, the industrial strength of São Paulo state is mitigated by the voting pattern within the CNI. This in turn results in a CNI position, which might be less favourable to FIESP and the industrial centre of Brazil, because CNI has to accommodate various – sometimes conflicting – interests across the entire Brazilian industrial sector. This has been exacerbated by the increasing liberalization as a result of not only global but also regional pressures, and the resulting pressures to increase competitiveness in certain sectors of the industry.

However, it is important to mention that the problems CNI is confronted with in relation to developing a common position of the Brazilian industry on often-controversial issues related to international trade agreements, for example, are repeated on the level of the state federations, too. Increasingly, FIESP has had problems in producing a trade-off between its various members, because the interests of the textiles sector, for example, vary considerably from the interests of the machine equipment manufactures or the many TNCs represented in the state of São Paulo. Within the textiles sector, for instance, cotton producers are very efficient and competitive and are waiting for the markets to open-up for export. The part of the textile sector which produces artificial fibres, for example polyester, however, is still important in terms of the number of people it employs and its industrial capacity. However, FIESP's strong interest lies in protecting the market and not to liberalize it too soon. This is the area where FIESP still has considerable influence, as it is backed by industrial sectors.

Other areas of the industry, for example the cellulose producers, the shoe and leather manufacturers and parts of the chemical sector, are very competitive and use modern equipment and production methods. However, these sectors try to balance modernization and the pressure to open their markets with the fear that they might ultimately lose market share to foreign competition. The reason for this is the current fragmentation of, for example, the domestic market for wood pulp, which is dominated up to 85 per cent by American or American-owned companies. The remaining 15 per cent of the market are shared by ten Brazilian producers, who are highly competitive but fear being driven out of the market in the event of increased foreign competition.[38]

This problem of mediating between differing interests towards regionalization and globalization makes it in turn difficult for FIESP to construct an efficient strategy and policy representation for its members *vis à vis* the Brazilian government and in relation to FIESP's position in the CNI towards the CIM and the BBC. However, it does also provide FIESP with some important leverage and influence based on the interests of its members and the need to be engaged in ongoing trade discussion. This is because the Brazilian market was liberalized more slowly and much later than the Argentine one. As a result, the rapid sell-off of state-owned or inefficient and non-competitive industries that marked the first two years of Carlos Menem's presidency in Argentina in 1992/93 was not mirrored in Brazil under President Fernando Enrique Cardoso. As a consequence, FIESP still has political capacity to influence the ongoing liberalization of the Brazilian market, rather than just accepting it. This in turn makes it more relevant to its members than its counterparts in Argentina.[39]

As a consequence of these often conflicting and overlapping interests on the domestic level in Brazil in relation to industry sectors and their interests in processes of regionalization and globalization, since the mid-1990s organized business in the form of not only FIESP, the CNI but also ABIQUIM, for example, have moved to become more directly relevant to its members in terms of providing direct technical assistance, regular updates on legal and trade related matters and also in providing training for its members in these areas.[40]

In relation to this, it is important to note that up until the 1990s the Brazilian business associations in general were not prepared to meet the challenge of regional or international trade negotiations. CNI, for example, had no Trade Department, and all trade-related work was co-ordinated by the Economics Department. By contrast, FIESP had a department dedicated to trade issues but similar to CNI, had no capacity to provide analytical support in strategic terms. With the emerging Mercosur agenda in the late 1980s and early 1990s, and the upcoming FTAA debate, the board of CNI decided to create the International Integration Unit not only to provide technical support but also to have sufficient analytical capability to follow the trade-related negotiations and the process of liberalization in the region.[41]

After pressure from its members, CNI agreed to initiate the previously mentioned BBC in order to coordinate trade and integration policies properly and to yield more influence in the related negotiations and also in relation to the Brazilian government. The agenda has also been broadened towards areas such as intellectual property rights, competition policies and government procurement among others. This need to broaden the expertise of CNI has resulted in a considerable increase in capacity building capabilities on the side of the business associations in Brazil.[42]

Table 3.2 Business interest associations in Brazil (selected)

	National Level	Federal State-level	Sectoral	Foreign
Corporatist	Confederação Nacional da Indústria (CNI) Confederação Nacional de Comércio (CNC) National Confederation of Agriculture (CNA) National Confederation of Financial Institutions (CNFI)	Federação das Indústrias do Estado de São Paulo (FIESP)		*Auslandshandelskammern* – German Chamber of Commerce Abroad (AHK)
Private	Brazilian Business Coalition (BBC) *Consejo Empresario de America Latina* – Congress of Latin American Businessmen (CEAL) Associação de Comércio Exterior do Brasil (AEB) Instituto Estudos para o Desenvolviemento Industrial (IEDI) Pensamento Nacional de Bases Empresariais (PNBE)		Brazilian Chemical Industry Association (ABIQUIM) Associação Nacional dos Fabricantes de Veículos Automotores (ANFAVEA)	American Chamber of Commerce (AMCHAM)

3.1.3   Summary

The national level of interest representation in the main Mercosur countries has changed fundamentally as a result of the unfolding processes of globalization and regionalization since the late 1980s and early 1990s. After an initial lack of engagement in the processes of regionalization and regionalism, business associations have increasingly become effective in influencing these processes, as outlined above. As a result, they have also increased their technical expertise in relation to trade agreements in general, thus strengthening their influence and competence in engaging with increasingly complex trade negotiations.

Moreover, when comparing Argentina and Brazil, it is very interesting to note the shift that has taken place in Argentina away from traditional forms of interest representation towards newly formed business associations, because associations such as the UIA did not adapt sufficiently to the reality of a regionalized and increasingly globalized economy. In Brazil, by contrast, the system of compulsory funding introduced in the 1940s has ensured that the level of professionalization of the CNI, for instance, was always relatively high. However, mandatory membership has also helped the business associations to increase their trade-negotiating capacity and to develop departments dealing with strategic trade analysis, before their members were starting to question the benefits of compulsory funding. By doing so, CNI and others anticipated and acknowledged the need to adapt to regional and global shifts in interest representation, thus maintaining their relevance to the processes and regaining the momentum lost at the beginning of the Mercosur process.[43]

3.2   The regional level of interest representation in the Mercosur: Building structures under conditions of regionalization and globalization

As mentioned in the previous part of this chapter, organized business in the Mercosur was characterized by a considerable lack of interest to engage actively with the integration process form the outset, despite various government efforts to consult the business sector. As a result, regional cooperation between business associations was often very limited, too. Thus, the following part of the chapter will analyse how regional interest representation has evolved in the context of the Mercosur.

The chemical industry of the Mercosur is the only industrial sector that developed close linkages through its respective business associations prior to the negotiations between Argentina and Brazil, which resulted in the PICAB, and also before the launch of the Mercosur project. From the point of view of the chemical industry, the Mercosur as a *political* project came *after*, rather than before *a business-driven integration* in the Southern Cone region.[44] Thus, it is important to note that especially the Argentine and Brazilian chemical industry cooperated by the end of the 1980s on issues such as technical standards and product classification, thus forming the nucleus of what later would become the CIQUIM.[45] Interest representation within the chemical sector can be seen as a direct result of the regionalization and globalization of the Southern Cone market, caused by, first, regional interests of domestic companies and, second, also by the role played by TNCs acting globally, thus supporting and in some respect even creating new forms of interest representation.

In addition to the regional level of interest representation in the chemical sector, the global interest organization, the International Council of Chemical Associations (ICCA), has also played a key role in shaping regional interest representation. Because of European resistance to Brazil as an individual country joining the ICCA, the ICCA suggested that Argentina, Brazil, Uruguay and Paraguay should join as a Mercosur block in the form of CIQUIM, rather than as individual associations. This Mercosur identity on the global level of interest representation strengthens in turn the regional identity of the chemical sector. Thus, the membership of CIQUIM in the ICCA is an example for the newly emerging regional and global levels of interest representation.[46]

Another regional business association, which could also be called an interregional association, will be analysed in more detail in Chapter 5 is the MEBF. The MEBF was formed by senior company executives in 1998. It held its first two conferences in Rio de Janeiro, Brazil and Mainz, Germany, both in 1999. The MEBF was set-up as a direct response to the emerging FTA negotiations between the EU and the Mercosur. Its aim was to conclude a FTA agreement by end of 2003. Although the MEBF to a large extent relies on individual company executives on the European side, on the Mercosur side representation is to a large extent channelled through national peak associations such as the CNI or other lobby groups such as the Consejo Interamericano de Comercio y Producción (CICYP). Increasingly, European peak associations such as the Union of Industrial Employers' Confederation of Europe (UNICE) and also other national peak associations have started to become involved in the MEBF process as the negotiations enter their final stage. This growing momentum for the MEBF process and the constant business support for it can be directly linked to keeping the Mercosur-EU FTA negotiations alive, despite the political tensions within the Mercosur. This is the case as the MEBF is providing vital input into the trade negotiations and reaffirming the interest of the business community in the conclusion of a trade deal.[47]

Therefore, the MEBF process as an interregional business association is another example of newly formed modes of interest representation in the Mercosur region. The involvement of peak associations, other business associations and individual companies in this process underlines the changing nature of organized business interest representation. Over and above that, it also highlights the increasing importance of organized business in keeping the Mercosur alive and in pushing it forward in recent years.[48]

Another regional business association which has its roots in the economic integration process of the Southern Cone region is the CEAL. It was founded as a direct response to processes of regionalization and globalization. Initially set up by businessmen from Argentina and Brazil, the CEAL has grown significantly and now encompasses the whole of the Americas, including Mexico. As a result, the CEAL is engaged in both the Mercosur as well as the FTAA process. Moreover, the Brazilian part of the organization is also part of the BBC. It is therefore involved closely with the other national business associations in Brazil. In many ways, the CEAL is better explained as a virtual network for the largest companies and investors in the whole of Latin America, and it organizes itself as a regional lobby and interest representation, which is not limited to certain industrial or commercial sectors.

The interesting aspect about the CEAL is the fact that its lobbying activity is more or less pursued behind closed doors, at luncheons or dinners organized around a guest speaker or a certain topic. Members of the CEAL interact with politicians informally in these fora, rather than the more formal meetings of the MEBF or the *Foro Empresarial de las Americas*, which always coincides with the Ministerial Meeting of the Americas and is formally part of the FTAA process. Nevertheless, the CEAL is also involved in the MEBF process, for example, where it took part in the MEBF conference in May 2002 in Madrid.

Moreover, it is important to note CEAL's significant contribution in its attempt to drive the Mercosur process forward. It is pushing for, among other things, a stronger institutional framework for the Mercosur, a stronger and better-resourced Secretariat, a more powerful Secretary-General, common pension systems in the Southern Cone region, common labour laws and generally a comprehensive and consistent agenda for economic and social reform across Latin America. Thus, the CEAL has continuously lobbied for a deepening of the Mercosur project, because 'the costs of going back are far higher than the costs of going forward'.[49]

In addition to the CIM mentioned before, another more formally institutionalized forum for the participation of organized business, is the *Foro Consultivo Economico y Social* (FCES), created in 1994 by the Protocol of *Ouro Preto*.

The decision to create the FCES was mainly based on the perception by the Mercosur governments of the need to engage various civil society actors in the process of economic integration.[50] However, from speaking to various actors involved in the FCES, it is important to note that the role of the FCES, as a means to provide access to the intergovernmental structures of the Mercosur, has been and still is not that important. This is due to the lack of formal influence the FCES can exert, but more importantly by the way in which the business associations and trade unions represented in the FCES fail to constructively engage with each other to move the process forward and to come up with a coherent response *vis à vis* the Mercosur member states. As one interviewee described it, 'it is a big freezer. If you want to stop something, put it in [the FCES]'.[51] The role of the FCES has also been sidelined by the MEBF, essentially a business-driven and business-organized process outside the institutional structures of the Mercosur. As a consequence, the role of alternative business networks and alliances in respect of the emergence of a genuine regional economic space with reference to the Mercosur cannot be underestimated.

Nevertheless, it is important to note that there are considerable differences in how the FCES is perceived in the various member

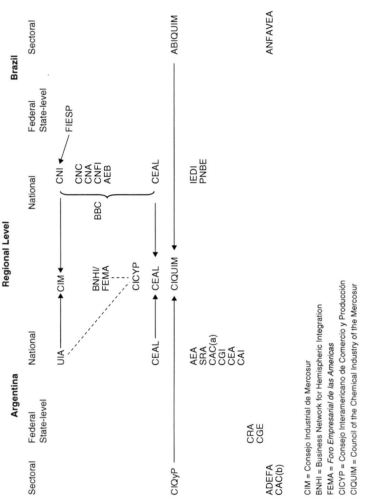

CIM = Consejo Industrial de Mercosur
BNHI = Business Network for Hemispheric Integration
FEMA = *Foro Empresarial de las Americas*
CICYP = Consejo Interamericano de Comercio y Producción
CIQUIM = Council of the Chemical Industry of the Mercosur

Figure 3.1 Overview of business interest associations on the national and regional level (selected).

states of the Mercosur. Whereas in Argentina and Uruguay the response to the usefulness of the FCES was predominantly negative or at least neutral, almost all interviewees in Brazil described the forum as useful in exchanging different views and in establishing links among the business associations of the various member states.[52] Thus, the following chapters will discuss these differences in more detail to shed light on these different perceptions.

Conclusion

As has been emphasized throughout this chapter, the emergence of the Mercosur as a political and economic reality has resulted in a fundamental shift in the way interests are represented on the domestic and on the regional level. This has been predated and later on accompanied by processes of internationalization and globalization, respectively, which are constitutive of the Mercosur as a political project aimed at locking in neo-liberal reforms in the region, particularly in Argentina.

On the domestic level established business association have either redefined and reorganized themselves to stay relevant in the increasingly regionalized and globalized markets of the Southern Cone, or they have seen their relative power and influence decline since the mid-1990s.

In addition to that, new forms of regional, trans-regional and interregional organized business representation have emerged in the form of the CIM, the CEAL and the MEBF, pushing for more cooperation and integration within the institutional framework of the Mercosur and beyond. Moreover, established regional business associations such as the CIQUIM or the CICYP have built forms of regional interest representation even *before* the foundation of the Mercosur or the signing of the PICAB.

This chapter has underlined the important change that has taken place in relation to domestic and regional interest representation in the Mercosur. Moreover, what has become clear is the fact that organized business is increasingly playing a larger role in pursuing regional integration in the Southern Cone region than is generally accepted in the literature. Especially since the economic crises of the late 1990s, the role of organized business on the domestic and the regional level, in its various forms has gradually become more important in facilitating processes of regionalization *and* regionalism within the Mercosur.

4
The Relationship between Domestic and Regional Organized Business Interests in the Mercosur: Conflict and Convergence

Introduction

The previous chapter has outlined in detail the changing nature of organized business in the Mercosur, both on the national and the regional level. Moreover, it has also introduced the main actors in this respect, to provide a 'gateway' to understanding the very complex nature of business interest representation in the Southern Cone and also to highlight both the adaptibility of some business organizations in contrast to the static nature of others.

Therefore, this chapter will take the analysis presented in Chapter 3 further, in the sense that it will focus on the conflicting as well as converging interests that exist between organized business on the national and the regional level. Empirically, as Chapter 3 has shown, the domestic and the regional arenas are the two levels of interest representation for the actors analysed in this book, as interest representation in the Southern Cone region has evolved significantly since the mid-1980s. More importantly, domestic interests have to be articulated on the regional level and *vice versa*, an issue which will be discussed in depth in this chapter.

The chapter is divided into three parts. The first part will look at the period from the mid-1980s until just before the launch of the Mercosur negotiations in 1989, mainly concentrating on the role played and the positions taken by domestic interests *before* the opening-up of the previously closed Southern Cone economies and explaining their resistance to it. The second part of the chapter will focus on the period from 1989 to 1995, when neo-liberal reforms, trade liberalization and regionalization started to transform the Mercosur economies, thus changing the perception of organized business interests and reshaping their involvement in the process. Finally, the third part will focus on the developments from the mid-1990s onwards, when new tensions and fault lines between the domestic and the regional level of interest representation in the Mercosur emerged. These in turn resulted ultimately in a strengthening of the role of organized business interests on the domestic and the regional level in the Mercosur.

Consequently, the central aim of this chapter is to present an empirical analysis of the role played by the various actors introduced in Chapter 3, in the relation to regional and global changes during the evolution of the Mercosur. It is important to note that by doing so this chapter will form the basis for Chapter 6, in which the empirical analysis presented in this chapter will be linked to the wider theoretical conceptualization of business interests in the Mercosur, to present a comprehensive theoretical and empirical analysis.

4.1 Transforming closed markets? Contextualizing the interests of domestic organized business

As mentioned in previous chapters, central to the understanding of domestic organized business interests from the mid-1980s until the launch of the Mercosur is the broader economic situation of the Southern Cone countries at that time. Coming out of a long period of Import Substituting Industries (ISI)-focused industrialization, combined with the occasional liberalization effort which was soon to be reversed, and a long history of military-led or military dominated authoritarian regimes, these economies faced the dual challenge of economic and political reform.

Thus, by the mid-1980s Argentina and Brazil, to focus on these two, were in a period of democratic transition while at the same time facing the need to deal with severe economic problems, notably low tax revenues, rising inflation, lack of job creation and an increasing fiscal deficit. It is, thus, important to look at the position of organized business on the national level prior to the inception of the Mercosur, but as mentioned before, with global and regional challenges emerging at the horizon at the outset of the 1990s.

As mentioned earlier, the economies of Argentina and Brazil as the Mercosur's most important members were dominated by the legacies of ISI and state-controlled companies and characterized by heavily protected industrial and commercial sectors. The former were, for example, not only public utilities or oil and steel-related companies (YPF in Argentina, e.g., or Petrobras in Brazil), but also financial institutions. The latter were sectors such as the automobile or the manufacturing sector.

From the beginning, domestic organized business was, to a large extent, opposed to any attempts to liberalize markets and to open them up to foreign capital investment at the same time. It is important to note that foreign capital investment has been part of ISI strategies in the chemical and the automobile sector, for example. Therefore, the resistance was not against foreign investment *per se*, but primarily against liberalizing markets to enable foreign capital to buy domestic companies, and against a reduction of tariff and non-tariff barriers. Under ISI-imposed conditions, TNCs often had to invest quite substantially, locally, as the high tariff and non-tariffs barriers in automobiles and electronics, for example, made importing goods prohibitively expensive.[1]

The main reason for the resistance of domestic business against FDI combined with unilateral trade liberalization in the case of Argentina was the memory of the ill-fated liberalization period between 1976 and 1981, which was marked by a drastic rise in imports due to trade liberalization from 1979 onwards. This policy shift marked a U-turn away from the ISI strategy of the past towards an attempt to liberalize the domestic market to achieve a more efficient economy and to reduce the role of the state in the economy. The main aim of this new economic policy was to reduce inflation through exchange rate controls, while at the same time liberalizing the interest rate. This in turn led to an overvalued *Peso*, because of the risk premium which was added to the interest rate due to the uncertainty in the financial markets, which in turn was caused by these policy changes. At the same time imports rose due to the strong *Peso*.[2]

In relation to the business sector in Argentina, it is important to note that as a result of the high interest rates and the rapid rise in imports, economic stagnation was endemic by the early 1980s. Moreover, external debt had increased significantly, as the high interest rates attracted foreign capital investment into the economy and thus resulted in a high level of external debt of the private sector. As a consequence of this 'debt crisis', organized business demanded the 'socialisation' of external debt, which in effect meant the nationalization of its accumulated debt. This happened through a so-called 'exchange-rate risk insurance' by 1982.[3] Consequently, it is important to point out that the closing of the Argentine economy in the early 1980s was largely due to macroeconomic restrictions imposed because of the debt crisis. Thus, protectionism was mostly used as an instrument of macroeconomic policy. This stands in sharp contrast to the use of protectionist policies under conditions of ISI in the 1960s and 1970s, for example.[4]

As a consequence, in the mid-1980s, attempts to open up the Argentine economy, for example, to more international competition were mainly understood by business actors as meaning trade liberalization, rather than a significant reduction of state activity in the economy or privatization of state-owned enterprises and public utilities. This partly explains their initial resistance to any liberalization programme.[5]

In Brazil, a strong commitment to the corporatist structure of the Brazilian state, which goes back to Getúlio Vargas' policy of an *Estado Novo* and continued under successive military regimes between 1964 and 1985, also created opposition towards liberalization programmes. The tight control of the corporate sector and the trade unions made possible by this corporatist structure enabled successive military governments to remain an important actor in the Brazilian economy by stifling opposition from within the business community to their economic policies.

However, this policy of corporatism combined with state-led development and a military regime came under pressure in the early 1980s, when the Brazilian trade unions and business federations, although the latter much slower than the former, started to gain more autonomy and started to strengthen their internal structures to become more democratic and, thus, more representative.[6]

Consequently, when democratization took place in the mid-1980s, domestic organized business interests were faced with domestic political, social and economic reforms. Moreover, the debt crisis, which spread from Mexico across most parts of Latin America in the 1980s, meant that access to external capital, used in the past to finance expensive state-led development projects not only in the 1960s and 1970s but also, in the case of Argentina, during the brief period of liberalization from 1976 until 1981, virtually dried up.

As a consequence, by the end of the 1980s, the first democratic administrations under Sarney in Brazil and Alfonsín in Argentina were faced with a deepening economic crisis, lack of capital and domestic resistance towards far-reaching economic and social reforms. In relation to this, it is important to mention that Alfonsín started to address the need for economic reform and a retrenchment of the state by freezing prices and wages, cutting public spending and introducing a new currency, the *Austral*, in June 1985 as part of the *Plan Austral*.[7] Towards the end of Alfonín's administration, there were also some attempts to privatize minority stakes in state-owned company, and by the 1988 trade liberalization was already under way.[8]

Support from business groups, however, was inconsistent and not very structured, as it was channelled through both formal channels and informal interest coalitions. Moreover, as discussed in Chapter 3, the Unión Industrial de Argentina (UIA) was dominated by a 'lowest common denominator approach' towards taking positions *vis à vis* government policies. The UIA was also split internally along the lines of Small and Medium-Sized Industries (SMI) and larger conglomerates such as Techint and Perez Companc, which complicated the situation further.[9]

In this context, it is important to remember the complex and contradictory history of organized business in Argentine politics. Historically, as Acuña argues,

> the structural characteristics of the Argentine economy and the nature of political struggle, particularly after 1955, fed intra-business conflict along the *entire* spectrum of business organisations.... This generated a pattern of permanent tensions horizontally (between sectors and branches) and vertically (within the same branch, between forward- and backward-linked producers).[10]

As such, the historical conflict between, primarily, the UIA and the Confederación General Económica Argentina (CGE), the latter representing regional business federations, product-specific and sub-sector associations, was linked to their respective positions within the Argentine political spectrum. Whereas 'the CGE was closely linked to Peronism and by the 1950s to certain sectors of the Radical Party', the UIA was favoured by consecutive military governments. As such, the UIA and CGE were repeatedly dissolved and reinstated, depending on the political climate at the time.[11]

It is important to note that the CGE lost its political influence after it was reinstated in 1983 when Argentina returned to civilian rule. The reason for this is the political shift away from state involvement in the economy towards gradual economic and structural reforms. These reforms started in the early 1980s, as will be discussed below, and stood in contrast to the high degree of state involvement in the economy favoured by the CGE, hence its loss of influence.[12] Over and above that, the economically disastrous effects of the last military government in Argentina, which was in power between 1976 and 1983, combined with extensive 'military intervention in its internal affairs', resulted in the UIA shifting its preference for military or authoritarian regimes towards the unfolding process of democratization.[13]

Argentina in the 1980s was marked by economic stagnation and a significant reduction in manufacturing output, a lack of policies to revive job creation at a time of rising unemployment, structural problems in the labour market and low levels of investment in the manufacturing industry. As a consequence, the economy did not manage to capitalize on the positive effects of the ISI period, that is, the building-up of an industrial base, the strengthening of infrastructure, and first and foremost, investment in knowledge and human resources.[14]

Combined with a difficult economic framework, as previously remarked, an agenda of comprehensive structural reform was virtually impossible to implement politically, and as noted earlier, it lacked the necessary support from organized business actors. In relation to this, it is important to point out that business actors had very different and often conflicting positions towards structural reforms. As López points out, 'privatisation was widely seen as desirable, especially by large firms. Labour reform was appreciated by all business organisations. Trade liberalisation, instead, was supported by a relatively small portion of the Argentine firms'.[15]

The situation in Brazil was comparable to the situation described in the previous paragraph in relation to Argentina. At the end of the 1970s and the beginning of the 1980s, the Brazilian industry was characterized

> by a high level of inter sectoral integration, diversified production and low specialisation, with marked inefficiencies of a technical and economic character, and low exposure (less than 10 per cent) to external competition.[16]

Moreover, there was much less willingness to liberalize imports while strengthening exports, a policy used by the Argentine government throughout the 1980s in an attempt to stimulate economic recovery and growth. In Brazil, the economy was highly protected through import quotas and high tariffs, making it eventually more sensitive to a potential liberalization of its economy.[17]

In addition to structural problems in the Argentine and Brazilian economy, hyper inflation was one of the main economic problems both countries tried to deal with unsuccessfully. The previously mentioned *Plan Austral* in Argentina and the *Plano Cruzado* in Brazil were both attempts to revive the domestic economy through the introduction of a new currency; however, both did not achieve their main aim, that is, to reduce inflation. The *Plano Cruzado*, introduced in February 1986, was almost identical to the *Plan Austral*, and imposed spending cuts, a price freeze, a new currency, public sector job cuts and started the privatization of the state sector. Nevertheless, as remarked above, inflation still spiralled out of control, as wage cuts could not be maintained due to electoral pressure. The servicing of the external debt for both countries was increasingly expensive, as the economic climate and with it the value of the *Austral* and the *Cruzado* came under pressure. Despite a growth in exports, tax revenues were not sufficient to finance the budgets, and the debt had to be refinanced through further borrowing, thus contributing to inflationary pressures. Thus, the deepening economic crisis in both countries resulted in general political uncertainty and increasing social tensions within the Argentine and Brazilian societies.[18]

> This situation, however, resulted in the fact that the governments in both countries faced similar conditions: on the one hand,

domestic opposition against policy reform or at least no consistent support for it by organized business and other societal groups, and, on the other hand, failed attempts to revive the economy through moderate economic and monetary reforms.[19]

In this context, it is important to note that domestic organized business in Argentina and Brazil was mostly against or at least ambivalent towards regional cooperation and integration, as remarked in Chapter 3. Even after the signing of the PICAB, the UIA and the Confederação National da Indústria (CNI), for example, were reluctant to support or actively engage with the integration process.[20]

Nevertheless, it is important to mention that on the sectoral level in Argentina and Brazil, especially the chemical and steel sector, bilateral coalitions emerged even before the PICAB, as a result of increasing cooperation in these sectors. As remarked previously, the chemical industry, for example, which will be analysed and discussed in depth in Chapter 5, explored regionalization well in advance of the politically inspired regionalist projects. Thus, in many ways this sectoral business support was central in strengthening the case for regional integration and could be credited with launching the idea of regional cooperation as such.[21]

Over and above that, it is important to note that Alfonsín and Sarney developed a close working relationship, because they faced similar challenges at home and saw similar policies fail in their respective countries, notably the *Plan Austral* and the *Plano Cruzado*. Thus, the *political* project of achieving domestic economic reform through the regionalization of the previously relatively closed and protected economies of the Southern Cone became a conclusive political rationale for the Argentine and Brazilian governments.[22] Consequently, the process of regionalization and regionalism that started with the PICAB was closely linked to presidential initiatives and agreements from the beginning, a characteristic which later on would become a problem for the Mercosur process as a whole, and contributed to the increased role of organized business interest in this context.

To summarize this part of the chapter, as outlined before, the domestic economic situation in the Southern Cone at the end of the 1980s was marked by economic and social instability, failed attempts to stabilize the markets and regain growth and a very mixed attitude of organized business actors towards further reform. Nevertheless, certain industrial sectors were actively involved in strengthening regional cooperation and in establishing a regional rather than a purely domestic framework for overcoming the economic problems of the so-called 'lost decade' in Latin America in general and the Southern Cone in particular. The launch of the PICAB marked a fundamental shift towards creating a regional space, initially pushed and developed by governments (regionalism), but nevertheless also envisaged by organized business, based on historical ties and previous cooperation (regionalization).[23] The next part of the chapter will take this analysis further, by focusing on the formation of the Mercosur until the mid-1990s, with an emphasis on how organized business, previously reluctant towards regionalization and regionalism, started to adapt to the changing regional framework. Thus, the following part will add the regional dimension to the analysis of the domestic level, to show how domestic and regional organized business interests started to conflict and converge.

4.2   Emerging realities and multiple challenges: Domestic and regional organized business interests in the Mercosur in the first half of the 1990s

The launch of the Mercosur as a regional project rather than a bilateral treaty between Argentina and Brazil coincided with the election of Carlos Saul Menem, as the new Argentine President in 1989, and Fernando Collor de Mello, as Brazilian President in 1990. In a time of economic crisis and widespread social unrest described earlier, both Presidents launched an ambitious liberalization programme.

   The Argentine President Menem, by contrast, was a member of the Peronist party, and as such supposedly closer to the interests of workers and the lower classes of the Argentine society.[24] Despite his working class credentials, Menem started to implement economic policies aimed at neo-liberal reform, a privatization of state-owned and state-controlled enterprises, a reduction of the bureaucracy, tight controls of the budget and a general retrenchment of the state. To define it more broadly, Menem set out to reform the Argentine political economy fundamentally, and to realign it with the broader economic changes demanded by what would later be called the 'Washington Consensus'. By doing so, Menem set out to form an alliance between the working class, a traditional supporter of

Peronism, the main Argentine domestic business interests and the more global neo-liberal reform agenda.[25]

Thus, Menem's economic reforms were based on liberalizing imports, wide-ranging privatizations and consequent deregulation of the financial markets in Argentina. Moreover, to bring inflation under control, Menem adopted the so-called *Plan de Convertibilidad* (Convertibility Plan) of Domingo Cavallo, as part of which the *Austral* was replaced by the *Peso*, but this time all the *Pesos* in circulation had to be backed by a similar number of *US Dollars* in form of central bank reserves. This was designed to avoid printing new money to finance public deficits and, more importantly, the newly found value of the *Peso* resulted in a gradual reduction of the average rate of inflation, which averaged in the later years of the *Plan de Convertibilidad* at 0.5 per cent, as money supply was severely restricted.[26]

In 1990 in Brazil, President Collor de Mello decided, in his first year in office, to abolish non-tariff barriers almost completely, thus opening-up the Brazilian market to unprecedented foreign competition virtually over night.[27] He reduced external tariffs to jump-start economic and structural reforms, imposed an austerity programme, froze business accounts and limited withdrawals from private bank accounts to reduce the money in circulation, thus attempting to bring inflation under control.[28] From 1990 to 1993, average tariff rates fell from 32.2 per cent to 14 per cent, a more than significant reduction and a measure of the rapid degree of trade liberalization to which the Brazilian economy was subjected. These reductions were intended to mark a break of the ISI policies and protected markets of the 1950s through to the 1980s, and were complemented by the abolishing of non-tariff barriers in 1990, as noted above, and further reduction in tariffs, with an average tariff of 12.4 per cent in December 2000.[29]

However, these measures, in turn, were also the main point of critique of Brazilian business in terms of their first exposure to international competition. At a time of hyperinflation, the business community did not feel able to compete, as they were also highly uncompetitive and, in many areas, inefficient. Thus, on the domestic level the increasing internationalization of the economy was mainly understood along these lines. As one interviewee explained,

> the fear of denationalisation was a major issue [in Brazil at the time, late 1980s early 1990s, combined with] concerns ... about

the capacity of the national companies to survive the waves of mergers and acquisitions by foreign capital that resulted from the necessity of being big to be able to deal with the opening of the economy and the increase of foreign investment.[30]

In relation to this, it is important to look at the specific nature and evolution of national interest representation in Brazil. Here, in contrast to Argentina, the corporatist structure of compulsory business interest representation in the form of national federations for industry, commerce and the banking sector on the federal and the state-level, combined with central wage bargaining between business federations and trade unions dating from the 1940s, has dominated the landscape of how business interests have been articulated and represented over time. At the end of the 1970s, however, a variety of independent and very diversified business associations outside the established corporatist structure emerged, mainly in the so-called 'modern' industries, that is, the automobile and auto parts sector, electronics, pharmaceuticals, the chemical sector and so on. The result of this emergence of independent associations was the creation of a dual structure of interest representation in Brazil, as most companies were members of their relevant compulsory federation *and* one of the newly founded business associations.[31,32]

It is important to note, however, that Brazilian business associations have always been relatively close to the state. This is particularly the case in relation to three main aspects of business government relationships. First, Brazilian business generally saw the state's role in relation to business mainly as a provider of subsidies, investment incentives and general support, in particular during the early 1980s.[33] The perceived need for active state support on the side of Brazilian business might be explained by the long history of corporatism and state-sponsored industrial policies in Brazil, much more than in other countries in the Southern Cone. This particular closeness of organized business interests and the state is very different from the difficult and often adversary relationship the UIA, for example, has experienced with the Argentine state, as mentioned in Chapter 3. Even the CEA and the *Fundación Invertir* in Argentina, which became important in supporting government polices on trade liberalization and privatization during the early years of Carlos Menem's presidency, were only important at a particular point in time and in relation to a specific set of policies.

Indeed this second reason for the closeness of the CNI to the Brazilian state is directly linked to the first one; CNI has an important role in administering the provision of certain social services for workers, again a legacy of Brazil's corporatist system of business-state relationships. Confederação National da Indústria is responsible, among other things, to run the *Serviço Nacional de Aprendizagem Industrial* (SENAI), an occupational training scheme for workers, the *Serviço Social da Indústria (SESI)*, a social support network covering education, health care, food provision and recreation for workers, and finally, the *Instituto Euvaldo Lodi* (IEL), which aims to accelerate cooperation between academic research and industry and also acts as some sort of think tank compiling related studies. As a consequence of these arrangements, CNI was closely integrated into the emerging corporatist structure of the Brazilian economy as part of Getúlio Vargas' *Estado Novo*. It is important to note, however, that CNI was not as closely regulated as the trade unions and the *Partido Trabalhista Brasileiro* (Brazilian Workers Party), which were both set up by the Brazilian government, and as such directly under the auspices of the government.[34]

The third reason for the historically close relationship between the Brazilian state and the leadership of CNI is the not well-known fact that the President of CNI is traditionally a member of the Brazilian Congress, either a Senator or a member of the House of Representatives. Only recently has a discussion emerged within the leadership of CNI whether this arrangement, which inevitably politicizes CNI's agenda and decision-making, should be changed to a mode of leadership selection which insures that the President of CNI is not a politician but a leading business representative.[35] Therefore, looking at it from a historical perspective warrants the claim that Brazilian organized business in the form of CNI has been quite successful in the 1930s and 1940s in pursuing its interests, and even from the 1960s onwards, the corporatist nature of Brazilian business interest representation ensured some degree of influence on the part of CNI.[36]

Form the mid-1980s, however, business interest representation in Brazil started to widen significantly beyond the corporatist arrangements established in the 1930s and 1940s. In this respect, it is important to note that despite the growth of voluntary business associations in Brazil since the 1960s, state corporatism under military rule with its associated high degree of control had ensured that this fragmentation would remain, thus weakening the political influence of organized business. Nevertheless, this started to change form the 1980s onwards, as noted above. As Weyland points out,

> since the early 1980s, Brazilian business has indeed increased its political activism and come to make demands on an ever wider range of issues. The private sector has not, however, been able to agree on a coherent development project for the country. The advent of civilian rule guaranteed the full autonomy of private sector organisations from government control.[37]

It is this coexistence of and the interplay between different forms of organized business interests that characterizes Brazilian business interest representation in the 1980s in particular. As Doctor explains further,

> in the 1980s, ... the industrial elite became more visible, often developed close links to the new technocracy and increased its activity in the legislature. The formal corporatist structure survived side-by-side with more pluralist organisation, corporatist networks co-existed with incipient policy networks and *meso* level neo-corporatist arrangements (depending on the sector).[38]

With the end of military rule in Brazil in 1985 and the related loosening of state control on the organizational structures of business interests, FIESP and to some extent, also CNI came under pressure to adapt to the changing political and economic landscape. The challenge came in the form of two new small-scale business association, the *Pensamento Nacional de Bases Empresariais* (PNBE) (established in 1987) and the *Instituto Estudos para o Desenvoliemento Industrial* (IEDI) (founded in 1989), which Klein describes as more comparable to think tanks than actual associations. Whereas the PNBE represents primarily small- and medium-sized companies from industry and commerce, the IEDI is an elite organization which started with only 45 of the most important companies of Brazilian industry as members. In addition to the PNBE and the IEDI, in 1983 the *Institutos Liberais* had been founded in Rio de Janeiro and later in São Paulo to promote the idea of a market economy and liberal economic values.[39]

The IEDI and the PNBE in particular were favoured by President Collor de Mello to limit the influence of FIESP.[40]

What is important to note however is the fact that the emergence of these new forms of interest representation was not perceived by the business community to be necessary to pressure the Brazilian government into liberalizing the economy and break-up protectionist structures. On the contrary, with the notable exception of the *Instituto Liberais*, the IEDI and the PNBE favoured a stronger and more active industrial policy by the state and a softer approach to liberalisation than the CNI or FIESP, for example. In 1990, FIESP published a policy paper in 1990 aimed at the newly elected government of President Collor de Mello entitled 'Livre para crescer', which advocated a reduction in tariffs and a general policy of reforming the Brazilian economy.[41] As such, the IEDI and the PNBE were in direct competition with FIESP. As Weyland notes, 'since 1987, ... [PNBE's] leaders have attacked the "oligarchy" of big business in FIESP and criticised its close connections to the state, which they see as an impediment to the forceful pursuit of private sector interests'.[42]

Following a similar line of argument, the IEDI, too, from the beginning called for a more balanced approach to trade liberalization which would also take into account wide-ranging reforms of the established corporatist system of managing business and labour combined with a reform of entrenched business structures. This would also include the setting-up of new institutionalized forms of managing the relationship between the government and organized business and also between capital and labour more generally. Combined with sustained investment in infrastructure such as telecommunications and transport, these measures would result in an internationally much more competitive Brazilian industry.[43]

Nevertheless, it is important to mention that such demands for a more active state by the IEDI and the PNBE were also combined with a general desire to reduce the tax burden on business in Brazil. In the 1990s, for example, when the Brazilian economy was gradually opened up to competition and trade was increasingly liberalized, the main complaints from business were related to high taxes, although the majority of the business community did not regard subsidies and investment incentives as sufficiently high to compete internationally. Thus, a demand for lower taxes was, paradoxically, combined with the desire to have access to more state support.[44]

From the mid-1990s onwards, however, IEDI and PNBE lost some of their influence. This was due to a wide range of changes taking place and opportunities missed. In 1994, for example, President Itamar Franco, who succeeded Collor, offered the Finance Ministry to IEDI's President Paulo Cunha, who in turn declined. Although this shows the high degree of relevance and to some extent also influence IEDI had at the time, its refusal to accept a position in government and to take responsibility for policy reforms led to the impression among some of its members and the media that its members were not fully committed to their cause.[45] Nevertheless, the membership of IEDI has stayed stable, although its overall profile in recent years has been relatively low.[46]

Despite these setbacks, the PNBE for example continues to be very active and has branched out with representations in several Brazilian states, representing primarily small- and medium-sized companies from both industry and commerce. Its stated aims of reforming the judicial system, strengthening civil society and encouraging citizenship and the involvement of citizens in local and regional decision-making and representation, for example, are still very relevant today, with the ongoing discussions about wide-ranging reforms of the judiciary and the possible break-up of the corporatist structure of interest representation in Brazil.[47] This last point is interesting, as the PNBE as well as the IEDI were founded in the late 1980s to provide a counterweight to the business interest representation in the form of FIESP, as previously mentioned.

It is important to note that the relative lack of profile of both organizations in relation to the Mercosur, for example, can be explained by the fact that PNBE and IEDI focus very much on developing new approaches to a national development strategy for Brazil, rather than a regional one, and as such the former President Collor de Mello aimed at including these new approaches into his policies, as remarked earlier. An example for this can be found in the early 1990s, when as a result of Collor de Mello's attempts to bring business, labour and the state together in an alternative forum to deal with domestic economic issues, the first sectoral accord in Brazil was signed, the so-called *câmara setorial* (sectoral chamber) for the automobile industry. This sectoral agreement marked the first successful attempt by the government to negotiate these kinds of agreements within a tripartite forum, in addition to the established corporatist structures and channels of interest representation. As Schneider points out,

> [the] *câmara setorial* (subsequently renewed several times) ... committed the government to reduce taxes; business to reduce profits and prices, maintain employment, and increase investment in restructuring the industry; and labour to wage moderation and no strikes.[48]

The main aim of these sectoral arrangements, which later also covered general topics such as taxation and increasing industrial competitiveness, was to help those sectors to adjust to the planned tariff reductions and generally to trade liberalization from the beginning of the 1990s onwards. In this respect, the *câmaras setoriais* were very much in line with the IEDI's and the PNBE's policies, aimed at softening the impact of trade liberalization measures. However, with the advent of the *Plano Real* from 1993 onwards, aimed at controlling government deficits and sustaining a stable Brazilian currency, the focus of the government as an important partner in the tripartite negotiations changed. As Doctor explains,

> the priority placed on macro-economic stability meant that industrial performance issues were focused on short-term trade policy concerns such as managing the trade balance and controlling prices rather than long-term strategic industrial policy planning.[49]

In relation to this, it is important to note that President Collor de Mello's intention was to break away from the established political elites and entrenched interests. As such, he was elected as an independent candidate with enough private wealth to be above corruption. Moreover, Collor de Mello wanted to be seen to be insulated from business interests in particular, to mark a shift from the Sarney government which had close business links and many of its ministers were government representatives.[50] Ironically, in 1992 Collor de Mello was impeached on charges of corruption and bribery. In the wake of this scandal a whole network of corruption at federal and state level in Brazil was uncovered. This marked a new starting point for dealing with the endemic corruption in Brazilian political life.[51] As will be mentioned later on with reference to Argentina, corruption in Brazil has been endemic for decades. As De Souza Martins notes,

> the tradition of political authority and the politics of favour have for a long time depended on being disguised behind the appearances and external trappings of a modern, contractual system. That is, patrimonial rule does not set itself up, in Brazilian tradition, as the rival of rational legal rule. On the contrary, it feeds off it and contaminates it.[52]

In the wider context of the research presented in this book, the transformation of Argentina and Brazil from ISI-dependent economies into liberal or neo-liberal economies focused on attracting FDI and achieving long-term economic growth, has important implications for the organization and articulation of organized business interests. In particular, FDI changed the nature of the domestic economies and of the emerging regional market, the Mercosur, fundamentally in the sense that domestic actors in terms of business interest articulation and representation were confronted with a new set of actors, either in the form of intra-Mercosur cross border investment or TNCs taking advantage of the large-scale privatization programme, first in Argentina and later in Brazil.

The increase in FDI was indeed more than significant. In Argentina, for example, a combination of privatization of state-owned or state-controlled companies combined with newly discovered monetary stability and the upcoming regional integration process with Brazil, resulted in an enormous influx of FDI.[53] In 1991, the year when the *Plano de Convertibilidad* came into force, foreign-owned companies represented only 25 per cent of the total sales of the 100 biggest companies operating in the Argentine market. In 2000, the year before Argentina was plunged into a severe financial crisis, this percentage had increased to roughly 50 per cent. Thus, the Argentine market was increasingly dominated by TNCs buying into the Argentine economy.[54]

Privatization included companies such as the national flag carrier, Aerolinas Argentinas, YPF, the former state petroleum company, Telefónica de Argentina and Empresa Nacional de Telecomunicaciones (ENTEL), the former state telecommunications monopolies, virtually all public utilities (electricity, water and gas distribution), Aeropuertos Argentina, the airport infrastructure provider, rail network providers, the Banco Unión Comercial e Industrial and the postal service, to name just a few. These privatizations were financed to a large part by foreign investors, although Argentine conglomerates also participated in the privatization process.[55]

Over and above that, FDI also played a role in a range of joint ventures, primarily in the financial services industry, the petroleum sector, commerce and infrastructure provision. Examples for this are Aceros Paraná, part of the metallurgic sector, which is a joint venture of Techint of Argentina and Chilean and Brazilian partners; a joint venture in natural gas transportation between Enron of the United States (now in liquidation) and the Argentine conglomerate Perez Companc, later bought by Petrobras of Brazil; Austral, the Argentine regional airline, bought by Merrill Lynch, Bankers Trust and the Spanish state-controlled investment fund SEPI; the Spanish bank BBVA bought Banco Francés; and Bansud was bought by BANAMEX of Mexico, to name just a few.[56] Overall, however, joint ventures were relatively uncommon in Argentina in the 1990s and local participation, if at all, was low. Moreover, primarily joint ventures took place in relations to the privatization of state-owned companies and were not very important in other sectors of the economy. Generally, Argentine partners sold their stake in those projects after a few years, rather than holding it as a long-term investment.[57]

It is important to mention these companies and joint ventures to highlight the importance of the privatization process and the enormous inflow of FDI in the 1990s in Argentina. Moreover, the willingness by TNCs and generally foreign investors to cooperate with Argentine companies and also by jointly financing these acquisitions marks a qualitative shift in terms of corporate strategies and transnational responses to the privatization process in Argentina, as it highlights the emerging transnationalization of the Argentine economy since the early 1990s.[58]

In Brazil, the unilateral tariff reductions that started under President Collor de Mello in 1990 were complemented in 1994 by the introduction of the *Plano Real* under the then Finance Minister Fernando Enrique Cardoso, who later became Brazil's President. Similar to the *Plan Austral*, the *Plano Real* was aimed at bringing inflation under control and improving the overall economic framework, to enable economic and social recovery, the refinancing of debt and also to regain access to foreign capital and capital investment. The *real* was initially fixed 1 to 1 against the *US Dollar*, although a small band for fluctuations was allowed. Thus, the plan closely resembled the Argentine strategy.

Similar to the Argentine economic programme, from 1990 onwards Brazil started to add an increasingly accelerated programme of privatizations of state-owned and state-controlled companies to the unilateral tariff reductions implemented under President de Mello and in addition to the increasing economic integration with Argentina.[59]

The privatization programme in Brazil also included a wide range of companies, for example, the telecommunications provider CIESP, Embraer and Petrobras, public utilities, for instance, the electricity provider Eletropaulo Metropolitan and CGI, CARD, the largest producer of iron ore in the world, steel maker CSN and the aircraft manufacturer Embraer. Between 1991 and 2002, Brazilian privatizations resulted in net gains of *US Dollar* 70.9 billion for the Brazilian government. In addition to that, privatizations on the state level resulted in net gains of *US Dollar* 34.7 billion.[60]

It is important to mention, however, that the privatization process in Argentina, in the way it was administered, was very different to the one in Brazil. In Argentina, with its highly personalized system of politics, privatizations were accompanied by a significant lack of accountability. Close associates of President Menem were often favoured when companies were privatized, or privatization terms modified after the bidding process had formally ended so the government could award the company to its preferred bidder. Certainly, this high level of discretionary decision-making enabled the Argentine government to conduct the privatization in a very short period of time in comparison to Brazil or Chile, for example.[61] Nonetheless, lack of accountability led to serious repercussions for the overall Argentine economy, as the significant net gains of the privatization process were either not accounted for or used for fiscal expansion.[62]

In Brazil, by contrast, privatization was overseen by the Brazilian Development Bank (BNDES) on both federal and state level. The proceeds were mainly used to reduce debt or reinvested.[63]

As a consequence, change has been twofold. On the one hand, reform took place to break away from the 'boom and bust' cycles of the past, where a few years of economic growth were quickly followed by rising fiscal deficits and increasing rates of inflation. On the other hand, privatization was also a means of ensuring additional revenue for the state in times of a lack of domestic and external credit.[64] Over and above that, privatization and a reduction in fiscal spending was accompanied by a comprehensive deregulation of foreign capital investment, ownership rules and regulations and the overall level of regulation of business and the economy by the state more generally.[65]

This discussion of FDI so far leads to an important point in relation to the overarching theme of this book, the role played by organized business interests in the Mercosur. When analysing the pattern of FDI investment and the level and areas of cooperation, it becomes clear that the domestic dimension of organized business interest representation was more and more complicated by the increasing importance, on the one hand, of TNCs and, on the other hand, of intra-regional investors in the domestic economy of Argentina and Brazil.

As noted in Chapter 3, especially TNCs felt themselves better represented by the American or German Chambers of Commerce, thus adding a competitive element to the interest representation on the domestic level in Argentina. Moreover, organized business represented by the UIA was less open to the newly favoured neo-liberal policies and the wide-ranging privatization process, as outlined before. Again, as discussed in Chapter 3, the CEA was specifically formed by parts of the Argentine industry which aimed to institutionalize business support for President Menem's reform process to counterbalance the UIA. In Brazil, too, the structure of organized business interest representation changed, with FIESP losing influence to rival organizations on the state level and to CNI at the federal level.[66]

To summarize very briefly, the analysis presented so far reflects the fundamental shift in the representation of organized business interests as a result of the opening-up of the Mercosur economies and the wider economic changes in the region. This shift became even more evident with the move of the Mercosur member states to create a customs union in 1995, thus strengthening regional economic integration further. This will be discussed in the next part of the chapter.

4.3   Conflict and convergence: 1995 to 2003

With the move of the Mercosur to become a customs union by 1995, the interest of organized business in the formulation and the evolution of the regional project increased significantly. The following part of this chapter will discuss how interest representation fundamentally changed at the national and regional level from the 1995 until 2002. This process of transformation started with the opening-up of the Southern Cone economies from the mid-1980s onwards, accelerated by the inception of the Mercosur in 1991 and culminated in 1995 when the customs union was formed.

Moreover, the previous discussion of the role played by FDI by bringing in new 'players' into the domestic and regional markets, and in creating new alliances between foreign and domestic companies, underlines the role played by the internationalization and regionalization of the Mercosur economies.

As previously mentioned, the increasing liberalization and internationalization within the Southern Cone region was primarily understood as trade liberalization by domestic companies. Thus, initially domestic business in Argentina, for example, was generally not aware of the fundamental challenges posed by increasing attempts to liberalize the economy and of the structural economic shifts taking place because of it.[67] Only later, as in the case of Brazil, domestic companies started to understand neo-liberal reform also as a means of acquiring new production techniques and of adopting total quality management and, consequently, increasing productivity across the business sector.[68]

As a consequence, this part of the chapter will first look at changes in Brazil from 1995 onwards and will then turn to Argentina.

In relation to Brazil, it is important to note that the main push towards privatizing the Brazilian economy started about five years later than it did in Argentina. In Brazil, the revenues from privatizations started to increase significantly from 1996 onwards, whereas in Argentina the process of privatization took place within a very short time frame of about two years and was more or less concluded by 1994, in relation to all-important industrial and commercial sectors.[69] Consequently, domestic economic reform in Brazil was also slower and with it the degree of FDI coming into the country, which only started to increase after important domestic reforms had taken place.[70] This in turn resulted in a slower adaptation of organized business interests in Brazil to the increasing internationalization and regionalization of the Brazilian economy.

From 1994 onwards, however, CNI and other domestic interest organizations increasingly became actively engaged with the regional and trans-regional trade negotiation process with reference to the Mercosur and the FTAA, respectively. As mentioned in Chapter 3, organized business in Brazil in the form of the CNI and the CNC, for example, is much better funded and has as a result much more technical expertise than in Argentina, for instance, due to compulsory funding through employer contributions. As such one could argue that Brazilian organized business was much more aware and, because of its high level of professionalization, much better equipped and prepared to adapt to regional and global issues.

Consequently, the CNI moved to organize the third *Foro Empresarial de las Americas* – Americas Business Forum (FEMA) in 1997 in Belo Horizonte. It initiated the BBC as a voluntary peak organization for the Brazilian business sector to strengthen its voice externally, in terms of trade negotiations and internally *vis à vis* the government. At the same time, the traditionally very strong FIESP came under pressure from above, as the CNI became increasingly focused on providing technical expertise and information for the industrial sector and thus strengthening its role; and also from below, as FIESP's representation of the interest of São Paulo state were increasingly challenged by other associations, which were more focused on sectoral rather than state-wide interests.[71]

It is important to note that in the case of Brazil sectoral organizations increasingly started to play a more prominent role, as trade negotiations in the FTAA and the Mercosur, for instance, affected commercial and industrial sectors rather than states.[72] Thus, the example of the chemical sector association ABIQUIM or the car manufacturers association ANFAVEA and their importance in their respective sectors underlines this. Especially ABIQUIM, ANFAVEA and sectoral associations from the electronics and the wood pulp sector were the most important and most coordinated sectors, as the number of companies in these industrial sectors is relatively small, thus making it easier to find a common negotiating position within the Mercosur and FTAA frameworks, in contrast to textiles, for instance. In addition to that, the shoe industry has increasingly tried with some success to come up with a common negotiating positions, also in response to cross-border investment taking place.[73]

Consequently, these sectors are characterized by a mix of Brazilian companies, TNCs and intra-Mercosur investment, the latter for example in the petroleum industry, where Petrobras bought the Argentine company Perez Companc or Repsol of Spain acquired YPF of Argentina in the early 1990s.

Thus, with the launch of the Mercosur as a customs union rather than a common market in 1995, organized business interests engaged significantly with the process, as outlined above. Moreover, even after the Brazilian devaluation in 1999, which resulted in widespread concerns in Argentina regarding a potential loss of its competitiveness, organized business in Argentina to a large extent did not support the former Argentine Minister of the Economy, Domingo Cavallo, who called for a suspension of the Mercosur in the aftermath of the devaluation and even contemplated turning it into a FTA rather than a customs union, so that Argentina could pursue a FTA with the US.[74]

For Brazil, the devaluation was necessary to relieve its economy from the pressure caused by the fixed exchange rate mechanism mentioned before. Moreover, the Asian crisis of 1997 and the Russian crisis of 1998 resulted in a much more sceptical assessment of the Brazilian economy and its domestic fiscal and economic policy pressures.[75]

Nevertheless, business in the other Mercosur member states demanded unilateral protection against anticipated 'cheap' Brazilian imports from their governments, as Argentina, for example, was not willing to end its currency peg to the *US Dollar* and to allow the *Peso* to float. After initial worries, however, the expected trade deficit for Argentina did not materialize.[76]

As the following part of this sub-chapter with reference to Argentina will show, the role and the transformation of organized business as an integral driving force in the Mercosur accelerated with the deepening economic crisis in Argentina. The resulting *political* lack of focus in relation to the future role of the Mercosur underlines the important role played by the business community in helping to sustain the regional project.

In Argentina, the UIA increasingly lost influence,[77] first to smaller and more specialized associations such as the CIQyP; and second to associations dominated by TNCs, for example ADEFA. As discussed in Chapter 3, business associations such as the CEA and the *Fundación Invertir* were founded to support, through lobbying and funding related research, the comprehensive privatization process under way in Argentina in 1991 and 1992.[78] Moreover, the UIA had to be pressured by the Argentine government to participate in the CIM, because it was worried that the divisions within the UIA would become public and to some extent paralyse the association in its position to the regional negotiations in the Mercosur, due to the very different interests of the various sectors of the Argentine industry. Thus, the early privatization process in Argentina also resulted in an early split of organized business interests, in the light of structural changes taking place on a regional level in relation to the Mercosur, and on a global level in terms of FDI and the reinsertion of the Southern Cone economies into the world markets.

As a consequence, by 1995 an increasing rift developed within the Argentine domestic business sector. On the one hand, Argentine companies such as Techint demanded more protection, as the Argentine market was subjected to increasing competition both from TNCs and also from other regional investors from Brazil and Chile, for example. On the other hand, TNCs, Argentine export-oriented companies such as Arcor, for example, and the increasing cross-border investment in the Mercosur, led to the emergence of another group of business actors, who actively supported closer cooperation and integration within the Mercosur and beyond.

The Consejo Interamericano de Comercio y Producción (CICYP), a virtual peak association encompassing all of the Americas, which also organizes the FEMA and is linked to the Business Network for Hemispheric Integration (BNHI), supports closer economic integration and policies aimed at attracting FDI. It is also closely engaged in the FTAA process, for example, and also advocates closer cooperation in terms of trade and investment.[79]

However, it is important to note the CICYP is a good example for the internal rift within the Argentine domestic business community. On the one hand, the UIA cannot agree on a common policy position because of the diverging interests of its members, thus reducing its own level on influence and participation in government policies over time. On the other hand, the UIA, the CAC and others are founding members of the CICYP, which supports and in many ways coordinates together with the BNHI regional policy issues, in particular in relation not only to the FTAA but also to the Mercosur.[80]

As a consequence, the analysis presented so far highlights the conflicting as well as converging interests that exits on the side of organized business in Argentina in relation to the Mercosur and the tensions this caused in terms of the effectiveness of business interests on government policies. With the previously mentioned devaluation of the Brazilian *real* in 1999, parts of the domestic business community advocated unilateral measures on the side of Argentina. However, as noted earlier, this policy was not supported by the majority of the Argentine business community due to the high degree of internationalization and regionalization already achieved by 1999.[81]

Moreover, as one interviewee stated, after the Argentine devaluation in the wake of the currency crisis in December 2001, which ended the link of the *Peso* to the *US Dollar*, nobody paid any attention to the Brazilian devaluation anymore, as the Argentine *Peso* fell to almost 3.9 *Peso* for 1 *US Dollar* on the foreign exchange markets. Combined with a related default on foreign currency denominated debt, a government decree converting all *US Dollar* denominated debt in Argentina into *Peso* and, in turn, all *US Dollar* deposits in Argentine banks into *Peso*, bringing about the economic and political collapse of the country, the Brazilian devaluation was no longer significant. Due to the devaluation, Argentina now had the competitive advantage in terms of exchange rates.[82]

On the positive side, Argentine exports regained competitiveness due to the forced devaluation and foreign companies, mostly from Brazil, started to invest in Argentina due to the devalued prices.[83] One example previously mentioned is the acquisition of the Argentine oil and gas conglomerate Perez Companc by Petrobras of Brazil.

Furthermore, the crisis in Argentina had an important effect on organized business in Argentina itself. In September 2002, the AEA was formed as a new peak organization for Argentine business, as discussed in Chapter 3. It was initiated by the CEA and the *Fundación Invertir* and gained rapid support from both 'national' companies such as Techint and Arcor, and also TNCs and companies owned by or with foreign participation such as IBM Argentina, Banco Rio, Droguería del Sud and Gas Natural Ban. At its inception, the main aim of the AEA was to stabilize the Argentine economy, to help to relaunch the IMF negotiations and to secure FDI. It also supported the nationalization of foreign debt to restart the Argentine economy and to inject fresh capital into the economy. This point is important both for domestic business to maintain its position and to reduce the threat of being taken over, but also for foreign-owned companies to avoid injecting fresh capital from abroad in the middle of a crisis.[84] In relation to this, it is interesting to note that the launch of a new peak association for Argentine business was discussed among business leaders in Argentina several months before it was formally set up, to push the UIA to become more open and to re-engage with the regional business interests.[85]

However, the decisions to go ahead with forming a new peak organization rather than reforming the existing one underlines the fundamental differences and points to the significant shift that has taken place in terms of a regionalization of domestic business interests under conditions of increasing global competition in Argentina.

As noted earlier, one of the main obstacles for an effective representation of business interests *vis à vis* governments in the Mercosur member states was the lack of professional lobbying capacity and a lack of focus on their members' needs. However, in Brazil for example, this has started to change in the wake of ongoing reforms in the way business associations, such as CNI and its affiliated federations in particular, try to push specific legislative proposals and institutional reform, as noted earlier. As Doctor argues,

> globalisation, market liberalisation and democratisation resulted not only in dismantling the developmentalist state and restructuring the production process, but also created new organisational imperatives for interest representation and business' articulation as a collective actor.[86]

Moreover, these changes have taken and are taking place within the wider context of long-term economic reform. Apart from a concentration of ownership through mergers and acquisitions within the Brazilian industry, productivity has improved significantly, as noted in previous chapters. The FDI has resulted in the internationalization of the majority of industrial sectors with foreign majority ownership becoming more and more important. Combined with

> the changing behaviour and improving performance of sectoral associations (for example, business associations upgraded their member services and switched away from their exclusive focus on the executive to also include the Congress in their lobbying activities).[87,88]

Since the mid-1990s, the Brazilian government, too, has shifted its policy preferences away from the policies advocated by the IEDI and the PNBE, for example, and towards policies aimed at managing gradual trade liberalization as such, rather than focusing primarily on industrial and social development, which explains the relatively low profile of both organizations on the national level in Brazil in recent years. In addition to that, a study prepared by CNI before the 2002 election as a consolidated version of policies favoured by Brazilian industry also advocates, among others, judicial reform, infrastructure investment, and most importantly, reforms to the system of business interest representation in Brazil.[89] As such, these policies are relatively close to those advocated by the IEDI, and to some extent, the PNBE mentioned before.

Over and above that, it is important to note that despite its focus on developing a national industrial development strategy for Brazil, in February 2003 IEDI published a working paper on the importance of the Mercosur and how it could be enhanced within the wider context of reforms and industrial policy in Brazil.[90] In this paper, IEDI advocates a whole range of policies which support the relaunch of the Mercosur as an integrationist project by the then newly elected Presidents of Brazil and Argentina, 'Lula' da Silva and Néstor Kirchner, respectively.[91] These policies included the strengthening of intra-Mercosur infrastructure to physically integrate the economies of its members more closely, something that has already started with various road-building projects and new cross-country electricity grids, the creation of a Mercosur Development Bank to finance projects aimed at strengthening integration, macro-economic policy coordination and the consequent implementation of Mercosur-related legislation. Following the IEDI paper, all of this should take place within the wider context of trade negotiations with NAFTA, the EU and within the context of the World Trade Organization (WTO) and the ongoing Doha round of trade talks.[92]

The policies advocated in this working paper not only mark the importance attributed to the Mercosur project by large Brazilian corporations, but it also underlines that the policies of fostering greater integration in the Mercosur find strong support within the business community.

Conclusion

The chapter analysed and discussed the wide-ranging changes that have taken place on both the domestic and the regional level in the Mercosur in relation to organized business interests. After outlining the domestic framework of Mercosur's two main economies, Argentina and Brazil, and its effect on organized domestic business interests in the 1980s, the chapter has then turned to show how these interests have been challenged and have been fundamentally altered by significant inflows of FDI, widespread privatization and structural reforms from the 1980s onwards. Consequently, the chapter has shown how regionalization, regionalism and, through TNCs, internationalization started to have a significant effect on organized business in the Mercosur, especially from the mid-1990s onwards. Moreover, what has become clear is the fact that initially conflicting domestic and regional business interests have increasingly been converging towards the regional market.

The CEAL, for example, founded in 1990, advocates closer regional integration, more cooperation, harmonization of pension and education, macro-economic coordination and policy reform to stabilize the Southern Cone economies and achieve sustainable development. Over and above that, the CEAL understands itself explicitly as an organization that brings together leading managers and Chief Operating Officers (CEOs) of domestic as well intra-regional companies, and TNCs. The CICYP, primarily engaged in the FTAA process, also favours more integration and cooperation across all of the Americas but has as its founding members the UIA and the CAC, for example, who represent it in Mercosur fora. The CIQUIM coordinates the interests of the chemical industry on a regional level and speaks for the Mercosur economies as a whole in the ICCA.

Moreover, the MEBF, also discussed in Chapter 3, is an example of the importance regional organized business has in supporting the EU-Mercosur FTA negotiations.

The launch of the AEA in Argentina, bringing together domestic companies as well as TNCs, underlines this shift towards, and increasing overlap between, the domestic and the regional arenas in terms of organized business interests in the Mercosur. In Brazil, the formation of a voluntary peak organization, the BBC, to engage comprehensively in regional and trans-regional trade negotiations also confirms this.

In all these organizations, domestic organized business interests conflict and converge with regional interests and global strategies, thus emphasizing that changes in the extent of business leadership, trade liberalization and regionalization have created different dynamics and highly complex relations at different points in time.

5
Two Case Studies of Interest Representation within Organized Business: The Chemical Industry in the Mercosur and the MEBF

Introduction

This mainly empirically focused chapter discusses and analyses two well-developed examples of the evolution of organized business interests in the Mercosur across countries and across time. Both the CIQUIM as well as the MEBF underline the importance and increasing relevance of these interests for the development and strengthening of the Mercosur as a regional integrationist project. By tracing the development of these two examples of organized business interests in the Southern Cone region, the chapter will aim to show two aspects regarding the evolution of these interests in the Mercosur, which are central to the main arguments advanced by this book.

First, in relation to the CIQUIM and the chemical industry sector of the Mercosur more generally, it will become clear in this chapter that the cooperation in this important industrial sector pre-dates the foundation of the Mercosur and even the PICAB itself. This is important as it contradicts to some extent the widely held view that cooperation between the business communities of the Mercosur member countries only emerged well after the signing of the PICAB and the formal launch of the Mercosur. In many ways, therefore, the chemical industry is a very special case, but it is nevertheless a very relevant and informative example for the effectiveness and the importance of organized business interests in the context of the Mercosur.

Second, it is a well documented fact that the Mercosur ran into political problems from the mid-1990s onwards, in particular in the wake of the Brazilian currency devaluation in 1999 and the related loss of competitiveness of Argentine exports to Brazil, as Argentina was still bound to the monetary constraints of its currency board and the related peg of the Argentine *Peso* to the *US Dollar*.

Consequently, many of the institutional reforms aimed at strengthening the Mercosur structure were not ratified or implemented, and member states unilaterally started to add products to the list of goods exempted under the so-called Common External Tariff (CET), originally designed as a corner stone of Mercosur's customs union. The overall political climate deteriorated considerably, and high-ranking Argentine officials such as the Minister of the Economy and architect of Argentina's currency board Domingo Cavallo publicly debated the possibility of a break-up of the Mercosur block for the first time. It is thus interesting that in 1998, shortly before the low point of Argentine–Brazilian economic relations, the MEBF was founded by a handful of companies with the aim to provide a business-driven initiative to launch negotiations between the Mercosur and the EU aimed at concluding an interregional Free Trade Agreement (FTA). This was underpinned by the launch of technical negotiations and working groups within the MEBF framework, providing much of the technical details and expertise needed to advance these negotiations.

This chapter is divided into two parts. First, it will focus on the emerging cooperation within the chemical industry of the Southern Cone region, culminating in the formation of the CIQUIM. Second, it will focus on the MEBF, which interestingly enough was originally initiated by the chemical sector of the EU, among others. Focusing on these two examples of organized business interests will show how these interests have been important in the evolution of the Mercosur and have helped in keeping the regional project on track in times of emerging political tensions between Mercosur's two biggest members, Argentina and Brazil. Over and above that, the chapter will also show how the increasing regionalization of the chemical industry has resulted in organizational change, and more importantly, it will highlight the emergence of the Mercosur region as a single investment area with increasing levels of intra-regional investment patterns. Processes of privatization and liberalization in the Southern Cone region have also facilitated this, as discussed in Chapter 4.

As a consequence, the theoretical framework employed by this book, connecting CPE and IPE, will also prove to be essential for under-standing and analysing the complex processes of change that have taken place since the early 1980s on both the domestic and the regional level. The repositioning and refocusing of the chemical industry in the region and the emergence of interregional business initiatives such as the MEBF, which in turn strengthen intra-regional coordination of business interests across countries and across sectors, underline the interplay of domestic, regional and to some extent global business interests. The focal point for these changes is the regional level, both from the point of view of domestic business interests as well as TNCs active in the Mercosur. Consequently, the following part of the chapter will focus on the CIQUIM, while the second part will focus on the MEBF to demonstrate and analyse the dynamics described above.

5.1 The CIQUIM: From regionalization to regionalism

What makes the chemical industry in the Mercosur an interesting object for the study of organized business interests and how these interests have changed across countries and over time is the fact that in the chemical sector two very important actors in the political economy of the Southern Cone region are present, probably even more so than in the often studied automobile sector.[1]

These actors are, first, national conglomerates and holdings, which have acquired a dominant status in their respective countries during the period of ISI in the 1960s and 1970s. More importantly, as these companies became increasingly competitive internationally, the chemical sector has seen a tendency to regionalize and internation-alize in line with the increasing regionalization, internationalization and globalization of the Mercosur economies.[2] Second, TNCs have also been substantially involved in the industrialization and the building-up of basic industries in Latin America from the 1950s onwards, as previously noted in Chapters 3 and 5.[3]

Taken together, this set of actors started to cooperate on a bi-national and, later on, on a regional level much earlier than the politically driven PICAB and the emerging Mercosur project.[4] To properly address the various actors and processes involved in the transformation of organized business in relation to the chemical industry in the Mercosur, the following subdivision will focus on the time period from the early 1980s until the mid 1990s. The second subdivision will then focus on the changes from the mid-1990s onwards, the difficulties of the Argentine chemical industry as a result of conflicting business interests after the devaluation of the Brazilian *Real* in 1999 and the corresponding changes in the interest representation of the chemical industry.

5.1.1 From regionalization to regionalism:
Emerging structures of interest representation
in the chemical industry

As noted earlier, the chemical industry in the Mercosur countries started to coordinate their policies much earlier than the politically driven bilateral and regional integration projects. Due to historical ties and previous cooperation, by the end of the 1980s, the Brazilian and Argentine chemical industry in particular were starting to cooperate in terms of product classification, standardization and so on.[5] Thus, economic cooperation in this case came before political decisions to attempt to create a common market and, later on, a customs union in the Southern Cone region.

This early cooperation was finally accepted by the governments of Brazil and Argentina as part of the PICAB and the launch of the Mercosur project later on. The CIQUIM subsequently institutionalized the existing cooperation in the chemical sector.[6]

In many ways, the chemical sector is a very good example of the structural changes that have accompanied the process of regionalization and the emergence of regional structures of interest representation. This took place alongside shifts in domestic interest representation and accompanied by an influx of FDI and the resulting internationalization and globalization of the Mercosur economies. Before going into the details of how the chemical industry was restructured in the early 1990s as a result of regional and global changes, it is important to give an overview about the main characteristics of this particular industrial sector.[7]

The chemical industry in Argentina, for example, emerged in the 1940s and started to develop fully by the 1950s, driven by small domestic plants of TNCs operating in the country at the time. Only from the 1960s onwards, chemical production expanded with the setting-up of two companies, Petroquímica General Mosconi (PGM) and Petroquímica Bahía Blanca (PBB). It is important to note that PGM and PBB were minority-owned by the Argentine state aimed at building-up a cluster of petrochemical companies to jump-start the Argentine petrochemical industry.

Brazil, by contrast, started out with larger chemical plant operations, due to its much larger domestic market, which were operated by TNCs and only smaller plants managed by the Brazilian state-owned oil company Petrobras. Only by the late 1960s, the Brazilian chemical industry emerged as an internationally competitive and technologically advanced sector, based on state-subsidized chemical industry operations clustered around Camacari in the federal state of Bahia and Triunfo in the state of Rio Grande de Sul. Generally, in both Argentina and Brazil, the chemical industry

> developed from broad and, in the Brazilian case, well-articulated state action, which included the definition of regulatory frameworks and the implementation of a combination of fiscal and credit stimuli and incentives. These sectoral policies developed under ISI and existed until the 1980s.[8]

The most important difference in the way the Argentine chemical industry was developed lies in the level of participation of TNCs in this process. In Argentina, national conglomerates emerged in the 1970s, to which TNCs licensed technologies and production techniques, but did not form strategic partnerships. In Brazil, by contrast, the country's corporatist system of interest mediation was successfully applied to the strategic development and strengthening of the domestic petrochemical sector. The so-called 'tripartite' model started to be implemented, which involved 'the participation of private capital, the state (through Petroquisa, the... [chemical industry] subsidiary of Petrobras) and foreign capital'.[9]

Consequently, FDI was used as a means to rapidly expand the capacity of the Brazilian chemical industry in line with growing domestic demand from the late 1960s onwards. This in turn resulted in a refocusing of FDI on the Brazilian manufacturing industry. As a consequence, FDI influx in the chemical and pharmaceuticals industry as a percentage of overall FDI inflows reached 18 per cent in 1976, 17 per cent in 1981 and 13 per cent in 1991 and 1995, reflecting the initial high levels on FDI in the early years of ISI.[10] Moreover, the chemical sector alone accounted for 12.8 per cent of all FDI in the 1995 census, with the entire industrial sector receiving 66.8 per cent of all FDI inflows over the same period.[11] By 2000, those figures declined to 5.9 per cent and 33.7 per cent, respectively.[12]

This also resulted in the fact that by 1992 a high percentage of sales of pharmaceuticals, plastics and rubber in the Brazilian market were produced by subsidiaries of TNCs, fertilizers were predominantly sold by domestic companies and tripartite companies dominated the market for petrochemicals. Moreover, the chemical and pharmaceuticals industrial sector accounted regularly for the highest percentage of all FDI inflows, underlining the overall importance of this sector for the Brazilian economy.[13]

In relation to this, it is important to point out that state involvement in the chemical and petrochemical industry in Brazil was largely restricted to the petrochemicals sector. State involvement in the tripartite companies was also not direct, but rather was exercised through Petrobras and Petroquisa. Moreover, a Brazilian private company and a foreign company were usually the majority shareholders, as each shareholder in a tripartite company would hold a third of the total shares.[14] Hence, tripartite companies were not state controlled.

Argentina, by contrast, witnessed a much lower lever of involvement in its domestic chemical industry by TNCs, despite some plants operated by TNCs in the 1950s and 1960s, aimed at primarily domestic consumption rather than the export market. From the 1970s onwards and through to the 1980s, production capacity by domestic companies increased significantly. This was achieved primarily by a high level of protection granted to the industry by the Argentine state. As Hasenclever, López and de Oliveira state,

> the state provided a substantial portion of the investment costs..., ensured favourable prices and the preferential provision of raw materials, protected the domestic market through tariff and non-tariff barriers, and regulated entry to the sector as a means of avoiding 'excessive' competition in the domestic market.[15]

As a result of this relatively closed market, Argentine conglomerates dominated the chemical industry in the country until the late 1980s, whereas the tripartite model in Brazil ensured the active participation of TNCs, last but not least in terms of technology transfer and competitiveness. Again, the significant size of the domestic Brazilian market also played a role in attracting FDI, but the tripartite regime created overall favourable condition for investment.[16]

By contrast, the overall level of mergers and acquisitions (M&A) with foreign participation in Argentina in relation to the petrochemical sector, for example, was extremely low with an average of 0.7 per cent of the total volume of M&A over the period 1990–1999. By contrast, during the same period the telecommunications sector accounted for 17.1 per cent of M&A activity, and the oil and gas exploitation sector saw the highest level of M&A transactions with an average of 33.5 per cent.[17] At the same time, however, the level of concentration in the Argentine industry increased considerably, although no reliable data exists on whether the high level of M&A activities has contributed to this trend. As Chudnovsky and López point out, in relation to the Argentine economy,

> the importance of large corporations has increased in a significant way in the 1990s.... In turn, in relevant sectors such as the iron and steel industry, the petrochemical industry and the banking sector one could observe an increase in the respective levels of concentration.[18]

It is important to note, however, that between 1994 and 1996 the chemical industry received 12.8 per cent of all FDI inflows into Argentina, making it the third largest recipient of FDI among major sectors of the Argentine industry.[19] These high levels of investment have clearly contributed to an increased capacity of the petrochemical industry in particular, as will be discussed later on.

5.1.2 Adapting to change: Interest representation and the chemical industry in the 1990s and beyond

What the chemical and petrochemical sectors of both countries had in common was the need to change their institutional and regulatory frameworks as well as the need to raise quality levels and technical expertise. This need arose during the 1980s and had accelerated considerably by the early 1990s. These fundamental changes took place in the context of, first, the increasing cooperation between ABIQUIM and CIQyP on matters such as standardization and technical norms from the 1980s onwards. This later resulted in the foundation of the CIQUIM.[20] Second, both business chambers started to promote actively changes within the chemical and petrochemical industry aimed at increasing the level of competitiveness and the overall quality of chemical and petrochemical products. As a consequence, the introduction of internationally recognized quality assurance schemes such as the by now well established ISO standards in relation to the overall management of the plants, environmental effects, social responsibility of companies and the quality level of products has been actively promoted by ABIQUIM and CIQyP since the early 1990s.[21]

What is important to note, however, is the fact that from the 1980s onwards, the chemical and petrochemical industry in the Mercosur has been driving the process of the Mercosur-wide harmonization of standards and norms in this sector. This is necessary for the domestic industries to be able to compete in the face of increasing internationalization and globalization of the Southern Cone economies, and also forms part of the membership of ABIQUIM and CIQyP in the ICCA through the CIQUIM.[22] Although this was mentioned before, it is important to keep in mind the fundamental changes within the chemical and petrochemical industry that have taken place in the region. The importance of TNCs in the chemical and petrochemical sectors in Argentina and Brazil alike underlines this and, consequently, strengthens the cooperation and integration process. Moreover, the standardization of norms in general is essential in creating a common market, as it forms the basis of product classification and so on. Consequently, the Mercosur Secretariat has gained new competences in monitoring and implementing those norms.[23] Over and above that, the wealth of expertise in terms of technical data and information specific to the chemical industry more generally has helped the CIQUIM and its members to be highly influential in relation to the design of policies and the drafting of laws aimed at the chemical sector.[24]

The level of cooperation in CIQUIM has inevitably increased since the early 1990s in line with the increasing regionalization of the Southern Cone economies. This cooperation was twofold.

First, the Mercosur is particularly beneficial for those parts of the chemical industry, which view the Southern Cone region as a single investment area covering Brazil, Argentina, Uruguay and Paraguay. Companies such as BASF, Dow Chemicals and others increasingly considered the Mercosur as a single investment area with a single market. The transfer of production lines from one Mercosur member state to another, similar to the automobile industry, makes economic sense in a single market.[25] This allows companies, among other things, to exploit the currency differentials between member states. The latter could of course be problematic, as mentioned before. By the end of the 1990s, Brazil's *Real* was a free floating currency whereas Argentina's *Peso* was pegged to the *US Dollar* until the end of 2001, with the well known consequences in terms of the relocation of companies from Argentina to Brazil due to lower production costs and higher export margins.

Second, the chemical industry in the Mercosur became a member of the ICCA through the CIQUIM rather than joining as individual countries, as European countries were reluctant to let Brazil join as a separate country.[26] Although the interviewee did not elaborate on the reasons for this, it becomes clear if one looks at the membership structure of the ICCA itself, where for example the North American Council of Chemical Associations and the European Chemical Industry Council represent North America and Europe, respectively. In a global business association such as the ICCA, it is by far easier to reach a consensus on an important issue, if regional blocks with an agreed consensus negotiate rather than individual countries.

Consequently, the regional identity of the chemical industry in the Mercosur was strengthened in line with the need to not only coordinate its policies in relation to Mercosur issues and policy proposals, but also in respect of interest representation on the global level. As noted in Chapter 3, this points to the emerging regional and global linkages in terms of how business interests are articulated on a regional and global level and how, as consequence, they are to some extent mutually re-enforcing.

Nevertheless, the chemical industry in the Mercosur has undergone fundamental changes since economic liberalization started in the early 1990s and the interplay of regionalization, internationalization and globalization with all its related dynamics started to unfold. As discussed in Chapter 4, similar to the automobile sector, the Brazilian chemical sector, for example, has a long history of TNC and MNC involvement dating back to policies in the 1950s and 1960s aimed at promoting ISI in heavily protected domestic markets. Consequently, when the domestic markets of the Mercosur economies were opened up in the early 1990s, competition increased and regional policies and strategies emerged as part of the new economic environment. The chemical and petrochemical industry within the region changed accordingly. Whereas in the case of Brazil, exports of industrial chemicals increased from US$ 1.925 billion in 1991 to US$ 3.05 billion in 2001, imports almost tripled from US$ 3.204 billion in 1991 to US$ 8.526 billion in 2001.[27] Similarly, exports of chemical products grew from 2.085 billion US$ in 1991 to 3.533 billion US$ in 2001, whereas imports of chemicals increased from 3.565 billion US$ in 1991 to 10.761 billion US$ by 2001. High levels of imports of chemical products and industrial chemicals point towards the growing domestic consumption in Brazil, which was to a large extent satisfied by importing chemical products from abroad rather than expanding and increasing production capacity in Brazil itself.[28]

This trend was even more pronounced in Argentina, where overall domestic production increased with a primary focus on exports within the Mercosur rather than on just producing for the domestic market. As a consequence, 41.3 per cent of Argentine petrochemical exports are sold into the regional market, whereas 33.5 per cent of Brazilian petrochemical exports are destined for the Mercosur market.[29]

It is important to note that the overall level of production in the chemical and petrochemical sector in both Argentina and Brazil from the early 1990s onwards has increased significantly in line with market opening and increased access to the world markets, in addition to a general tendency to restructure domestic markets and overhaul regulatory regimes. Argentina in particular has seen some large-scale investment by TNCs in the chemical and petrochemical industry, which explains the significant increases in exports to the Mercosur, and here primarily to Brazil. This expansion has been made possible by the comprehensive restructuring of the Argentine chemical and petrochemical industry in terms of vertical integration of production, investment in new equipment and, last but not least, the deregulation of the domestic market. The latter was particularly important, as it resulted in, first, a concentration of local suppliers and the emergence of a few large conglomerates such as Perez

Companc and YPF, now owned by the Spanish company Repsol and renamed as Repsol YPF. Second, large foreign investors such as Dow Chemicals were attracted to the Argentine market due to the Mercosur, and thus a guaranteed access to the Brazilian market without tariff restrictions. Both domestic and international producers also had in common either their access to raw materials essential for chemical and petrochemical production processes or access to the international capital markets to finance their investment. Examples for this are not only Perez Companc and Repsol YPF but also Dow Chemicals and BASF, respectively.

In relation to this, it is important to note that especially industrial chemical production is very capital-intensive, so access to relatively cheap capital is important, in particular in the light of the economic reforms and the related reduction in the availability of cheap loans from, for example, state-owned banks.[30] As a consequence, the Argentine market for chemicals and petrochemicals is today characterized by a mixture of local conglomerates and TNCs, which are focusing on the regional market and have also developed a significant international expertise.[31]

In the context of Brazil, however, it is worth mentioning that increased liberalization and the reduction in tariffs has resulted in reduced levels of capacity utilization in the Brazilian chemical and petrochemical industry. Whereas capacity utilization in industrial chemicals averaged 88 per cent in 1999, by 2001 this fell to 75 per cent of the total installed industrial capacity.[32] Consequently, capacity growth in the chemical and petrochemical industry has been significantly lowered and has also been affected by the large increase in imports noted above.

It is important to note, however, that some of the imported chemicals and petrochemicals are used to produce products for exports. Moreover, the increasing level of competition within the Brazilian domestic market has not resulted in a significant reduction in the market share of domestic companies. Rather, competition has helped to reduce prices and bring them more in line with the international market. This happened both in relation to chemical and petrochemical products as such, but also in relation to raw materials, for example petrochemical base products produced by the state-owned oil monopoly Petrobras. Nevertheless, capacity growth has slowed in line with reduced capacity utilization and has reduced considerably the expansion of the Brazilian chemical and petrochemical industry despite strong export growth to other Mercosur member states, as previously noted.[33]

As trade liberalization and the deregulation of the economy was pursued much slower in the context of Brazil, as discussed in Chapter 4, Brazil has not seen the same levels of internal restructuring as discussed earlier with reference to Argentina. Although the Brazilian chemical and petrochemical industry has focused successfully on maintaining and increasing its competitiveness from 1990 onwards, domestic consumption of petrochemical products, for instance, is still relatively low compared to other markets. For example, per capita consumption of plastics averages 100 kilos in the United States, 80 kilos in the EU, 30 kilos in Argentina, but only 22 kilos in Brazil.[34,35] Although this low level of consumption shows the potential for growth within the Brazilian markets, it also underlines at the same time the weakness of domestic consumption in Brazil.

This weakness is primarily caused by the enormous differences in income distribution among the Brazilian population. The widespread poverty and the state's inability to close the widening gap between the urban population on the one hand and the rural population on the other hand, have not been reduced by the privatizations pursued during the 1990s. As Skidmore and Smith point out with reference to the early 1990s and in the wake of the *Plano Real*,

> with the spectre of hyper-inflation gone, many poorer Brazilians could now buy consumer durables previously available only to the wealthy and the middle class. For much of the country, however, the familiar problems remained: hunger illiteracy, and ill health.[36]

Nevertheless, it is important to point out that also within the urban population of Brazil significant differences exist, which make the fight against poverty such an important political issue in the country. For example, only 50 per cent of the population in urban areas is connected to a sewage treatment system of some sort.[37] Driving through Rio de Janeiro with its *favellas*, as the run-down and extremely poor shanty towns in the city are known, which cover some of the sweeping hillsides amid the surrounding apartment blocks, increases the visibility of poverty in Brazil much more than in, say, Buenos Aires.[38] Even in Buenos Aires, however, where the poorer areas are primarily located in the suburbs of the city, the amount of people living below the poverty line has increased rapidly in the wake of the increasing economic problems since the end of the currency convertibility regime in December 2001.

It is important to mention, however, despite this relative weakness of the Brazilian market in particular, it is nevertheless considered an important investment area. Indeed, several TNCs in the chemical and petrochemical industry have relocated their research and development (R&D) activities to Brazil, rather than to Argentina, due to the size of its internal market and, simultaneously, its access to the wider Mercosur market.[39] Moreover, although the privatizations during the 1990s have not resulted in the same degree of deregulation than in Argentina, as remarked earlier, a concentration and restructuring of the ownership structure has taken place, with TNCs and local conglomerates acquiring privatized companies to strengthen their respective position within the domestic market and with a view towards the enlarged regional market in relation to the Mercosur.[40]

5.1.3 Summary: The 'logic of membership' and the 'logic of influence' – organized business interests in the chemical industry in the Mercosur

What is important to point out when summarizing the previous discussion of how the organizations and the organizational structures of the chemical industry of the Mercosur have evolved over time is the concept of the so-called 'logic of membership' and the 'logic of influence'. As Martinelli argues,

> the logic of membership requires an articulated organisational structure that is capable of adapting to fragmented and segmented interests. The logic of influence, by contrast, requires an organisational structure that is capable of providing a unified representation of business interests *vis à vis* institutional counterparts such as unions, government agencies, consumer associations and environmental lobbies.[41]

If one applies these two theoretical concepts to interest representation in the chemical industry in the Mercosur, then the logic of membership is high in relation to both ABIQUIM and CIQyP.

Both business interest organizations have managed to adapt to the changing environment within both their domestic markets and the wider regional and global context. The creation of the CIQUIM and the membership of the ICCA are both good indicators for this. Moreover, the chemical industry with its need for economies of scale for both domestic producers and TNCs has not encountered the same internal divisions as, for example, the UIA in Argentina or, to a much lesser extent, the CNI in Brazil. Of course, sectoral organizations tend to have a higher degree of homogeneity than multi-sector associations, especially in capital-intensive industries such as the chemical industry. Nevertheless, despite the need for domestic companies to adapt to a changing and much more competitive domestic environment in the late 1980s and early 1990s, the emergence of a regional economic space by the mid-1990s has not resulted in significant internal divisions. The comprehensive deregulation of the chemical industry in Argentina and the historically close cooperation between domestic producers, TNCs and the state under the tripartite regime in Brazil have both contributed to that. More importantly, however, the chemical sector can be considered a special but very relevant case, as it is highly internationalized and concentrated with relatively few members, in comparison to other industrial sectors. A similar case could be made for the steel sector, which can also be described as highly internationalized and integrated.[42]

Consequently, ABIQUIM and CIQyP have evolved into much more than simply lobbying organizations. They provide a wide variety of services for their members, ranging from training seminars on international trade to training in health and safety.[43] This is one aspect, which CNI and FIESP in Brazil have also focused on providing, to enhance the value of membership for their member companies.[44]

It is important to mention, however, that ABIQUIM and CIQyP in relation to their traditional lobbying role work both through their industrial federation, in the case of ABQIUIM this is the CNI, in the case of CIQyP this is the UIA. In addition to that, on the domestic level both interest organizations engage with their respective governments directly to influence legislation, which affects the chemical and petrochemical industry.[45]

As a consequence, the logic of influence in relation to the chemical sector can also be considered high, especially if one takes into account the high degree of coordination among the member associations in the CIQUIM and the ICCA. By achieving this high degree of consensus to present a common position *vis à vis* governments on the domestic and the regional level, the chemical industry in the Mercosur has successfully created various avenues of access to governments on all policy levels.[46] Moreover, the evolving linkages between interest representation on the domestic and the regional level that have emerged in the Mercosur underline the central argument of the book. These new forms of interest representation and coordination within domestic and regional policy arenas, also taking into account the newly emerging global linkages, can only be properly understood within a wider theoretical framework applying theories of both CPE, coming from below, and IPE, coming from above. The regional level, consequently, is the level of analysis where both theoretical concepts meet. The regionalization of interest representation in the chemical industry in the Mercosur, discussed in this part of the chapter, is an example for this.

Over and above that, the CIQyP, for example, is actively studying how the interaction between the public and private spheres of interest in Argentina can be redesigned to enhance the interaction of both sides in relation to trade policies. A consultation paper suggests, among other issues, a structured process aimed at producing results and overcoming differences among the actors involved; a formal negotiating structure, which nevertheless allows for flexibility if required by trade negotiations, for example; transparency; and clearly defined topics. Moreover, the paper calls for a wide range of actors to be involved in the negotiations, to achieve broad support for the outcome of trade negotiations. In addition to that, a law governing trade negotiations should be passed to ensure that the consultation process is adhered to.[47]

Consequently, this study is one example of how organized business interests are actively engaged in attempts to reshape and redefine the ways in which domestic interest representation and the formulation of public policy have to be adapted to respond to regional and global changes faced by the various actors involved. The following part of the chapter, focusing on the MEBF, will offer yet another example of the changing role and increasing importance of organized business in relation to supporting the evolution of the Mercosur and the strengthening of regionalism.

5.2   The MEBF: Regionalization as a supporting process for regionalism

As noted in the introduction of this chapter, the chemical industry, and in particular BASF of Germany with its long-standing business interests in Brazil, was one of the key sectors behind the push for a Mercosur-EU trade agreement.[48] As a consequence, Jürgen Strube, Chief Executive Officer (CEO) and Chairman of the Board of BASF until November 2003, Carlos Bulgheroni, Chairman of the Argentine Bridas Corporation, a company that specializes in oil and gas exploration and exploitation and Roberto Teixeira da Costa of Banco Sul América (Brazil) were among the first co-chairmen of the MEBF.[49] Thus, on the European side, the project was promoted primarily by the German chemical industry, on the Brazilian side, it was supported mainly by the banking sector but also by the Brazilian Ministry of Foreign Affairs and on the Argentine side, the energy sector was one of the main driving forces. Indeed, leadership for the MEBF on the side of the Mercosur was initially provided by Argentina through the Club Europa-Argentina.[50] The Club Europa-Argentina was founded in 1992 to promote economic ties between Argentina and the EU, thus attracting FDI and technology to the Argentine market.[51]

Initially envisaged in 1998, the MEBF was formally launched in 1999. It runs in tandem with the ongoing Mercosur-EU FTA talks, which also started in 1999 in time for the first EU, Latin America and the Caribbean Summit.[52,53] Consequently, the MEBF acts as an important input mechanism for the business community in relation to the official trade negotiations. Moreover, from the beginning the MEBF was designed as a business-driven lobby for the Mercosur-EU association agreement, to coordinate the responses of the EU and Mercosur business communities towards trade liberalization and issues such as market access, investment and privatization and also services. As such, in relation to the EU, the MEBF is the only business-driven lobby group for the Mercosur-EU association and is thus central for articulating the interests of organized business in the EU towards an agreement with the Mercosur.[54] The main aim of the organization is to negotiate among the business communities before presenting common positions to both the EU and Mercosur governments, thus facilitating the Mercosur-EU FTA negotiations. The strategy is thus similar to the one applied to intra-Mercosur negotiations by the chemical industry in relation to the CIQUIM. Over and above that, there are also strong similarities between the MEBF process and the Trans-Atlantic Business Dialogue (TABD), founded in 1995 by the EU Commission and the US State Department. The TABD has a bi-regional structure similar to the MEBF and represents CEOs of large US and European companies with a strong interest in transatlantic business relations. It provides high-level policy input to both the EU Commission and the US government on areas that affect transatlantic trade, such as standards and regulatory policy, business facilitation and SMEs.[55]

Overall, the MEBF is structured around a bi-regional structure, that is a co-chairman from both the Mercosur and the EU for the overall MEBF structure, and two co-chairmen from both regions for each of the three working groups, that is market access and market facilitation, investment, privatization and financial services and service, cooperation and special projects. Each of these working groups provide detailed proposals for their respective areas of expertise, and the work in both the Mercosur and the EU is also coordinated by a regional coordinator. The coordinators act as facilitators to ensure a timely preparation of proposals.

An initial problem of MEBF negotiations was the different expectations of both the European and the Mercosur business community in relation to how these negotiations should proceed. At the beginning of the MEBF process in 1998, the Mercosur members of the MEBF favoured a 'nothing is agreed until everything is agreed' approach to any Mercosur-EU trade agreement. The EU members of the MEBF, by contrast, favoured a gradual approach, which would yield results earlier and facilitate Mercosur-EU trade before the formal conclusion of a trade agreement. The negotiating position of the Mercosur members of the MEBF changed, however, and during the MEBF conference in Buenos Aires in December 2001, business facilitation measures were agreed on and, following the Madrid Summit of Heads of State and Government of the EU, Latin America and the Caribbean in May 2002, accepted and implemented by the Mercosur governments and the EU.[56] The MEBF process is thus following the same model of close interaction between business conferences and political summits, which was already discussed in Chapter 2 in relation to the FEMA and the related FTAA process.

The problems in relation to the MEBF and Mercosur-EU trade negotiations prior to 2001, mentioned above, could to some extent be attributed to unfolding economic crisis in the Southern Cone, in particular with reference to Brazil's currency devaluation in 1999 and the emerging monetary and fiscal crisis in Argentina, mentioned before.

As a consequence, the support of the business community and the ongoing MEBF negotiations and working papers were vital in keeping the Mercosur-EU trade agreement on track by providing important input into the negotiating process. In this respect, it is also important to mention that the EU Commission generally considers the involvement and the input of civil society groups (in addition to business, for example, human rights groups, labour unions and environmental groups) as important to justify pushing forward trade agreements such as the Mercosur-EU FTA. The MEBF also agreed in Madrid to aim to move the MEBF negotiating agenda to its third stage by initiating negotiations on the sectoral level. This will in turn enable the MEBF to engage in detailed negotiations to help speeding the Mercosur-EU FTA negotiations.[57] An exception to this is the chemical industry, which did not accept proposals for sectoral negotiations, but only agreed to share information with the European Chemical Industry Council (CEFIC) and to discuss business facilitation measures.[58]

The MEBF plenary meeting in Brasilia in 2003 not only reaffirmed the goals of the Madrid declaration, but has also underlined the need to overcome the issue of agriculture, which is one of the main stumbling blocks for reaching an agreement between the EU and the Mercosur, as noted earlier also in relation to the chemical industry.[59] The MEBF plenary meeting in Lisbon in October 2007 reaffirmed the commitment of the business sector to put pressure on the political actors on both sides to achieve a timely conclusion to the Mercosur-EU FTA negotiations.[60]

It is important to note, however, that the MEBF process was initially set up by only a handful of companies, as already mentioned in the introduction to this part of the chapter. Thus, the process was accompanied initially by a high degree of scepticism, as the MEBF was, first, not considered to be very relevant to a wide range of businesses due to the fact that formal negotiations for a Mercosur-EU FTA had not yet been decided on. Second, CNI and a large part of the organized business sector, in particular in Brazil, resisted the fact that only a few large corporations dominated the MEBF process, and that the Brazilian Foreign Ministry was involved in choosing Roberto Teixeira da Costa as the Brazilian representative. Although the CNI was asked to support the MEBF by the Brazilian government, its members were very reluctant to do so and openly complained about the lack of direct involvement of a broader range of companies in the MEBF process. This changed only when Mercosur-EU negotiations were formally launched at the end of 1999, and consequently the MEBF emerged as the main channel of business influence on the negotiating process. The Madrid summit in particular, where CNI for example was present with over fifty representatives, gradually changed the perception of the MEBF as a relatively closed process in comparison to the FTAA, for example, and Brazilian business, for instance, felt more comfortable participating in it.[61]

Nevertheless, the tensions within the Brazilian business community in relation to the initial phase of the MEBF underline the differences that exist generally between, on the one hand, companies and CNI staff focusing on the purely technical aspect of these agreements, and on the other hand individual CEOs of large corporations, who develop an economic as well as political interest in these projects. As such, the initial lack of transparency in the MEBF process is indicative of that.[62]

What is also interesting to compare in case of the MEBF is the very different nature of the key actors involved in the process. To begin with, in the EU the main driving force behind the MEBF from the start have been individual companies. Thus, on the European side individual companies with a strong interest in a Mercosur-EU trade agreement and with a high degree of investment in the Southern Cone region dominate the organization.[63] Examples for this are not only the above mentioned BASF, but also Siemens, Repsol YPF and the steel producing companies Arcelor and Corus.[64] In relation to this, it is interesting to mention that European companies tend to see the Mercosur as a destination for FDI in terms of building-up production, and using its internal market as a platform from which to export to other parts of Latin America and to North America. American companies, by contrast, tend to focus on the Mercosur primarily as an export market or have invested in the 1990s in infrastructure companies and service providers, for example in the telecommunications sector.[65]

On the side of the Mercosur, by contrast, the picture is more mixed. As noted earlier in this chapter, at the beginning of the MEBF process it was primarily driven by individual CEOs, and in many ways that is still its main difference in comparison to the FTAA, for example. In this instance, the MEBF is closer to the TABD, as discussed earlier, than the FTAA, as business associations are overall much more important in the FTAA than individual companies or CEOs.[66] From 2000 onwards business associations such as the CNI in Brazil have become more involved in the MEBF process due to its increased economic and political relevance, as remarked earlier.[67] Other regional business associations are also involved in the MEBF. One example for this is the CICYP, whose members are business associations throughout the Americas and which is also linked to the Business Network on Hemispheric Integration (BNHI), itself closely involved in the FTAA process through the FEMA. The CEAL, which is supported by individual businessmen, is also important in relation to the MEBF, as it attended the Madrid conference.[68] Moreover, the CEAL is also engaged in the FTAA process, again, similar to the CICYP and the BNHI, through the FEMA.[69]

Consequently, it is important to note that the speed of the negotiations in the MEBF is closely linked to the degree of progress made in the FTAA, last but not least because several of the actors and several of the areas sensitive in relation to the MEBF are also central to the FTAA process.[70] As such, the involvement of the CNI and the CICYP, for example, in both the MEBF and FTAA point to the closeness of the two processes and the overlapping interests of organized business in both projects. Over and above that, very often the same individuals present business interests in both the MEBF and the FTAA, creating an even closer relationship not simply in organizational terms but also in relation to ideas and issues discussed in both projects.[71,72]

Nevertheless, companies in the EU have also increasingly been successful in involving national peak associations in the individual EU member states and also on EU level, for example the *Bundesverband der Deutschen Industrie* (BDI), which supported the MEBF early on due to BASF's role in it, Confindustria of Italy and UNICE, respectively.[73]

In relation to this, it is interesting to note that the *Auslandshandelskammer* (AHK) São Paulo was also directly involved in preparations for the MEBF conference in Madrid in 2002, acting as the coordinating chamber for all AHKs in Brazil. If one adds to this the formation of a Mercosur Council of all the AHKs in the Mercosur member states, then this underlines the importance attributed to the Mercosur as an investment area by German commerce and industry generally.[74]

Nevertheless, it is important to mention that the involvement of the AHKs in the MEBF process not only underlines the interest of German companies in the wider Mercosur market, but it also highlights the role of the AHKs in representing domestic business interests. The AHKs, similar to the American Chambers of Commerce (AMCHAM), also represent a wide range of domestic companies. These companies are not necessarily export-oriented companies or companies with a special interest in, say, the German or American Market. Rather, they come from all sectors of the industry and use the professional services offered by the chambers, in particular in relation to the network of AHKs in the Southern Cone. As a result of the increasing cross-country investment that has taken place in the wake of the Mercosur, Argentine companies, for example, have invested in Brazil, either in the form of production facilities or in the form of trading companies. In turn, these corporations are then interested in being represented and obtaining advice and services in Brazil, something the AHKs or also AmChams in the region can offer within the same organizational framework. As a consequence, not just TNCs and domestic conglomerates and holding companies are members of the chambers, but also a large number of Small and Medium-Sized Enterprises (SMEs).[75]

All of these factors taken together make the involvement of the AHKs in the MEBF process a logical conclusion, as they represent the various domestic and foreign companies as well as companies involved in cross-border investment.

Conclusion

The two case studies analysed and discussed in this chapter provide the empirical evidence for the theoretical framework employed in this book, the synthesis of CPE and IPE. Consequently, the main purpose of this conclusion is to bring the empirical threads presented in this chapter together with the theoretical threads and hypotheses presented in Chapter 2.

First, empirically this chapter has demonstrated the importance of organized business interests for the evolution of the Mercosur.

Starting off with the chemical industry, it has become clear that cooperation between national business associations, which pre-dated the politically driven integration process in the Southern Cone, has over time been institutionalized and strengthened the capacity of the chemical industry to influence policy-making processes through the CIQUIM, both on the domestic and, later on, also on the emerging regional level. This cooperation was enhanced by both regional dynamics and by global currents, in particular the membership of the ICCA, to which national associations could not become individual members but only collectively through the CIQUIM. The cooperation on the regional level has resulted in lobbying on both the national level, either directly by ABQUIM and the CIQyP or indirectly through CNI and the UIA respectively, or on the regional level through the CIQUIM.

In this regard it is also important to note that the high degree of cooperation in the chemical industry in the Mercosur has not only strengthened the sector's capacity to influence the policy-making process, as mentioned above, but has also enhanced the usefulness of organized business for policy makers on the domestic level by providing, for example, leadership on the design and implementation of Mercosur-wide industrial standards and technical norms, as discussed earlier in this chapter.

Second, the MEBF has highlighted a similarly increasing relevance of organized business in relation to the policy-making process within the Mercosur, primarily in relation to an interregional FTA with the EU. Apart from this, the MEBF was also the main vehicle to draw the business community into the trade negotiation process and its membership was successfully broadened after it increased its credibility in the eyes of the business community, particularly in Brazil, as discussed earlier in the chapter. By doing so, the MEBF provided a highly useful input mechanism for organized business into the Mercosur-EU negotiations and has over and above that managed to maintain the *economic* rational for a Mercosur-EU FTA despite the political turmoil in the region in the aftermath of the Brazilian devaluation followed by the crisis in Argentina.

Theoretically, both the case study of the chemical industry in the Mercosur and the MEBF have demonstrated the need to connect CPE and IPE to explain the evolution of the regional level of interest representation in the Mercosur and its linkages with both the national and the global level of governance. Namely, from CPE the 'varieties of capitalism' debate and the discussion of interest group formation on the national level, and from IPE theories of regionalization, regionalism and globalization.

In particular, new and evolving avenues of access and consultation mechanisms on the regional, interregional and global level have supplemented the reconfiguration of channels of access to the policy-making process on the domestic level. Taken together, as emphasized in Chapter 2, only a synthesis of CPE, coming from below, and IPE, coming from above, is able to capture adequately the regional level of governance in the Mercosur.

To summarize, this chapter adds two very relevant and inform-ative case studies to the empirical analysis presented in this book, by looking in detail at the chemical industry in the Mercosur and the role played by organized business in the formation and evolution of the Mercosur-EU FTA through the MEBF. As such, it demonstrates how organized business interests have been able to influence to a degree, and at different points in time drive and support, processes of regionalism through regionalization.

In this respect, it is important to remember that in the case of the chemical industry, cross-country cooperation emerged even before the politically driven PICAB and the formal launch of the negotiations to create the Mercosur.

Over and above that, this chapter has also pointed out the multitude of actors that exist in relation to organized business interests in the Southern Cone, as emphasized in Chapters 3 and 4. This diversity of actors, the variety of avenues of access for business associations, indi-viduals and corporations for shaping trade negotiations, for example in relation to the CIQUIM and the MEBF, underlines this.

Both the chemical industry in the Mercosur and the MEBF consequently provide very useful examples of how established business associations can transform and refocus themselves and how new forms of interest representation have emerged, respectively. This has happened in response to changes in the political economy on both the national and the regional level as a result of processes of internationalization, regionalization and globalization.

Overall, therefore, a picture has emerged which clearly supports the relevance and increasing importance of organized business within the context of the evolution of the Mercosur. The linkages between the domestic and the regional level, both in the case of the chemical industry and the MEBF, also empirically support the theoretical framework employed by this book. Namely, emphasizing the need to connect both CPE and IPE to provide an adequate theoretical context for the conducted research. Moreover, the example of the MEBF also underlines the emerging interregional dimension of organized business interests.

6
The Regionalization of Organized Business Interests in the Mercosur: A Theoretical and Empirical Analysis

Introduction

Organized Business interests in the Mercosur have undergone fundamental changes since the late 1980s as a result of various economic and political reforms in the member countries. In addition to that, the increasing internationalization, globalization and regionalization of these economies have also resulted in important changes in the way business interests are represented and, over and above that, on what level. As such, the domestic framework of political and economic analyses has been firmly linked to new regional and global frameworks, which all interact with each other and which affect, differently at different points in time, the way organized business interests are articulated. One of the main findings in this respect is that these interests, their shape, extent and influence vary greatly across countries and across time. As such, organized business interests on the domestic level have undergone many changes, while at the same time interest representation on the regional level has been strengthened or at least has increasingly gained in importance.

The previous three chapters have discussed the empirical evidence for the comprehensive changes that have taken place on the domestic and the regional level in relation to organized business interests in the Mercosur. They have highlighted how the regional level has increased in importance, and as a result organized business interests have realigned themselves to reflect this reorientation, have lost influence on the domestic level as a result of not responding to these changes or new forms of interest representation on the domestic and the regional level have been created. As a consequence, the landscape of organized business representation has been fundamentally altered both on the domestic and the regional level. With it, organized business interests have been strengthened to become increasingly important in influencing the governance agenda with reference to the ongoing evolution of the Mercosur. Over and above that, the FTAA process and the MEBF negotiations have increased the outside pressure on organized business to present a coherent voice within the Mercosur framework.[1]

The central purpose of this chapter is to bring together the empirical analysis presented so far with the theoretical framework introduced in Chapter 2. By doing so, the chapter will clearly position the empirical research within the wider theoretical context of CPE and IPE. It will show how important a theoretical framework is which combines the domestic as well as the regional level, by taking into account the broader implications of internationalization, globalization, regionalization and neo-liberal reform in the Southern Cone region. Only by bringing together both theoretical lines of analysis, one can adequately discuss the role played by organized business interests in the evolution of the Mercosur, and also account for the fundamental changes that have taken place with regard to these interests on both the domestic and the regional level. Moreover, as Chapter 4 has shown, domestic and regional forms of interest representation are inextricably linked.

Rather than following a chronological chapter structure similar to Chapter 4, this chapter will be structured around three central themes to draw on the empirical material to question the various theoretical approaches introduced in Chapter 2. These central themes are the domestic arena, the global arena and the regional arena. The chapter will clearly address the strengths as well as the limitations of each theoretical approach discussed in the respective theme. This will reaffirm the need to adopt a theoretical framework that encompasses both CPE and IPE theories in the analysis of organized business in the Mercosur. This is emphasized throughout the book.

6.1 The domestic arena

The discussion of CPE theories in Chapter 2 started with an analysis of the 'varieties of capitalism' debate, with which CPE is commonly associated. This debate is very relevant for the research presented in the previous chapters as we have seen different models of capitalism and interest representation develop in both Argentina and Brazil. In particular, this difference has given rise to variations in the organization and levels of influence of organized business interests, as discussed in detail in Chapter 4.

Consequently, the emphasis in CPE in the 1970s and early 1980s on the revival of neo-corporatist arrangements in Western Europe provides important theoretical insights into the development of interest representation in Brazil. Importantly, although reforms to the corporatist system of interest representation are debated and indeed supported by the CNI as discussed in Chapter 4, these attempts have so far yielded no tangible results. Over and above that, as the discussions in Chapters 3 and 4 have also demonstrated, organized business interests in the Mercosur can only be understood in the context of their domestic evolution and the structural changes that have taken place on the domestic level since the mid-1980s, first as a result of the internationalization of the Mercosur economies and later as a result of the increasing regionalization and globalization.

Of equal importance, however, are the ways in which changes in the international political economy from the mid-1980s onwards have interacted with these interests. This has resulted in a fundamental shift in the way business interests are represented in the Mercosur on both the national and the newly emerging regional level.

In this context, the well-established distinction between insider and outsider groups as a possible way of explaining the influence exerted by some groups in the context of the Mercosur, but not by others, provides a useful starting point for the study of the domestic level of interest representation. Although, as remarked in Chapter 2, the insider/outsider model is not strictly related to CPE and is equally valid in relation to lobbying on the regional and supra-regional level, it nevertheless will be discussed in this part of the chapter, because it is most applicable to the domestic level of interest representation in the context of the Mercosur.

Looking at the empirical evidence assembled so far, it has become clear that despite Pages' criticism of the insider/outsider analysis as being 'at best an oversimplification, and at worst simply misleading', in the context of interest group articulation in the Mercosur the distinction between insiders and outsiders provides a useful starting point for analysis.[2]

In Argentina during the 1980s, for example, business associations such as the UIA, the CAC and in particular sectoral associations such as the CIQyP were consulted on the PICAB and the related integration measures by the government, thus making them clear insiders in the negotiation process.[3] The same was the case in Brazil, where the previously noted closeness of the Sarney government to Brazilian business circles, in particular from São Paulo, and the fact that several business leaders were actually government ministers in the Sarney administration ensured business participation in the PICAB, albeit indirectly and with somewhat limited effect.[4]

However, in this respect it is important to remember that organized business across the Mercosur was generally not interested in regional integration or at least assumed it would simply be a political project without any 'real' economic dimension to it. Moreover, when business associations in Argentina and Brazil realized that the Mercosur process was generating very 'real' and tangible economic challenges and thus generated complex issues for these association to deal with, they attempted to engage with the process. However, this was mainly aimed at securing exemptions from trade-liberalization measures between the Mercosur members, rather than being actively involved in the integration process or trying to actively shape its direction.[5]

In this respect, it is important to note that governments, too, were interested in conducting consultations with the associations and other interested business groups. When the trade-liberalization negotiations affected the chemical and automobile sector, for example, and the government required technical expertise and specific industrial and sectoral knowledge in this respect, this led to the involvement of business associations in these areas.[6] As a consequence, one of the main aspects of the insider/outsider distinction is the important role played by state actors in choosing their preferred 'partners'. From the perspective of organized business interests it is reaffirmed in the context of the Mercosur and is to a large extent still valid today.[7]

This brings us to another important element of government/ business relations, the structural power inherent in business actions. Following Lindblom, what is important to state is that in addition to the changing nature of business representation aimed at gaining or regaining influence on government policies, organized business interests exercise a certain degree of structural power.[8] As Haggard, Maxfield and Schneider point out, 'any discussion of business-government relations must bear in mind the structural power of capital and remember that business need not be organised to exercise influence'.[9]

Essentially, therefore, if one relates this argument to the analyses and observations presented in this book so far, the structural power of capital results in a basic level of influence for organized business that exists independently of any variations in the extent of the organization of these interests or their direct or indirect access to the state, for example. What is essential for the definition of structural power if applied to the study of organized business interests, in particular with reference to corporatist and so called private-interest government structures, is the assertion that 'capital as a social relation, depends on the power of the state to define, shape and be part of a regime of accumulation'.[10,11] As Gill and Law argue,

> capital as a social relation ... [is] the contrast between those with a substantial or even privileged ownership, control or access to both financial and/or physical assets, in contrast to the bulk of the remainder of society (most of labour and their dependents).[12]

Following this neo-Gramscian understanding of the power of capital, organized business interests have a certain and underlying degree of influence *per se*, simply because of the fact that they can withhold investment or invest abroad rather than at home. In this respect, governments have to build a relation of trust or at least demonstrate some degree of reliability for business to sustain a viable economic environment for investment.[13]

Empirically, if one applies this to Brazil, then what becomes obvious is the ability of the government, through a corporatist system virtually unchanged since the 1940s, to dominate at least formally the decision-making process and structural organization of business. On the other hand, the state did not prevent business interests from flourishing outside of the official structure by allowing the setting-up of entities such as the IEDI and the PNBE and, at times, attempting to draw them into the policy-making process, as discussed earlier. To some extent, this was of course in the interest of the Brazilian state, as a fragmented business sector is less able to promote its interests, thus enabling the state to sideline it more easily than would otherwise be the case. Thus, as we have seen in Western Europe, organizational coherence strengthens organized business as a force to be reckoned with considerably.[14] On the other hand, as Evans notes, 'disorganised states lead to disorganised business communities and vice versa. Investors flounder in the absence of coherent public policy. Without an organised business community, even an organised state cannot promote structural change'.[15] An example for this would be Argentina, where the government pushed through privatization, for example, with a minimum of transparency and accountability, thus emphasizing individual access of interested companies or individuals and consequently a weakening of organized business, over a strengthening of a reliable and predictable government strategy in this regard.

In Brazil, by contrast, the government has been very successful in shaping and reviving organized business interests when it considered these interests to be necessary to implement government policy, a point referred to previously in this chapter with reference to the *câmaras setoriais* during the first half of the 1990s. Theoretically, one could link this to the previously discussed insider/outsider distinction, as the state is in effect in a position to 'choose' the actors as well as its preferred channels of access.[16]

In this respect, it is important to note, however, that Weyland does not consider the Brazilian state as highly organized and influential in its ability to influence organized business. Ultimately, it was the fact that the business community and the Brazilian government had a shared interest in reviving the *câmaras setoriais*, most notable in the automobile industry, which made them achievable and ultimately successful. As Weyland notes with reference to the relative strength, or better weakness of the Brazilian state,

> the state ... has suffered from rampant bureaucratic politics, which has paralysed it and limited its autonomy from the private sector. Business groupings have also maintained multiple (though

dispersed) channels to the state, which have allowed them to block serious threats to their interests. Since entrepreneurs have not faced any profound danger, they have not deemed it necessary to resort to broadly encompassing collective action.[17]

This is important as far as it underlines the claim made at the beginning of this part of the chapter. Although organized business interests in Brazil and in Argentina have been relatively fragmented in organizational terms, and until recently without an encompassing peak organization to represent them, they have certainly had sufficient influence to block proposals detrimental to them. This does not mean, however, that they were necessarily able to exert power to push the government in a specific, and from the point of view of the business community *positive* direction. As Schneider notes with reference to Mexico, 'structural power of business as capital is not necessarily matched by organised, proactive input into policy formulation .... In other words, business exercises structural veto power but cedes policy initiative to the state'.[18]

What is important, however, is the change business–state relations have undergone in the mid-1990s as a result of the newly found interest of the Brazilian state in working together with organized business to soften the impact of trade liberalization policies and to improve the overall competitiveness of the Brazilian industry. As discussed in Chapter 3, it is important to recall that the CNI, the CNC, the CNA, the CNIF, the AEB and the CEAL formed the BBC only *after* the Brazilian government asked them to host the 1997 FEMA in Belo Horizonte. Thus, the government was forcing the business sector to reorganize itself through the need to represent a coherent response to the ongoing trade talks, which in turn created an encompassing and voluntary peak association *outside* the established channels of corporate interest representation for the first in Brazil. Since then the BBC has gained momentum and has been the main vehicle for organized business to conduct trade negotiations in Brazil, even in respect to the Mercosur.

As a consequence, it was the interplay between the state's desire to push for more organizational coherence on the side of the business community which in turn resulted in a restructuring and strengthening of organized business. This then made the influence of organized business interests in Brazil overall more responsive to the needs of its members and started successive changes in the way CNI and others have been increasingly using the advantage of their mandatory funding to increase the effectiveness of their lobbying activity, as remarked earlier. As Evans summarizes,

> the extent to which states can promote transformation depends on the character of the business community with which they have to work. If states succeed in changing the character of the business community, that changed character must in turn have an impact on the state. The state and business reshape each other in reciprocal iteration.[19]

As a consequence, what one can witness in the Southern Cone during the first decade since the 1980s is the fundamental change that has taken place in the way interests are articulated, both inside and outside established systems of interest representation. As Argentina has not had anything comparable to Brazil's corporatist system of interest representation, organized business interests in Argentina tended to be nominally weaker, and a few companies developed privileged access to the government, especially during the Menem years, or the private sector was reluctant to engage with the state during the late 1980s in relation to the first liberalization attempts. As discussed in Chapter 4, the significant influx of FDI into Argentina, particularly during the first half of the 1990s, has fundamentally altered the fabric of Argentine industry and commerce. This resulted in newly emerging complex and partially overlapping structures and levels of interest representation, in which companies or specific interest groups within business interest organizations shifted their preference for certain policies relatively often and with varying degrees of success.[20]

What is important to mention, however, is the fact that while the 1980s saw an opening of previously closed markets (internationalization) combined with an increasingly neo-liberal policy set-up (the Washington Consensus), at least in Argentina under Menem, the early 1990s witnessed the emergence of regionalization and regionalism. As remarked earlier, the latter was primarily designed to preserve the former by creating cross-border investment and an enlarged market. By the mid-1990s, however, internationalization was in the process of transforming into globalization, and domestic and regional business interest representation started again to shift. It is this acceleration of internationalization – globalization – which will be the focus of the next part of this chapter. Incidentally, with the emerging economic crisis in Argentina in 2002, the 'reality' of globalization and the ongoing FTAA and Mercosur-EU trade talks was increasingly combined with the emergence of a post-Washington consensus debate and attempts to strengthen the Mercosur.[21] As a consequence, the following empirically informed but theoretically focused debate of the various theoretical approaches to globalization is particularly relevant.

6.2   The global arena

The second part of this chapter focuses primarily on the changes organized business interests in the Mercosur have undergone since the mid-1990s in the wake of an increasing internationalization and globalization of the markets of the Southern Cone region. As noted before, it is important to distinguish between internationalization and globalization to be able to distinguish properly between the different responses and consequences both had on organized business. As a consequence, it will start with some theoretical observations regarding the nature of internationalization and globalization in CPE and IPE, in particular to the changes analysed so far in this book in relation to not only domestic but also regional interest representation. This is followed by a brief historical analysis of the political economy of Latin America, which again is important for the understanding of the wider context of how internationalization and globalization are perceived in the Southern Cone region. Finally, this part of the chapter will turn towards the recent changes in domestic and regional interest representation and will put these changes into the context of the overall analysis presented so far.

What is essential when looking at internationalization and changes in domestic interest representation is what Milner and Keohane call 'internationalisation and domestic politics'. It is this internationalization of the domestic arena that in essence provides the bridge between the two theoretical approaches employed in this book, CPE and IPE. As Milner and Keohane argue, 'the central proposition ... is that we can no longer understand politics within countries ... without comprehending the nature of the linkages between national economies and the world economy, and changes in such linkages'.[22] And as Underhill summarizes, 'an international relations theory which fails to conceptualise the role of non-state actors in general and of organised business in particular is not an international relations of the real world, and were it a boat it wouldn't float'.[23]

What is important, however, is not necessarily to *merge* CPE and IPE, but rather to draw attention to the core assumptions and principles of both approaches. This is to show that in an ever-more integrating world economy, changes in the way domestic business interests develop, and regional organized business interests are defined, the interplay between them and the multitude of actors, levels and avenues of interest representation can only be fully conceptualized theoretically and understood empirically when bringing together domestic theories of interest representation with international political economy concepts.

As mentioned in Chapter 2, Susan Strange defined IPE as 'the study ... that ... concerns the social, political and economic arrangements affecting the global systems of production, exchange and distribution, and the mix of values reflected therein'.[24] As the discussion in this chapter and the previous chapters of the changes that have taken place in relation to business interest representation on the national and regional level in the Mercosur since the mid-1980s has shown, these global changes analysed by IPE theories are directly affecting domestic institutions, markets and social networks. Moreover, once the regional dimension is added to this analysis, providing an additional level of interest formulation and mediation, it becomes clear that IPE and CPE are intrinsically linked, although they both start from very different premises. This chapter previously referred to the notion of structural power in relation to the underlying influence business interests have in the political sphere of a state, a region or globally. Susan Strange's definition of structural power within the world economy can also be directly linked to this previous analysis. She argues,

> structural power ... confers the power to decide how things shall be done, the power to shape frameworks within which states relate to each other, relate to people, or relate to corporate enterprises. The relative power of each party in a relationship is more, or less, if one party is also determining the surrounding structure of the relationship.[25]

As it becomes clear, this definition of structural power within IPE can also be applied to the previously mentioned analysis of structural power, making the link between CPE and IPE analyses in relation to organized business interests even more clear. Moreover, as Milner argues,

> domestic politics matter because the state is not a unitary actor. Groups within it have *different policy preferences* because they are differentially affected by government policies. Any change in policies, as might occur because of international co-operation, has domestic distributional and electoral consequences.[26]

As noted above, a possible synthesis as opposed to a merger of CPE and IPE is what this book intends to argue for.[27] The emphasis is on how both sets of theories complement each other when applied to the study of the regional level of governance. What is important in this regard is the observation that the study of organized business interests has so far been neglected by mainstream IPE, although there is a growing body of literature on the EU and to some extent on North America, as discussed in Chapter 2. Generally, the study of organized business and its role on the national and regional level outside the EU and North America has not been widespread.[28]

Furthermore, Greenwood argues,

> even the very phrases coined by international relations of 'non-state actors', or 'societal interests', belies its failure to adequately address the role of corporate interests in world politics. Indeed, within 'alternative' international relations, studies of business interests have lagged behind study of the role of institutions and regimes, or ... to those of non-governmental organisations.[29]

Jacek argues along similar lines by stating,

> the significant, if not primary, role of organised business associations continues to be neglected. Mainstream international relations does not significantly encapsulate the specific role of organised business associations in the process of regional and global integration. In the world of capitalism, business is the key interest.[30]

Consequently, this book aims to contribute to this debate by widening it and attempting to explain how organized business has changed and has been altered by regional and global changes, while at the same time pointing out the close linkages between the domestic, the regional and the global in this respect. Moreover, with reference to the research pursued in this book, it is important to note that the role of organized business in these regional and global arrangements is a relatively recent phenomenon. The increasing internationalization of the world economy since the late 1960s is often seen as the starting point of what later would be called globalization.[31] This provides the backdrop for the emerging discussion about the relationship between the state and the market, or, to relate it more closely to the analysis presented in this chapter, between the state and business interests more broadly. This is exemplified by the 'states and markets' and 'rival states, rival firms' paradigms employed by Strange and Stopford, respectively.[32] As a consequence, this chapter has attempted to link the emerging changes in the domestic political economy of the Mercosur countries from the mid-1980s onwards to the wider changes that have taken place from the 1960s and 1970s onwards on the global level, especially in relation to the expansion of trade and investment.

The previous, relatively brief discussion of IPE and organized business interests is, of course, embedded into the wider theoretical debate regarding the emergence of internationalization, regionalization and globalization. What is important for the empirical analysis of the changing and emerging role of organized business in the Mercosur is the increasing internationalization of business from the 1960s onwards, as remarked earlier. In many ways, the point in time to define as the starting point of internationalization and globalization is one of the most contentious points in the ongoing debate on the nature and the extent of globalization. As previously noted, Scholte points out,

> if conceived as the growth of supraterritorial spaces, then global-isation has unfolded mainly since the 1960s. Although transworld relations are not completely novel, the pace and scale of their expansion has become qualitatively greater during the last four decades of the twentieth century.[33]

Hirst and Thompson, by contrast, point out that 'the history of the internationalization of business enterprises is a long one and not something confined just to the period since 1960'.[34]

As remarked earlier in this chapter, the distinction between internationalization and globalization, and the assumption that, to some extent, economic liberalization is not necessarily linked to internationalization and globalization, is central to the understanding of the role of organized business in emerging regional and global processes. Indeed, as discussed in Chapter 4, business actors in the Mercosur understood the opening-up of their economies in the late 1980s and early 1990s as internationalization rather than globalization, a term introduced only later into the economic and political analysis.[35]

Nevertheless, the internationalization of Latin American economies, along the lines of Hirst and Thompson, goes back to the late seventeenth- and earlyeighteenth-century, culminating during the first decades of the twentieth century, when exports of beef, natural rubber, coffee, copper and cane sugar, primarily to the United States and Europe, increased rapidly. These exports created the wealth which enabled countries such as Argentina and Brazil to import manufactured goods in return, and a wave of immigration from Europe to Latin America started in the 1880s to increase the workforce. The per capita income in Argentina, for instance, during the early twentieth century was comparable to that of Germany and The Netherlands and higher than that of Switzerland or Sweden. However, there was also significant FDI from abroad. British investment, for example, mainly in rail infrastructure and mining, accounted for roughly two-thirds of all FDI investment into the region by 1913 and at one time Britain owned around eighty per cent of the rail infrastructure in Argentina.

However, a combination of a lack of support for the building-up of a domestic industrial production capacity combined with the world economic crisis of the 1930s resulted in rising unemployment and social tensions when exports started to dry up during the 1930s and virtually collapsed with the start of the Second World War. The integration of Latin American economies into the world trading system, the internationalization of investment from Western Europe and North America and the dependence on imports of labour and capital goods, all made possible by the support of Latin American elites for liberal economic policies, came increasingly under pressure. A worsening of the terms of trade for agricultural exports, combined with repeated devaluations of the Argentine currency, increases in import duties and currency controls resulted in an increase of the costs of imports by the late 1920s. For example, from the mid-1930s onwards, the percentage of imports in relation to GDP in Argentina started to fall from 25 per cent between 1925 and 1929 to 15 per cent. By the late 1920s and early 1930s, the political landscape, and with it the economic and social context for development, started to change. Increasingly, expensive imports were substituted, and a refocusing on the domestic economy with a particular emphasis on rapid industrialization and the strengthening of the domestic market took place. For the time being, the era of liberal market economics combined with free trade and high inflows of FDI was over.[36]

This, admittedly very brief, overview of the political and economic background of economic and social development in Latin America was necessary, because it connects directly to introduction of corporatist structures in Brazil from the mid-1930s onwards and also helps to explain the relative weakness of organized business in Argentina.

With the emergence of ISI as the dominant political ideology from the 1930s through to the early 1980s, a central role for the state in Latin American business and politics emerged and was seen as central to a successful economic and social development of the region. The intellectual basis for ISI was provided by the first director of the Central Bank of Argentina, Raúl Prébisch, who later on became the Executive Secretary of what is known today as the Economic Commission for Latin America and the Caribbean (ECLAC) and was also the first Secretary-General of the United Nations Conference on Trade and Development (UNCTAD). Prébisch advocated economic development based on national development strategies, with a central role for the state as the main initiator and planner for development. His analysis of the structural dependence of Latin America on imports of manufactured goods and machines from the industrialized North, similar to the structural power discourse referred to earlier in this chapter, combined with a worsening of the terms of trade for agricultural products and primary goods, provided the blue print for what would later be known as the dependency theory of development. This theory, mainly developed in the 1960s and 1970s by Fernando Enrique Cardoso, until 2003 the President of Brazil, and

André Gunder Frank, for example, is essentially a neo-Marxist analysis of the structural dependency of Latin America within the world economy. Following dependency theory, ISI enables national industrial development and is thus aimed at ending the reliance of Latin American countries on imports of manufactured goods.[37]

Despite some initial success of industrialization in the 1960s, partly also caused by FDI as discussed in Chapter 3, in the 1970s multiple pressures emerged, both from within the region and from outside. The need to finance investment in the economy and high domestic demand for import goods combined with the cheap availability of foreign credit resulted in massive over-borrowing towards the end of the 1970s and early 1980s, and gave rise to successive debt crises, as discussed in Chapter 4. Dependency on external borrowing, however, made structural reforms less likely. As Teichman points out,

> Latin America, with the notable exception of Chile, proved stubbornly resistant to this new international policy culture [globalisation] .... Indeed, the opportunities for foreign borrowing made possible by the increase in price and demand for petroleum probably prolonged the resistance to change in ... the region.[38]

As a consequence, the economic and social situation deteriorated rapidly. As Fanelli et al. put it,

> in most ... countries of the region [Latin America], the external shock of the early 1980s was ... severe. The initial impact was exacerbated by different propagating mechanisms. The result was a highly uncertain economic environment with destabilising tendencies ... and extreme volatility of ... level of activity, rate of inflation, key relative prices, public internal debt, degree of monetization.[39]

By the mid-1980s, however, the external economic environment had changed fundamentally. The so-called 'embedded liberalism' of the 1950s and 1960s gave way to 'disembedded liberalism', accompanied by the increasing internationalization and transnationalization of capital markets and the manifestation of neo-liberal economic policies by the end of the 1980s.[40] This emergence of the internationalization of the global economy combined with an increasing emphasis on liberal and later neo-liberal economic and social reforms and the end to military rule in Brazil and Argentina, for example, resulted in fundamental changes in the region, as previously discussed in Chapters 3 and 4. In theoretical terms, what is important, as noted earlier, is the distinction between liberalization, internationalization and globalization, previously discussed in Chapter 2.[41]

Latin America witnessed internationalization and liberalization, followed by ISI and an increasingly closed market. During ISI, however, markets in the region were still internationalized in the sense that they attracted significant amount of external financing which resulted in over-borrowing, as discussed above, and FDI aimed at sectors which benefited from near monopolies as a result of ISI policies, for example the chemicals and automobile sectors. From the late-1980s onwards, the newly elected democratic governments of the region embarked again on liberalizing their economies to reintegrate them into the global economy (except Chile under the military dictatorship of General Pinochet, who started to liberalize the Chilean economy form the early 1980s onwards). This was followed in the early 1990s by high levels of FDI and access to foreign capital, as discussed in Chapter 4.

The third part of the chapter will therefore turn to the regional level as the nexus between the national and the global level of governance. As previous chapters have demonstrated, the regional level within the Mercosur has emerged as an important point of reference for organized business interests.

6.3   The regional arena

The previous brief discussion of the economic history and the intellectual mind set of Latin America and the Southern Cone countries in particular in combination with the emerging global changes from the 1960s onwards was necessary, because it explains to some extent the scepticism of large parts of the business community towards the emerging regionalization and globalization of the Mercosur economies by the early 1990s. Since the mid-1990s, however, organized business has increasingly tried to increase its input into the regional and trans-regional trade negotiations as well as the institutional strengthening of the Mercosur. In addition to that, the Mercosur project itself has for the first time created significant trade flows between its members, who historically traded mostly with North America and Western Europe. As a consequence, we have seen attempts on the side of the business community to actively strengthen processes of regionalization *and* regionalism, as discussed in previous chapters.[42]

Theoretically, what we have seen in the context of the Mercosur is that regionalism and regionalization in the pre-Mercosur and early Mercosur years had been driven by governments and were aimed at reintegrating the Southern Cone economies into the world market and strengthening their democratic framework in the context of the region. Only later, from the mid-1990s onwards, when obstacles to this politically driven approach to regionalism and regionalization emerged, did organized business interests increase their efforts to create a regional economic and political space, in line with the restructuring of those interests and the emergence of new forms of interest representation on the national and regional level. Mainly the exception to this is the previously discussed chemical industry of the Mercosur, which cooperated and co-coordinated their efforts and lobbying activities well before the politically driven process of regional integration. Overall what we have seen in the context of the Mercosur, is an interplay between regionalization and regionalism being driven by governments and business interests alike, at different points in time and with varying degrees of focus and intensity. It is important to point out that this support by governments and business associations for a strengthening of regional institutions and the acceleration of the Mercosur is mainly twofold.

First, it might be to some extent attributable to the prospect of wide-ranging trade liberalizations on the horizon in 2003 in relation to the trade negotiations, co-chaired by the United States and Brazil, aimed at concluding a FTAA by 2005, and the parallel talks between the EU and Mercosur on a bilateral trade agreement between the two blocks. At the time, the moves of the Brazilian and Argentine governments during the Mercosur summit in Asunción to strengthen Mercosur internally to present a coherent negotiating position combined with increased flexibility on the side of Brazil with reference to what these trade deals might cover in addition to the trade in goods point to the increasing relevance of the Mercosur as a vehicle to engage in comprehensive trade deals.[43,44] The fact that this is also increasingly realized and actively supported by organized business supports the general argument of the book.[45] Moreover, for the first time Argentina and Brazil agreed on a common position paper for the FTAA negotiations, overcoming past problems based on differing policy preferences of both countries.[46]

Second, successive reforms at CNI and FIESP, for example, since the mid-1990s have made these organizations much more flexible and responsive to business input. At the same time, the emerging trade talks within the FTAA and later the Mercosur-EU trade talks have led to a general refocusing of how organized business will approach these negotiations. As a consequence, the setting-up of the BBC in Brazil as an attempt to overcome the structural rigidities of the compulsory system of corporatism and the associated lack of an encompassing peak associations, as discussed in Chapters 3 and 4, confirm this. The related strengthening of trade negotiating capacity on the side of the CNI aimed at using the BBC as a common platform to present the collective interest of Brazilian organized business underlines this analysis. In addition to that, CNI also calls for a greater institutional coherence of the Mercosur, in particular in relation to a timely implementation of the recent decision to set up a permanent tribunal for settling trade disputes and also in relation to the necessary strengthening of the technical capacity of the Mercosur Secretariat.[47]

In Argentina too, changes in interest representation because of the internationalization, regionalization and globalization of its trade combined with high inflows of FDI have resulted in a realignment of business interests away from the UIA. This realignment has resulted in a shift of the representation of organized business towards the sectoral chambers, for example in the chemical and automotive industries, and alternative forms of interest representation such as the MEBF, the CICYP, the CEAL and, more recently, the AEA. Again, all of this has been mentioned in the previous two chapters; however, it is important to reiterate these observations as they relate directly to the analysis presented above.

Finally in July 2003, during a meeting of high-ranking officials from Argentina and Brazil in Buenos Aires, the so-called *Grupo Brasil*, an influential business group representing Brazilian companies with significant business interests in Argentina, called for a strengthening of the Mercosur and the creation of strong supra-national institutions to enforce Mercosur trade rules and treaties.[48] This underlines the increasing regionalization of the Southern Cone economies and the growth of cross-border investment.

The previous discussion also points to the importance of Sandholtz and Zysman's argument introduced in Chapter 2, who argue that a fundamental shift in global economic power relations resulted in a rethinking on the side of European elites in respect of their position within an evermore-globalizing world economy.[49] Thus, a refocusing of the political and business elites within the Mercosur towards the strengthening of the wider regional space and beyond should come as no surprise.

As noted earlier in Chapter 2, theories commonly used to explain regional integration in the context of the EU, such as Mitrany's functionalism, Haas and Lindberg's neo-functionalism or Marks' multilevel governance approach, have had only very limited power of explanation in the context of the Mercosur.[50]

However, new forms of national, regional and interregional business interest representation and lobbying are emerging, as discussed in particular in Chapters 3 and 4. As a consequence, Moravcsik's refined version of Hoffman's intergovernmentalism, liberal intergovernmentalism has also only very limited abilities to explain these new forms of interest group formation on the regional level in the Mercosur, as discussed in Chapter 2.[51] As a consequence, as Schirm argues, '[in liberal intergovernmentalism] the formation of "national interests" occurs in an analytical vacuum: there are explanations of *how* interests are articulated...but none of *why* interests emerge and *which* interests succeed in becoming driving forces'.[52]

Conclusion: bridging the divide, connecting CPE and IPE

This chapter intended to map out the complex and often-overlapping structures of business interest representation on both the domestic and the regional level in the Mercosur. Rather than focusing just on the empirical analysis, the main aim of this chapter was to integrate the empirical analysis presented so far with the theoretical framework developed in Chapter 2. As a consequence, the chapter has discussed in detail the various forms of interest representation and the various avenues taken by business to access government and to influence policy decisions. Moreover, it has placed these forms of interest representation into the wider context of the internationalization and globalization of the Mercosur economies. By doing so, the chapter has used both theories of CPE and IPE to describe and analyse the complex nature of how organized business interests have evolved across countries and across time, and the various pressures these interests were subjected to.

Above all, what has emerged from the analysis presented in this chapter is the sheer complexity and multitude of interests, both in terms of levels of access and actors involved. As Lopéz puts it,

> I think that these processes are very complex and not even fully understood by those who participate in them. In my opinion it is difficult to trace a clear dividing line between those who favour trade liberalisation (or regional integration) and those who do not (perhaps, the same firm that in some period is against trade liberalisation, may change its opinion later in other macroeconomic and international context).[53]

In many ways, throughout the book the answer to the Schirm's theoretical puzzle mentioned above, why certain interests emerge and which interests succeed in influencing policy-making and the emerging regional governance agenda, has been central to the empirical and theoretical debate presented so far. Following Schirm's argument, globalization has fundamentally altered the economic reality of domestic economies, thus changing the perceptions of state and business elites alike and ultimately resulting in the emergence of regional integration schemes such as the Mercosur.[54] Nevertheless, it is also important to remember the essentially uneven nature of globalization, as discussed in Chapter 2.[55]

However, theoretically as well empirically, how interest group formation has taken place and still continues to take place on the domestic level is also a complementary and therefore necessary element to an analysis based on the importance of global economic changes on the distribution of power among domestic business and elites and the formation of new forms of regional interest representation.

As has been demonstrated in this chapter, the particular national conditions of interest group access to government and policy-making circles are embedded into domestic and regional economic and political changes. As states are an important actor in the Mercosur, domestic interest group analysis remains an important tool in understanding the role played by organized business interests in processes of regionalization and regionalism in the Southern Cone region. Thus, a theoretical framework, as presented in this chapter, which encompasses both CPE and IPE theories is essential in describing and analysing domestic and regional changes in the structures of interest representation under conditions of globalization.

7
Organized Business Interests in the Mercosur: Conflict, Convergence and Influence

The book started off with the observation that the role played by, and the evolution of organized business interests in the context of the regional cooperation and integration, which has unfolded in the Southern Cone region of Latin America since the late 1980s, is a neglected area of study. Grant points out, 'neglect is, of itself, not a justification for the study of a subject: some subjects are justifiably neglected, and there are others which have been studied which might have been better left neglected'.[1] However, the neglect in this case has been due to the language barrier for the English-speaking world, and as many interviewees have pointed out, a lack of funding in their part of the world.

The discussion in the book has demonstrated that organized business interests have undergone many changes. Some organizations have lost influence to other business associations and entirely new forms of interest representation have emerged. The previously so dominant domestic level of interest representation has been complemented by regional, interregional and global levels as important fora for interest representation and mediation. Over and above that, this transformation of avenues of access for organized business on all levels has strengthened the influence and policy-making capacity of these interests over time.

Two central themes run through this book. First, organized business in the Mercosur has been under-researched both in terms of its evolution and underestimated in relation to the role it is playing in the regional integration process. Second, the emerging regional dimension of business interest representation and its linkages with domestic and global levels of governance cannot be adequately conceptualized by either CPE or IPE alone. Rather, the regional level has emerged as a level of governance where the theoretical insights of CPE and IPE complement each other to understand the ongoing processes of change at this level.

When discussing the evolution and the role played by organized business as an actor within the context of the Mercosur, it is import-ant to remember that with the exception of the chemical industry, the business community was not very concerned with contributing to the process of regional integration in the Southern Cone from the late 1980s onwards in a *positive* way. However, this does not mean that business was not involved or did not contribute to the PICAB and later on the Mercosur negotiations. Business indeed participated in these negotiations, but this was mainly aimed at securing tariff exemptions and limiting competition from trade liberalization.

However, when the Mercosur in 1995 moved to become a customs union and in the wake of the considerable rise in intra-regional trade, organized business started actively to engage with the regional project. In relation to this it is important to recall the global economic context in which this re-engagement took place. The Mercosur was, among other things, designed to enable its member states to reinsert their economies into the global economy and to lock-in processes of neo-liberal reforms. By doing so, however, what can be witnessed in the Southern Cone region is the reconfiguration of the state towards an explicitly neo-liberal project, rather than the active developmen-talist and ISI-focused actor of the 1950s, 1960s and 1970s. As a consequence, the wide-ranging privatizations of state-owned and state-controlled assets, for example in Argentina and later on also in Brazil, and the high levels of FDI in the region have reshaped the domestic economies of the Mercosur member states fundamentally and have given rise to what Phillips calls the Southern Cone model of regional capitalist development.[2]

This reorganization and reconfiguration of the state in the context of the Mercosur gives rise to 'a process by which a form of political authority is crystallising and being articulated at the regional level', and this has resulted in the reorganization and reconfiguration of organized business, too.[3] Whereas business interests initially had to be brought into the regional project by state actors, as remarked earlier, later on organized business started to change its organizational structures and channels of access to governments in the light of the new regionalization of the Mercosur economies. As the previous empirical chapters have discussed in depth, organized business at the domestic level in the Mercosur member states has undergone fundamental changes, in particular with the aim of strengthening organizational structures and to consolidate or regain political influence in the regional integration process. Similarly, new regional business associations have been created in response to both the emerging regional economic structures and the increasingly important interregional dimension in the form of the Mercosur-EU trade negotiations and the FTAA process. Thus, when the Mercosur as a political project ran into trouble in the aftermath of the Brazilian currency devaluation in 1999 and the economic and political crisis in Argentina in 2001/02, organized business interests on both the national and the regional level were instrumental in maintaining the economic rational of economic cooperation and regional integration.[4] Organized business interests in the Mercosur have constantly been under pressure to change and adapt to maintain both 'the logic of membership' and the 'the logic of influence' for their respective associations. Overall, therefore, those business interest associations that have responded to the need to reconfigure and redefine their activities have seen their relevance to the political and social processes of regional integration in the Mercosur increase.[5]

In this context, it is helpful to recall the discussion in Chapter 2 of Phillips' notion of controlled eclecticism in political economy and the move to a synthesis of CPE and IPE guided by the controls of parsimony, internal coherence of the method, and relevance, to understand the regional level of governance in the context of the Southern Cone. On the one hand, the domestic level of interest representation is very different in terms of political and institutional structures in Brazil and Argentina, emphasizing CPE with its focus on the 'varieties of capitalism' approach. On the other hand, the regional level of interest representation is an increasingly important level of interest articulation. It is analytically distinct from both the domestic and the global level, while at the same time being an important interlocutor between both levels. Thus, the domestic and the regional level of interest representation are the two levels on which organized business interest are articulated, whereby the domestic level is still the most important point of access for business interest associations. Both levels are also influenced by the neo-liberal nature of the Mercosur project within the context of reinserting the Southern Cone economies in the global markets, hence the need for IPE in the context of this book.

7.1   Recent developments in Argentina

At this point it is quite helpful to reflect on some of the more recent political and economic developments in Argentina.

With the election of Néstor Kirchner as Argentine President in May 2003, Argentina has gone through a period of political realignment combined with a remarkable economic recovery, the latter supported by substantial tax revenues on the back of high prices for commodities, primarily soy, corn and wheat but also hydrocarbon products, its main exports, on the world market, and a policy of keeping the value of the Argentine *Peso* low to stimulate exports. Economically, the changes in the domestic and global economic environments have helped the Argentine government to follow Brazil in paying back its remaining debt to the IMF and, after defaulting on government bonds in the wake of 2001/02 financial crisis, to restructure its debt with private investors in 2005, thereby reducing the nominal size of the debt to about one-third of its original value. Politically, the changing economic policy has been accompanied by a political realignment away from the pro-US stance and neo-liberal policy priorities under Menem in the 1990s to a policy that supports a more left-wing political agenda. This is exemplified not just by seeking financial independence from the IMF and restructuring the remaining private debt through enforcing substantial write-downs, as mentioned above, but also through political support for Venezuela's President Hugo Chávez. This has not only resulted in the purchase of Argentine government bonds by Venezuela, but also in Argentina's support for Venezuela's membership of the Mercosur, which will be discussed later on in this chapter.

In terms of Argentina's and also Brazil's recent economic development, both countries have seen substantial rates of economic growth in recent years, growing at an annual rate of 8 per cent and 6.4 per cent in 2007 respectively.[6] Whereas high rates of economic growth have been accompanied by a policy of rising interest rates and combating inflation in Brazil, Argentina under Kirchner has used the increasing tax revenues to support a substantial increase in government spending and public works projects, in particular in the run-up to the Presidential election in October 2007.[7] Combined with a policy of keeping the value of the *Peso* down, as mentioned above, these economic measures have not only led to strong economic growth, but have also stoked inflation, which is now (2007/08) estimated at running between 16 and 20 per cent annually.[8] To address the situation, the government imposed price controls in late 2005 on a wide range of products, from milk to beef, and also limited the amount of produce that could be exported to increase availability in the domestic market. This policy has led to a shortage of staple foods without significantly reducing inflation, as local producers simply refuse to sell at government-stipulated prices.[9] In addition, five years of economic growth since 2003 combined with price freezes imposed on utility companies in the wake of the 2001/02 economic crisis discouraged necessary infrastructure investment in energy production and distribution. This has led to power shortages during periods of peak demand, that is in winter and during the summer months.[10]

In addition to price controls, the government has embarked on a policy of changing the way the official inflation figures are calculated, thus potentially undermining the credibility of government data and thus risking medium to long-term damage to the trust in local currency deposits, a key reason for the financial and banking crisis of 2001/02.[11]

Therefore, it remains to be seen how Argentina might deal with a, albeit at the moment unlikely, significant fall in global commodity prices and the effects that might have on its domestic economic model and the corresponding necessary adjustment. The decision of the newly appointed minister – only in July 2007 – of the economy, Miguel Peirano, not to be part of the government of Argentina's new President, Cristina Fernández de Kirchner, Néstor Kirchner's wife, elected in October 2007 might be significant in this respect. Mr Peirano, who was a significant figure at the UIA, was brought into the government to improve the relationship between the government and parts of the business community in the wake of the price controls and the government's attempts at changing the calculation of inflation data.[12] His decision not to continue in his post supports the argument that the government does not intend to deal with the root causes of the inflationary pressures building-up in the Argentine economy, in particular a relatively loose fiscal policy combined with price freezes, export controls and, consequently, a lack of investment and low productivity growth. In addition, the monetary policy aimed at keeping the *Peso* artificially weak could also be seen as contributing to the overall level of inflation by encouraging a loose monetary policy.[13]

7.2   Emerging trends in the region

The following part of the chapter will reflect on some of the changes that have taken place in relation to the regional and global trade negotiations that are affecting Latin America generally and the Southern Cone region in particular.

An area of particular interest is, first, the interregional level of business interest representation not just in the context of the Mercosur-EU trade agreement, but also in relation to the FTAA negotiations. The relationship between the Mercosur and the FTAA is dominated, first, by sub-regional rivalry between Brazil, by far Mercosur's biggest member, and the United States (US). In 2004, the US rejected a proposal launched by Brazil to negotiate a 4 + 1 agreement between the Mercosur as a block and the US, to avoid separate negotiations within the FTAA framework. However, Washington is determined to push the FTAA rather than a possible deal outside the FTAA framework.[14] Whereas for the Brazilian government the Mercosur provides a very useful regional trade agreement centred on its own trade preferences, for the US the Mercosur should eventually become part of the larger FTAA to encompass the whole of the Americas. As such, there have been continuing tensions between Brazil and the US as the co-chairs of the FTAA, primarily about the issues of agriculture (where Brazil in line with many other countries with a highly competitive agribusiness sector wants a firm commitment by the US, in the long term, to eliminate tariffs on agricultural products and eventually eliminate its very generous domestic farm subsidies) and intellectual property rights (where the US wants tougher measures to retaliate against the violation of intellectual property rights).[15] As such, the problems in the FTAA mirror those encountered in the WTO's Doha Development Round of trade negotiation and as such, the success or failure of both projects is closely linked.[16]

In contrast to the FTAA negotiations, the Central American Free Trade Agreement (CAFTA) is on track to be ratified after supporters of the agreement won a referendum in October 2007 in Costa Rica. As Costa Rica is the only remaining country that still has to complete the ratification process, the outcome of the referendum in favour of the trade agreement removes the final obstacles to CAFTA's implementation.[17] Although CAFTA has avoided some of the problems of the FTAA process in the sense that the US Congress granted fast-track negotiating authority to the US administration and CAFTA was concluded in only one year of negotiations, its submission to the US Congress was initially put on hold until after the US Presidential elections in 2004.[18] Nevertheless, as CAFTA is seen as a means to pave the way for the ratification of a still to be concluded FTAA agreement, failure by the US Congress in particular to ratify CAFTA would have been interpreted as a severe blow to the prospect of concluding the FTAA any time soon.

Although the FTAA project itself has seen no progress since the Mar de la Plata Summit in 2005, there is considerable scope for an analysis of the involvement of organized business in the hemispheric trade negotiations. This is also underlined by the forthcoming completion of the ratification for CAFTA and the increasing concerns of the Brazilian business community in particular of losing ground to US companies in terms of access to Central American markets as a result of the failure to advance the FTAA project.[19]

Second, a pertinent theme is also the bilateral negotiations the Mercosur is currently conducting. Important in this regard is the recent decision to merge the Mercosur with the Comunidad Andina (CAN) by 2008 to form the Unión de Naciones de Suramérica (UNASUR), previously known as the Comunidad Sudamericana de Naciones (CSN).[20] The overall aim is to create an organization modelled along the lines of the EU and covering the whole of Latin America, thus providing a counter weight to any future efforts to resuscitate the FTAA process. It remains to be seen to what extent this new integration initiative will bear fruit, particularly as the CAN has only recently started to negotiate its own FTA with the EU, thus somewhat challenging Mercosur's own – albeit in recent years very indecisive – efforts in this area.[21] To complicate matters further in terms of future trade negotiations, Mercosur has recently decided to admit Venezuela as a new member, although the formal ratification of its accession to the block has been delayed in the Brazilian Congress due to President Chávez's treatment of media outlets opposed to the government. As a consequence, Venezuela has now threatened the withdrawal of its membership application and Venezuela's role as well as its future in the Mercosur might be re-evaluated in the near future.[22]

Finally, outside the region the Mercosur signed a Preferential Trade Agreement (PTA) with India in March 2004.[23] The Mercosur-India PTA is beneficial not just because India is an important and growing market for Mercosur's exports of vegetable oil, petroleum, manufactured goods and precious and semi-precious stones, among others, but the trade deal also gives Mercosur leverage in terms of the FTAA and Mercosur-EU negotiations, as it helps to diversify the destination of its exports (Mercosur's main export markets are the EU and the US). Moreover, the Mercosur-India trade agreement helps to strengthen the cooperation between Brazil and India as the spokespersons for the developing countries in the WTO's Doha Development Round.[24] Furthermore, in December 2004, the Mercosur signed a PTA with the Southern African Customs Union (SACU), which, similar to the agreement with India, might eventually lead to a FTA. As a consequence, the possibility of a three-way trade agreement between SACU, the Mercosur and India was also mentioned as a possibility to strengthen South-South trade.[25] Early in 2005, the Mercosur has also signed an agreement with the Gulf Cooperation Council, formed by the United Arab Emirates, Bahrain, Qatar, Saudi Arabia Oman and Kuwait. Negotiations aimed at concluding a FTA are under way and a successful deal would provide the business sector in the Mercosur with preferential access to a well-developed export market. In addition, in December 2007, the Mercosur finally concluded its FTA negotiations with Israel, marking the first FTA negotiated and signed by the bloc with a country or bloc outside the region.[26]

Concluding remarks

The analysis presented in this book has demonstrated the sheer complexity of, fluidity of, and overlap and conflict between organized business interests in the Mercosur. As remarked previously, for López maintains,

> I think that these processes are very complex and not even fully understood by those who participate in them.... It is difficult to trace a clear dividing line between those who favour trade liberalisation (or regionalisation) and those who do not (perhaps, the same firm that in some period is against trade liberalisation, may change its opinion later in other macroeconomic and international context).[27]

The institutional and organizational strengthening of business interest associations combined with a significant increase in capacity building in relation to intra- and interregional trade negotiations will most likely, over time strengthen the influence of those interests. This has to be seen in the context of the continuing development of formal consultation processes with state actors, as these processes are still weak in the context of the Southern Cone.[28] Moreover, state actors have suffered and are to some extent still suffering many of the organizational weaknesses and lack of technical expertise that business interest associations had to overcome in the 1990s, to engage and influence policy-making on both the national and regional level in the Mercosur. Thus, it is important to emphasize the need for transparency and structured channels of access to the policy-making process for organized business interests, among others.[29] This is important and should help to sustain support for regional integration and interregional trade negotiations beyond the *political* uncertainties of regional cooperation and integration.

Notes

1 Organized Business Interests in the Mercosur: Setting the Scene

1. The term 'Southern Cone' describes the countries of Southern Latin America, that is Brazil, Argentina, Uruguay, Paraguay, Bolivia and Chile. As a result, the Mercosur is also referred to as the Southern Cone Common Market.
2. For a detailed definition of organised business in the context of this book, please see Chapter 2.
3. Winston Fritsch and Alexandre A. Tombini, 'The Mercosur: An Overview', in Roberto Bouzas and Jaime Ros, eds, *Economic Integration in the Western Hemisphere* (Notre Dame and London: University of Notre Dame Press, 1994), 83.
4. Roberto Bouzas, 'El proceso de integración en el Mercosur', in Bernardo Kosacoff, Gabriel Yoguel, Carlos Bonvecchi y Adrián Ramos, eds, *El desempeño industrial argentino – Más allá de la sustitución de importaciones* (Buenos Aires: Naciones Unidas – CEPAL, Oficina de Buenos Aires, 2000), 177; email correspondence with Andrés López, Researcher, Centro de Investigaciones para la Transformación (CENIT), 26 February 2003.
5. For a detailed discussion and definition of IPE in the context of this book, please see Chapter 2.
6. For a detailed discussion and definition of CPE in the context of this book, please see Chapter 2.
7. I am grateful to Nicola Phillips for suggesting to focus on a theoretical framework that draws on insights from both CPE and IPE.

2 Studying Organized Business Interests in the Mercosur: A Theoretical Framework for Analysis

1. The book is particularly interested in economic globalisation without discounting the other equally relevant aspects of the globalisation debate, for example, the cultural dimension.
2. See for example: Geoffrey R. D. Underhill, 'Conceptualising the Changing Global Order', in Richard Stubbs and Geoffrey R. D. Underhill, eds, Political Economy and the Changing Global Order (Don Mills, Ontario: Oxford University Press, 2000), 4–6; Nicola Phillips, *The Southern Cone Model – The Political Economy of Regional Capitalist Development in Latin America* (London and New York: Routledge, 2004), 15; Frederik Söderbaum, *The Political Economy of Regionalism: The Case of Southern Africa* (Basingstoke: Palgrave

Macmillan, 2004); Nicola Phillips, ed., *Globalising International Political Economy* (Basingstoke: Palgrave Macmillan, 2005); Nicola Phillips, 'Special Section: The State Debate in Political Economy: Bridging the Comparative/ International Divide in the Study of States' *New Political Economy* 10(3) 2005, 335–43; Amanda Dickins, 'The Evolution of International Political Economy' *International Affairs* 82(3) 2006, 479–92.

3. Dickins, 'The Evolution of International Political Economy', 481 [emphasis in the original].

4. José Maria Fumagalli, 'Interacción pública y privada en el diseño de políticas comerciales' (CIQyP, Buenos Aires, July 2002; internal document, not published), 1–26.

5. Phillips, *The Southern Cone Model – The Political Economy of Regional Capitalist Development in Latin America*, 215–16.

6. Interview with Felix Peña, Director, International Trade Institute, Fundación Bank Boston, 12 April 2002.

7. The term 'Southern Cone' describes the countries of Southern Latin America, that is Brazil, Argentina, Uruguay, Paraguay, Bolivia also Chile. As a result, the Mercosur is also referred to as the Southern Cone Common Market.

8. Interview with Santiago González Cravino, Director, Secretaría Administrativa del Mercosur, 9 April 2002 and interview with Alberto Pfeiffer, Director Ejecutivo, Consejo Empresario de America Latina (CEAL), 26 August 2002.

9. Thomas E. Skidmore and Peter H. Smith, *Modern Latin America* 5th ed. (New York and Oxford: Oxford University Press, 2001), 3.

10. Richard Higgott, 'The Political Economy of Globalisation in East Asia – the Salience of "Region Building"' in Kris Olds, Peter Dicken, Philip F. Kelly, Lily Kong and Henry Wai-chung Yeung, eds, *Globalisation and the Asia-Pacific – Contested Territories* (London and New York: Routledge in Association with the Centre for the Study of Globalisation and Regionalisation, University of Warwick, 1999), 96–98.

11. Björn Hettne and Frederik Söderbaum, 'Theorising the Rise of Regionness' *New Political Economy* 5(3) 2000, 461.

12. *The Oxford English Dictionary*, 2nd ed., Vol. XIII (Oxford: Oxford University Press, 1989), 510.

13. Wyn Grant, *Business and Politics in Britain*, 2nd edition (Houndmills, Basingstoke and London: Macmillan, 1993), 3.

14. The book will use the term TNCs rather than Multi-National Corporations (MNCs), because this defines the increasingly transnationalised nature of firm activity much better than MNCs without discounting the debate about distinguishing the truly transnational corporations from MNCs.

15. See for example, Peter A. Hall and David Soskice, 'An Introduction to Varieties of Capitalism' in Peter A. Hall and David Soskice, eds, *Varieties of Capitalism – The Institutional Foundations of Comparative Advantage* (Oxford: Oxford University Press, 2001), 1; Jan Erik Lane and Svante Ersson,

Comparative Political Economy – A Developmental Approach, 2nd edition (London and Washington: Pinter, 1997), 1–2.

16. Phillips, *The Southern Cone Model – The Political Economy of Regional Capitalist Development in Latin America*, 18.
17. Peter J. Katzenstein, 'Introduction: Domestic and International Forces and Strategies of Foreign Economic Policy', in Peter J. Katzenstein, ed., *Between Power and Plenty – Foreign Economic Policies of Advanced Industrial States* (Madison, Wisconsin and London: The University of Wisconsin Press, 1978), 22.
18. Philippe C. Schmitter, 'Still the Century of Corporatism?' *The Review of Politics* 36(1) 1974, 93; see also the entry on corporatism by Wyn Grant in Iain McLeod, ed., *Oxford Concise Dictionary of Politics* (Oxford and New York: Oxford University Press, 1996), 112–15.
19. Schmitter, 'Still the Century of Corporatism?', 103.
20. Peter J. Katzenstein, *Small States in World Markets – Industrial Policy in Europe* (Ithaca, New York: Cornell University Press, 1985).
21. Peter J. Katzenstein, 'Small States and Small States Revisited' *New Political Economy* 8(1) 2003, 25.
22. Wolfgang Streeck and Philippe C. Schmitter, 'Community, Market, State – and Associations? The Prospective Contribution of Interest Governance to Social Order' in Wolfgang Streeck and Philippe C. Schmitter, eds, *Private Interest Government – Beyond Market and State* (London, Beverly Hills and New Delhi: Sage Publications, 1985), 16.
23. Streeck and Schmitter, 'Community, Market, State – and Associations? the Prospective Contribution of Interest Governance to Social Order', 15 [emphasis in the original].
24. Colin Crouch and Wolfgang Streeck, 'Introduction: The Future of Capitalist Diversity' in Colin Crouch and Wolfgang Streeck, eds, *Political Economy of Modern Capitalism – Mapping Convergence and Diversity* (London, Thousand Oaks and New Delhi: Sage Publications, 1997), 17.
25. David Coates, *Models of Capitalism – Growth and Stagnation in the Modern Era* (Cambridge: Polity Press, 2000), 19 [emphasis in the original].
26. Katzenstein, 'Small States and Small States Revisited', 25–26.
27. Hall and Soskice, 'An Introduction to Varieties of Capitalism', 8.
28. Hall and Soskice, 'An Introduction to Varieties of Capitalism', 37.
29. Hall and Soskice, 'An Introduction to Varieties of Capitalism', 62–66.
30. This was until recently the case in Brazil, for example, where the Federation of Industries of São Paulo state (Federação das Indústrias do Estado de São Paulo – FIESP) used to dominate business representation on the national level despite the existence of the Confederação Nacional da Indústria (CNI), the national business association; see Kurt Weyland, 'The Fragmentation of Business in Brazil' in Francisco Durand and Eduardo Silva, eds, *Organized Business, Economic Change, Democracy in Latin America* (University of Miami: North-South Center Press, 1998), 77; John Lucas, 'The Politics of Business Associations in the Developing World' *The Journal of Developing Areas* 32(Fall 1997), 84.

31. 'Paraguay to remain in Mercosur despite corporate sector pressure to leave' *AFX Europe*, 20 June 2001.
32. For a very good overview over the main types of interest groups, their strategies and their various levels of access within the political system consult Wyn Grant, *Pressure Groups and British Politics* (Houndmills, Basingstoke: Macmillan Press Ltd., 2001); Wyn Grant, *Business and Politics in Britain,* 2nd edition (Houndmills, Basingstoke: Macmillan Press Ltd., 1993).
33. Throughout the book the term 'EU' will be used to refer to the European Communities in their various stages of evolution to avoid confusion.
34. Mancur Olson, *The Logic of Collective Action* (Cambridge, Massachusetts: Harvard University Press, 1965), 2.
35. Olson, *The Logic of Collective Action*, 2 [emphasis in the original]; see also 126–27.
36. Olson, *The Logic of Collective Action*, 3, 127.
37. It is important to note that the insider/outsider distinction cannot just be applied to lobbying on the national level within CPE. It is equally valid for analysing lobbying activities on the regional and supra-national level and is thus not strictly related to CPE.
38. Grant, *Pressure Groups and British Politics*, 19.
39. Edward C. Page, 'The Insider/Outsider Distinction: an Empirical Investigation' *British Journal of Politics and International Relations* 1(2) 1999, 212.
40. Page, 'The Insider/Outsider Distinction: an Empirical Investigation', 212.
41. Page, 'The Insider/Outsider Distinction: an Empirical Investigation', 211–12.
42. Grant, *Pressure Groups and British Politics*, 29–32.
43. Grant, *Pressure Groups and British Politics*, 20.
44. Jeremy Richardson, 'Government, Interest Groups and Policy Change' *Political Studies* 48(5) 2000, 1010.
45. Richardson, *Political Studies*, 1010.
46. Nina Fishman, 'Reinventing Corporatism' *The Political Quarterly* 68(1) 1997, 31, 40.
47. Peter Munk Christiansen and Hilmar Rommetvedt, 'From Corporatism to Lobbyism? Parliaments, Executives, and Organised Interests in Denmark and Norway' *Scandinavian Political Studies* 22(3) 1999, 196.
48. Jens Blom-Hansen, 'Still Corporatism in Scandinavia? A Survey of recent Empirical Findings' *Scandinavian Political Studies* 23(2) 2000, 157–59; Christiansen and Rommetvedt, 'From Corporatism to Lobbyism? Parliaments, Executives, and Organised Interests in Denmark and Norway', 195–96.
49. Wayne Sandholtz and John Zysman, '1992: Recasting the European Bargain', in Brent F. Nelsen and Alexander C.-G. Stubb, eds, *The European Union – Readings on the Theory and Practice of European Integration,* 2nd edition (Boulder, Colorado and London: Lynne Rienner Publishers, 1998), 196.

50. David Coen, 'The European Business Lobby' *Business Strategy Review* 8(4) 1997, 18.
51. Coen, 'The European Business Lobby', 18.
52. Eduardo Silva and Francisco Durand, 'Organised Business and Politics in Latin America', in Francisco Durand and Eduardo Silva, eds, *Organized Business, Economic Change, Democracy in Latin America* (University of Miami: North-South Center Press, 1998), 1–2.
53. Skidmore and Smith, *Modern Latin America*, 389; see also Melissa H. Birch, 'Mercosur: The Road to Economic Integration in the Southern Cone' *International Journal of Public Administration* 23(5–8) 2000, 1395–96.
54. Monica Hirst, 'Mercosur's Complex Political Agenda', in Riordan Roett, ed. *Mercosur – Regional Integration, World Markets* (Boulder, Colorado and London: Lynne Rienner Publishers, 1999), 39.
55. Monica Hirst, 'Mercosur and the New Circumstances of Its Integration' *Cepal Review* 46, 1992, 146–47.
56. Hirst, 'Mercosur and the New Circumstances of Its Integration', 147.
57. Leonardo Campos Filho, *New Regionalism and Latin America: The Case of Mercosul* (London: University of London, Institute of Latin American Studies Research Papers, 1999), 32–33.
58. Hector E. Schamis, 'Distributional Coalitions and the Politics of Economic Reform in Latin America' *World Politics* 51(2) 1999, 268.
59. Donald G. Richards, 'Dependent Development and Regional Integration – A Critical Examination of the Southern Cone Common Market' *Latin American Perspectives* 24(6) 1997, 113, 150–51; Nicola Phillips, 'Global and Regional linkages' in Julia Buxton and Nicola Phillips, eds, *Developments in Latin American Political Economy: States, Markets and Actors* (Manchester: Manchester University Press, 1999), 81.
60. Paul Bowles, 'Regionalism and Development after (?) the Global Crisis' *New Political Economy* 5(3) 2000, 449; Skidmore and Smith, *Modern Latin America*, 389.
61. Interview with José Maria Fumagalli, Executive Director of the Chamber of the Chemical and Petrochemical Industry of Argentina (CIQyP), Secretary of the Mercosur Department of the Industrial Union of Argentina (UIA) and Secretary of CIQUIM, 12 April 2002.
62. For example, see Karl Kaltenthaler and Frank O. Mora, 'Explaining Latin American Economic Integration: The Case of the Mercosur' *Review of International Political Economy* 9(1) 2002, 72–97.
63. Héctor Alimonda, 'Brazilian Society and Regional Integration' *Latin American Perspectives* 27(6) 2000, 27–28.
64. Lia Vas Pereira, 'Toward the Common Market of the South: Mercosur's Origins, Evolution, and Challenges' in Riordan Roett, ed. *Mercosur – Regional Integration, World Markets* (Boulder, Colorado and London: Lynne Rienner Publishers, 1999), 11.
65. 'Mercosur threat' *Financial Times* 4 April 2001, 22; 'Some realism for Mercosur' *The Economist* 31 March 2001, 15–16; 'Another blow to

Mercosur' *The Economist* 31 March 2001, 67–68; Tom Holland, 'ASEAN: Latin Lesson' *Far Eastern Economic Review* 28 December 2000, 109; 'Latin trade' *Financial Times* 15 December 2000, 16; Jean Grugel and Marcelo de Almeida Medeiros, 'Brazil and Mercosur' in Jean Grugel and Wil Hout, eds, *Regionalism across the North-South Divide – State Strategies and Globalisation* (London and New York: Routledge, 1999), 57–61.

66. The most significant change in relation to a strengthening of the institutional structure of the Mercosur has been the Protocolo de Olivos (Olivos Protocol), signed during the Mercosur Summit in February 2002. The Olivos Protocol established a *Tribunal Permanente de Revisión* (Permanent Review Tribunal) for Mercosur trade disputes, thus replacing the previous ad-hoc tribunals. For a discussion of the Olivos Protocol consult Phillips, *The Southern Cone Model – The Political Economy of Regional Capitalist Development in Latin America*, 129.

67. Jeffrey Cason, 'On the Road to Southern Cone Economic Integration' *Journal of Interamerican Studies and World Affairs* 42(1) 2000, 24; Pamela Druckerman, 'Argentina's Plan to rescue Its Economy Annoys Brazil – Mercosur Members Will Lose Some Prized Privileges Under Cavallo's Proposal' *The Wall Street Journal* 5 April 2001.

68. 'Mercosur's trial by adversity' *The Economist* 27 May 2000, 69.

69. Emilio J. Cárdenas and Guillermo Tempesta, 'Arbitral Awards under Mercosur's Dispute Settlement Mechanism' *Journal of International Economic Law* 4(2) 2001, 339.

70. Robert Pearce and Ana Teresa Tavares, 'Emerging Trading Blocs and Their Impact on the Strategic Evolution of Multinationals' *Managerial Finance* 26(1) 2000, 26; Mark Milner, 'Peugeot questions Nissan aid decision' *The Guardian* 2 February 2001, 26; Charles Thurston, 'BASF bolsters Latin American investments and e-commerce' *Chemical Market Reporter* 15 May 2000; Tim Burt and Victor Mallett, 'French lessons from "Le Cost-Killer" of Nissan'.

71. Danny M. Leipziger, Claudio Frischtak, Homi J. Kharas and John F. Normand, 'Mercosur: Integration and Industrial Policy' *The World Economy* 20(5) 1997, 599.

72. Proof for this argument would be to look at the list of sponsors of the meeting of the Business Forum of the Americas (BFA) in April 2001 in Buenos Aires. The list included, among others, AOL, Bank Boston, Deutsche Bank, DuPont Argentina, Federal Myers, Ford Argentina, IBM Argentina, Movicom Bell South, Procter & Gamble, The Exxel Group, Visa Argentina and Wal Mart Argentina (http://www.vi.fema-abf.org.ar/instipa2.html, 9 September 2001).

73. The interviewee requested anonymity for this remark.

74. Ian Katz, 'Adios, Argentina' *Business Week* 17 January 2000; 'Brazilian business association says 2bn US$ investments in Argentina at risk' *AFX Europe* 9 July 2001.

75. Cason, 'On the Road to Southern Cone Economic Integration', 35.

76. 'Just through Mercosur, Argentina will get strengthened in the FTAA' Interview with Alfredo Neme Scheij, President of the Mercosur Committee

at the Argentinean House of Representatives, 23 April 2001 (http://www.mercosur.com/info/articuloimp.jsp?noticia=7646, 27 May 2001); 'US Trade Representative invites Mercosur to discuss FTAA with USA' BBC Monitoring Service – United Kingdom 24 August 2001; Raymond Colitt, 'EU extends proposal to infighting Mercosur' FT.com site 10 July 2001; 'EU presents trade liberalisation proposal to Mercosur' BBC Monitoring Service 7 July 2001.

77. 'The Business Sector vis à vis the FTAA negotiations' VI Foro Empresarial de las Americas (http://www.vi-fema-abf.org.ar/pressrelease.html, 9 September 2001).

78. Kaltenthaler and Mora, 'Explaining Latin American Economic Integration: The Case of the Mercosur', 92–93.

79. The term 'region' will be used in accordance with the previously given definition of the term, thus referring to the supranational level of the EU as the regional level. It is important to note that in the terminology of EU integration studies 'regional' refers to the sub-national level of governance in the EU.

80. Wolfgang Streeck and Philippe C. Schmitter, 'From National Corporatism to Transnational Pluralism: Organised Interests in the Single European Market' *Politics and Society* 19(2) 1991, 134.

81. Streeck and Schmitter, 'From National Corporatism to Transnational Pluralism: Organised Interests in the Single European Market', 134.

82. Streeck and Schmitter, 'From National Corporatism to Transnational Pluralism: Organised Interests in the Single European Market', 135.

83. Desmond Dinan, *Ever Closer Union?* (Houndmills, Basingstoke and London: The Macmillan Press Ltd., 1994), 27–28; George Ross, 'European Integration and Globalisation', In Roland Axmann, ed. *Globalisation and Europe – Theoretical and Empirical Investigations* (London and Washington: Pinter, 1998), 165; Helen Wallace, 'Politics and Policy in the EU: The Challenge of Governance' in Helen Wallace and William Wallace, eds, *Policy-Making in the European Union*, 3rd edition (Oxford: Oxford University Press, 1996), 9.

84. David Mitrany, 'A Working Peace System' in Brent F. Nelsen and Alexander C.-G. Stubb, eds, *The European Union – Readings on the Theory and Practice of European Integration*, 2nd edition (Boulder, Colorado and London: Lynne Rienner Publishers, 1998), 99–111.

85. Ernst B. Haas, *The Uniting of Europe – Political, Social and Economic Forces 1950–1957* (Stanford, California: Stanford University Press, 1958), xxxiii.

86. Ernst B. Haas, *The Uniting of Europe – Political, Social and Economic Forces 1950–1957*, 2nd edition (Stanford, California: Stanford University Press, 1968), 16.

87. For the role of interest groups and organised business interests in promoting the Single Market project consult Sandholtz and Zysman, '1992: Recasting the European Bargain', 197.

88. Andrew Hurrell, 'Explaining the Resurgence of Regionalism in World Politics', *Review of International Studies* 21(4) 1995, 349.

89. Knud Erik Jørgensen and Ben Rosamond, 'Europe: Regional Laboratory or a Global Polity?' CSGR Working Paper No. 71/01, 9.

90. Elizabeth Jelin, 'Dialogues, Understandings and Misunderstandings: Social Movements in Mercosur' *International Social Science Journal* 51(159) 1999, 42.

91. For a more detailed analysis of the nature of integration in reference to neo-functionalism consult Leon N. Lindberg, 'Political Integration: Definitions and Hypotheses' in Brent F. Nelsen and Alexander C.-G. Stubb, eds, *The European Union – Readings on the Theory and Practice of European Integration*, 2nd edition (Boulder, Colorado and London: Lynne Rienner Publishers, 1998), 147–150.

92. Stanley Hoffmann, 'Obstinate or Obsolete? The Fate of the Nation-State and the Case of Western Europe' in Brent F. Nelsen and Alexander C.-G. Stubb, eds, *The European Union – Readings on the Theory and Practice of European Integration*, 2nd edition (Boulder, Colorado and London: Lynne Rienner Publishers, 1998), 168.

93. Robert O. Keohane and Stanley Hoffmann, 'Conclusions: Community Politics and Institutional Change' in William Wallace, ed., *The Dynamics of European Integration* (London: The Royal Institute of International Affairs, 1992), 276.

94. Andrew Moravcsik, 'Preferences and Power in the European Community: A Liberal Intergovernmentalist Approach' in Michael O'neill, ed., *The Politics of European Integration – A Reader* (London and New York: Routledge, 1996), 297–300; Andrew Moravcsik, 'Negotiating the Single European Act: National Interests and Conventional Statecraft in the European Community' in Brent F. Nelsen and Alexander C.-G. Stubb, eds, *The European Union – Readings on the Theory and Practice of European Integration*, 2nd edition (Boulder, Colorado and London: Lynne Rienner Publishers, 1998), 223–24.

95. Gary Marks, 'Structural Policy and Multilevel Governance in the EC' in Alan W. Cafruny and Glenda G. Rosenthal, eds, *The State of the European Community (Vol. 2) – The Maastricht Debates and Beyond* (Boulder, Colorado: Lynne Rienner Publishers, Inc. and Harlow, Essex: Longman Group U.K. Ltd., 1993), 401; see also Wayne Sandholtz, 'Membership Matters: Limits of the Functional Approach to European Institutions' *Journal of Common Market Studies* 34(3) 1996, 412; Strange, by contrast, argues that the state has lost authority to the sides or 'downwards', but not to supranational institutions; see Susan Strange, *The Retreat of the State – The Diffusion of Power in the World Economy* (Cambridge: Cambridge University Press, 1996), 179.

96. Nicola Phillips, 'Governance after Financial Crisis: South American Perspectives on the Reformulation of Regionalism' *New Political Economy* 5(3) 2000, 387.

97. Justin Greenwood, *Interest Representation in the European Union* (Houndmills, Basingstoke and New York: Palgrave Macmillan, 2003), 96–104.

98. Sonia Mazey and Jeremy Richardson, 'Agenda Setting, Lobbying and the 1996 IGC' in Geoffrey Edwards and Alfred Pijpers, *The Politics of European Treaty Reform* (London and Washington: Pinter, 1997), 234–35; Paul Betts, 'The quiet knights of Europe's round table' *Financial Times* 20 March

2001, 16; Paul Betts and Brian Groom, 'Industry urges faster EU reform' *Financial Times* 20 March 2001, 1; Sandholtz and Zysman, '1992: Recasting the European Bargain', 212–13; Alec Stone Sweet and Wayne Sandholtz, 'European Integration and Supranational Governance' *Journal of European Public Policy* 4(3) 1997, 309.

99. *Grant, Business and Politics in Britain*, 171.

100. For an interesting overview about the ERT consult: Bastiaan van Apeldoorn, 'The European Round Table of Industrialists: Still a Unique Player?' in Justin Greenwood, ed., *The Effectiveness of EU Business Associations* (Houndmills, Basingstoke and New York: Palgrave Macmillan, 2002), 194–205.

101. For a current analysis of the state and future development of EU business associations consult Justin Greenwood, ed., *The Effectiveness of EU Business Associations* (Houndmills, Basingstoke and New York: Palgrave Macmillan, 2002).

102. Phillips, *The Southern Cone Model – the Political Economy of Regional Capitalist Development in Latin America*, 129.

103. Deisy Ventura, 'First Arbitration Award in Mercosur – A Community Law in Evolution' *Leiden Journal of International Law* 13, 2000, 458.

104. Cárdenas and Tempesta, 'Arbitral Awards under Mercosur's Dispute Settlement Mechanism', 350–51.

105. Ventura, 'First Arbitration Award in Mercosur – A Community Law in Evolution', 457.

106. Bela Balassa, *The Theory of Economic Integration* (London: Allen & Unwin Ltd., 1965), 2; for an earlier version of the argument consult Bela Balassa, 'Towards a theory of economic integration' *Kyklos* 14(1) 1961, 1–17.

107. Robert L. Allen, 'Integration in less developed area' *Kyklos* 14(3) 1961, 314–15 [emphasis in the original].

108. Shaun Breslin and Richard Higgott, 'Studying Regions: Learning from the Old, Constructing the New' *New Political Economy* 5(3) 2000, 344.

109. Peter C. Chow, 'Asia Pacific Economic Integration in Global Perspective' in James C. Hsiung, ed., *Asia Pacific in the New World Politics* (Boulder, Colorado and London: Lynne Rienner Publishers, 1993), 195.

110. Richard Higgott, 'The Pacific and Beyond: Apec, Asem and Regional Economic Management' in Grahame Thompson, ed., *Economic Dynamism in the Asia-Pacific* (London: Routledge, published for The Open University, 1998), 337 [emphases in the original]; for a more complex definition of regionalisation and regionalism see also Richard Higgott, 'The Political Economy of Globalisation in East Asia – the Salience of "Region Building"' in Kris Olds, Peter Dicken, Philip F. Kelly, Lily Kong and Henry Wai-chung Yeung, eds, *Globalisation and the Asia-Pacific – Contested Territories* (London and New York: Routledge in Association with the Centre for the Study of Globalisation and Regionalisation, University of Warwick, 1999), 91–94.

111. Mark Beeson and Kanishka Jayasuriya, 'The Political Rationalities of Regionalism: APEC and the EU in Comparative Perspective' *The Pacific Review* 11(3) 1998, 317.

112. Beeson and Jayasuriya, 'The Political Rationalities of Regionalism: APEC and the EU in Comparative Perspective', 333.
113. Christopher Brook, 'Regionalism and Globalism' in Anthony McGrew and Christopher Brook, eds, *Asia Pacific in the New World Order* (London: Routledge, published for The Open University, 1998), 231.
114. 'Argentine foreign minister sees trade talks with USA as "fundamental landmark".' BBC Monitoring Service, 3 September 2001.
115. Walter Mattli, 'Explaining Regional Integration Outcomes' *Journal of European Public Policy* 6(1) 1999, 3; for a similar argument see also Moravcsik, *The Choice For Europe – Social Purpose & State Power From Messina to Maastricht* (London: University College London Press, 1998), 3–4.
116. John Zysman, 'The Myth of a "Global" Economy: Enduring National Foundations and Emerging Regional Realities' *New Political Economy* 1(2) 1996, 160–62.
117. Zysman, 'The Myth of a "Global" Economy: Enduring National Foundations and Emerging Regional Realities', 161–62.
118. Zysman, 'The Myth of a "Global" Economy: Enduring National Foundations and Emerging Regional Realities', 164; for the role played by the state in the process of globalisation consult also Eric Helleiner, 'Explaining the Globalisation of Financial Markets: Bringing States Back In' *Review of International Political Economy* 2(2) 1995, 315–41.
119. Marianne H. Marchand, Morten Bøås and Timothy M. Shaw, 'The Political Economy of New Regionalism' *Third World Quarterly* 20(5) 1999, 900 [emphasis in the original].
120. Marchand et al., 'The Political Economy of New Regionalism', 900.
121. Marchand et al., 'The Political Economy of New Regionalism', 900 [emphasis in the original].
122. Marchand et al., 'The Political Economy of New Regionalism', 900.
123. David Floyd, 'Globalisation or Europeanisation of Business Activity? Exploring the Critical Issues' *European Business Review* 13(2) 2001, 113.
124. Zysman, 'The Myth of a "Global" Economy: Enduring National Foundations and Emerging Regional Realities', 157; consult also Susan Strange, 'Globaloney?' *Review of International Political Economy* 5(4) 1998, 704–20; Bob Jessop, 'Reflections on Globalisation and Its (il)logic(s)' in Kris Olds, Peter Dicken, Philip F., Kelly, Lily Kong and Henry Wai-chung Yeung, eds, *Globalisation and the Asia-Pacific – Contested Territories* (London and New York: Routledge in Association with the Centre for the Study of Globalisation and Regionalisation, University of Warwick, 1999), 19–38.
125. Grugel and de Almeida Medeiros, 'Brazil and Mercosur', 59.
126. Kenichi Ohmae, *The End of the Nation State – The Rise of Regional Economies* (London: Harper Collins Publishers, 1996), 80.
127. Ohmae, *The End of the Nation State – The Rise of Regional Economies*, 80.
128. Mittelman by contrast argues that small states promote sub-regional integration to maintain their economic competitiveness by gaining access to lower-cost and lower-skilled labour; see James M. Mittelman,'

The Globalisation Challenge: Surviving at the Margins' *Third World Quarterly* 15(3) 1994, 436.

129. Paul Hirst and Grahame Thompson, *Globalisation in Question* (Cambridge: Polity Press, 1996), 49; for a historical analysis of globalisation consult Samir Amin, 'The Challenge of Globalisation' *Review of International Political Economy* 3(2) 1996, 216–59.

130. Hirst and Thompson, *Globalisation in Question*, 184.

131. Hirst and Thompson, *Globalisation in Question*, 183.

132. Linda Weiss, *The Myth of the Powerless State – Governing the Economy in a Global Era* (Cambridge: Polity Press, 1998), 211 [emphasis in the original]; consult also her article for a more compact version of her argument, Linda Weiss, 'Globalisation and the Myth of the Powerless State' *New Left Review* 225, 1997, 3–27. See also Linda Weiss, ed., *States in the Global Economy – Bringing Domestic Institutions Back In* (Cambridge: Cambridge University Press, 2003).

133. Weiss, The Myth of the Powerless State – Governing the Economy in a Global Era, 210–11; for a similar argument consult David Armstrong, 'Globalisation and the Social State' *Review of International Studies* 24(4) 1998, 461–78.

134. Jonathan Perraton, David Goldblatt, David Held and Anthony McGrew, 'The Globalisation of Economic Activity' *New Political Economy* 2(2) 1997, 257.

135. Perraton et al., 'The Globalisation of Economic Activity', 274.

136. Perraton et al., 'The Globalisation of Economic Activity', 274–75.

137. Stephen Gill, 'Globalisation, Market Civilisation, and Disciplinary Neoliberalism' *Millennium: Journal of International Studies* 24(3) 1995, 399; see also Stephen Gill and David Law, 'Global Hegemony and the Structural Power of Capital' in Stephen Gill, ed., *Gramsci, Historical Materialism and International Relations* (Cambridge: Cambridge University Press, 1993), 93–124; Vicki Birchfield, 'Contesting the Hegemony of Market Ideology: Gramsci's "Good Sense" and Polanyi's "Double Movement"' *Review of International Political Economy* 6(1) 1999, 27–54.

138. Stephen Gill, 'Epistemology, ontology, and the "Italian school"' in Stephen Gill, ed., *Gramsci, Historical Materialism and International Relations* (Cambridge: Cambridge University Press, 1993), 32–33.

139. Gill, 'Globalisation, Market Civilisation, and Disciplinary Neoliberalism', 419.

140. Richard Devetak and Richard Higgott, 'Justice Unbound? Globalisation, States and the Transformation of the Social Bond' *International Affairs* 75(3) 1999, 483; for the need to develop a new social context in the light of globalisation consult also Richard Falk, 'State of Siege: Will Globalisation Win Out?' *International Affairs* 73(1) 1997, 123–36; Philip G. Cerny, 'Globalising the Political and Politicising the Global: Concluding Reflections on International Political Economy as a Vocation' *New Political Economy* 4(1) 1999, 160–61.

141. Andrew Gamble and Anthony Payne, 'Conclusion: The New Regionalism' in Andrew Gamble and Anthony Payne, eds, *Regionalism and World Order* (Houndmills, Basingstoke and London: Macmillan, 1996), 258.
142. Hartmut Sangmeister, 'Im Labyrinth der Modernisierung – Lateinamerika zwischen Globalisierung und Regionalisierung' *Internationale Politik* 54(5) 1999, 23.
143. Sangmeister, 'Im Labyrinth der Modernisierung – Lateinamerika zwischen Globalisierung und Regionalisierung', 22–23.
144. Sangmeister, 'Im Labyrinth der Modernisierung – Lateinamerika zwischen Globalisierung und Regionalisierung', 18.
145. Grugel and de Almeida Medeiros, 'Brazil and Mercosur', 61.
146. Roberto Bisang, 'The Responses of National Holding Companies' in Bernardo Kosacoff, ed., *Corporate Strategies under Structural Adjustment in Argentina* (Houndmills, Basingstoke and London: Macmillan Press Ltd., 2000), 150–51.
147. The case of Arcor is analysed in detail in Bernardo Kosacoff, Jorge Forteza, María Inés Barbero, F. Porta and E. Alejandro Stengel. *Going Global from Latin America: The Arcor Case* (Buenos Aires: McGrawHill Interamericana, 2002).
148. Wil Hout, 'Theories of International Relations and the New Regionalism' in Jean Grugel and Wil Hout, eds, *Regionalism across the North-South Divide – State Strategies and Globalisation* (London and New York: Routledge, 1999), 27.
149. Jan Aart Scholte, *Globalisation – a Critical Introduction* (Houndmills, Basingstoke and New York: Palgrave Macmillan, 2000), 48–49.
150. Scholte, *Globalisation – a Critical Introduction*, 49 [emphasis in the original].
151. Scholte, *Globalisation – a Critical Introduction*, 49.
152. Scholte, *Globalisation – a Critical Introduction*, 59 [emphasis in the original].
153. Scholte, *Globalisation – a Critical Introduction*, 50.
154. I am grateful to Wyn Grant for pointing this out to me.
155. From the plethora of theoretical approaches within CPE and IPE, she has chosen an intersection of four specific literatures as her controlled eclecticism within the context of the political economy of the Southern Cone. Namely, 'from CPE the models of capitalism debate and strands of development theory; and, from IPE, the study of globalisation and the study of regionalism and regionalisation'. See Phillips, *The Southern Cone Model – the Political Economy of Regional Capitalist Development in Latin America*, 15.
156. See also Dickins, 'The Evolution of International Political Economy', 481.
157. A. Flew, ed., *A Dictionary of Philosophy* (New York: St. Martin's Press, 1979) as quoted in Anthony Bottoms, 'The Relationship between Theory and Research in Criminology', in Roy D. King and Emma Wincup, eds, *Doing Research on Crime and Justice* (Oxford: Oxford University Press, 2000), 23.
158. Longman's Dictionary of the English Language as quoted in Bottoms, 'The Relationship between Theory and Research in Criminology', 23.

159. See for example Söderbaum, *The Political Economy of Regionalism: The case of Southern Africa*, 5.
160. Susan Strange, 'The Future of Global Capitalism; or Will Divergence Persist Forever?' in Colin Crouch and Wolfgang Streeck, eds, *Political Economy of Modern Capitalism – Mapping Convergence and Diversity* (London, Thousand Oaks and New Delhi: Sage Publications, 1997), 184.
161. Susan Strange, *States and Market*, 2nd edition (London and Washington: Pinter, 1994), 18.
162. Phillips, *The Southern Cone Model – the Political Economy of Regional Capitalist Development in Latin America*, 13 [emphasis in the original]. 13.
163. Marchand et al., 'The Political Economy of New Regionalism', 897.
164. For an overview see Geoffrey R. D. Underhill, 'State, Market and Global Political Economy: Genealogy of an (Inter?) Discipline' *International Affairs* 76(4) 2000, 805–24; James A. Caporaso, 'Across the Great Divide: Integrating Comparative and International Politics' *International Studies Quarterly* 41, 1997, 563–92.
165. Simon Hix, 'The Study of the European Union II: The "'New Governance" Agenda and Its Rival' *Journal of European Public Policy* 5(1) 1998, 38–65; Jean Blondel, 'Then and Now: Comparative Politics' *Political Studies* 47(2) 1999, 152–60.
166. Andrew Hurrell and Anand Menon, 'Politics Like Any Other? Comparative Politics, International Relations and the Study of the EU' *West European Politics* 19 (2) 1996, 386–402; Michael Jachtenfuchs, 'Theoretical Perspectives on European Governance' *European Law Journal* 1(2) 1995, 115–33.
167. Hurrell and Menon, 'Politics Like Any Other? Comparative Politics, International Relations and the Study of the EU', 400.

3 Structures of Business Interest Articulation in the Mercosur: The National and the Regional Dimension

1. Chapter 5 refers to the CIQUIM in more detail and the role it played in fostering a Mercosur-wide coordinated policy response of the chemical industry to the Mercosur process.
2. Fritsch and Tombini, 'The Mercosur: An Overview', 83.
3. Bouzas, 'El proceso de integración en el Mercosur', 177; email correspondence with Andrés López, Researcher, 26 February 2003.
4. Email correspondence with Andrés López, 26 February 2003.
5. Interview with Felix Peña, Director, International Trade Institute, Fundación Bank Boston, 12 April 2002.
6. Interregional in this context refers to new forms of regional organised business representation, for example the Mercosur-EU Business Forum (MEBF) or the Foro Empresarial de las Americas (FEMA) encompassing North, Central and South America.
7. Interview with Antonio Estrany y Gendre, President, Consejo Interamericano de Comercio y Producción (CICYP), 26 March 2002.

8. The percentage of intra-bloc trade rose from very low levels to 16 per cent in 1991, shortly after the inauguration of the Mercosur, and now averages at 20 per cent (when taking into account the slump in intra-bloc imports and exports during the financial crisis in Argentina in 2001/02, this indicator drops to as low as 12%); consult Indicadores Macroeconómicos del Mercosur, Julio 2002, No. 906, Montevideo: Secretaría Administrativa del Mercosur; Economic Survey of Latin America and the Cartibbean 2001–2002 – Current Conditions and Outlook August 2002 (Santiago de Chile: CEPAL, 2002), 15.
9. Wolfram F. Klein, *El Mercosur – Empresarios y Sindicatos frente a los Desafiós del Proceso de Integración* (Caracas: Editorial Nueva Sociedad, 2000), 79; email correspondence with Andrés López, Researcher, 26 February 2003.
10. Julio Magri, 'La Asociación Empresaria para estatizar la deuda externa' (http://www.po.org.ar/po//po757/la.htm, 4 November 2002).
11. Interview with Andrés López, 10 April 2002.
12. Interview with Andrés López, 10 April 2002.
13. Ben Ross Schneider, 'Business Politics and Regional Integration: The Advantages of Organisation in NAFTA and Mercosur', in Victor Bulmer-Thomas, ed., *Regional Integration in Latin America and the Caribbean: The Political Economy of Open Regionalism* (London: Institute of Latin American Studies, 2001), 178.
14. Interview with Felix Peña, 12 April 2002.
15. Interview with Felix Peña, 12 April 2002.
16. Email correspondence with Andrés López, Researcher, 26 February 2003.
17. Klein, *El Mercosur – Empresarios y Sindicatos frente a los Desafiós del Proceso de Integración*, 176–77.
18. Interview with Felix Peña, 12 April 2002.
19. Observations made during a two-month visit to Brazil, summer 1991, during the time of hyper-inflation and just before the formal inauguration of the Mercosur.
20. Roberto Luchi and Marcelo Paladino, 'Improving Competitiveness in a Manufacturing Value Chain: Issues Dealing with the Automobile Sector in Argentina and Mercosur' *Industrial Management and Data Systems* 100(8) 2000, 349; 'Buy, buy, buy' *The Economist* 4 December 1997; information and available data from the Ministerio di Economía y Produccíon, Republica Argentina (www.mecon.gov.ar/peconomica/informe/anteriores. htm, 5 January 2005); Statistical Yearbook for Latin America and the Caribbean 2003 (Santiago de Chile: CEPAL, 2004), chapter 2/V, table 279 (www.eclac.cl/badestat/anuario_2003, 5 January 2005); Anuario 1998 (Buenos Aires: ADEFA, 1999), II/2 (www.adefa.com.ar, 29 December 2004).
21. This kind of flexibility, however, put Mercosur under pressure, as especially Argentina was suffering since the devaluation of the Brazilian real in 1999 from a massive shift of FDI away from the Argentine economy to Brazil. Because of the devaluation of the Argentine Peso, due to the end of the currency board and the related collapse of the Argentine financial system and economy more generally in 2001/02, the Argentine economy

started to recover, albeit slowly; for background information consult 'Trouble in Eldorado' *The Economist* 11 December 1997; 'Double parked' *The Economist* 7 January 1999; Ian Katz, 'Adios Argentina' *Business Week* 17 January 2000; Statistical Yearbook for Latin America and the Caribbean 2003, chapter 2/V, table 279.

22. Interview with Lars Grabenschröer, Abteilungsleiter Volkswirtschaft, Deutsch-Brasilianische Industrie- und Handelskammer (AHK Brasil), 28 August 2002.

23. ADEFA's members are Volkswagen, Toyota, Scania, PSA Peugeot Citroen, Daimler Chrysler, Renault, Iveco, General Motors, Ford and Fiat. ANFAVEA's members are, in addition to the one mentioned for ADEFA, Volvo, Nissan, New Holland, Case, Agco, Mitsubishi, Komatsu, Caterpillar, John Deere, Karmann Ghia and Honda.

24. Interview with Andrés López, 10 April 2002.

25. Spain has also increasingly played an important role through significant investment in the banking, telecommunications and oil and gas exploitation.

26. Daniel Chudnovsky y Andrés López, 'La inversión extranjera directa en el Mercosur: un análisis comparativo', in Daniel Chudnovsky, Andrés López, Mariano Laplane, Gustavo Bittencourt, Fernando Massi, Rosario Domingo, Fernando Sarti, Célio Hiratuka and Rodrigo Sabbatini eds, *El boom de inversión directa en el Mercosur* (Madrid: Siglo Veintiuno and Red de Investigaciones Económicas del Mercosur, 2001), 1–2.

27. Interview with Reinhold Meyer, Sub-director, Argentine-German Chamber of Industry and Commerce (CADICAA), 11 April 2002.

28. Email correspondence with Andrés López, 26 February 2003.

29. Email correspondence with Andrés López, 26 February 2003.

30. Interview with Andrés López, 10 April 2002.

31. Interview with Andrés López, 10 April 2002.

32. 'En medio de la crisis, crean una poderosa agrupación empresaria' Clarín. com (http://old.clarin.com/diario/2002/05/29/e-01601.htm, 4 November 2002); see also www.aeanet.net for more information on the AEA.

33. In this respect, it is worth mentioning that Paraguay still has an economy heavily dependent on agriculture and agricultural exports, which explains their relative weakness and the limited resources of the UIP.

34. Business Organisation for Participation in International Negotiations (Brazilian Business Coalition, November 2000), 5.

35. The AEB and the CEAL, by contrast, are voluntarily funded by their respective members. Ironically, the AEB is quite protectionist about their trade-related policies, despite being the exporters' federation.

36. The analysis of the CNI and the changes within the domestic business associations in Brazil are based on a two and a half hour-long interview with Sandra Polónia Rios, the Coordinator of the International Integration Unit of the CNI, 2 September 2002. The statements made in this interview have been substantiated by the interview with Christian Lohbauer, 28 August 2002.

37. The analysis of FIESP in the following paragraphs is based on a two hour-long interview with Christian Lohbauer, Gerente de Relações Internacionais, Federação das Indústrias do Estado de São Paulo (FIESP), Centro das Indústrias do Estado de São Paulo (CIESP), 28 August 2002. The statements made in this interview have been substantiated by the interview with Sandra Polónia Rios, 2 September 2002.
38. Interview with Christian Lohbauer, 28 August 2002.
39. Interview with Sandra Polónia Rios, 2 September 2002.
40. Interview with Sandra Polónia Rios, 2 September 2002.
41. Interview with Sandra Polónia Rios, 2 September 2002.
42. Interview with Sandra Polónia Rios, 2 September 2002.
43. Interview with Sandra Polónia Rios, 2 September 2002.
44. Interview with Guilherme Duque Estrada de Moraes, Executive Vice-President and CEO, Brazilian Chemical Industry Association (ABIQUIM), 26 August 2002.
45. As mentioned before, Chapter five refers to the CIQUIM in more detail and the role it played in fostering a Mercosur-wide coordinated policy response of the chemical industry to the Mercosur process. It is also important to note that the chemical industry generally is highly inter-nationalised, and in the case of the Southern Cone this dates back to pre-Second World War intra-industry agreements.
46. Interview with Guilherme Duque Estrada de Moraes, 26 August 2002.
47. The interviewee requested anonymity for this remark.
48. Interview with Lars Grabenschröer, 28 August 2002.
49. The analysis of the CEAL is based on an interview with Alberto Pfeiffer, Director Ejecutivo, Consejo Empresario de America Latina (CEAL), 26 August 2002.
50. For a comprehensive survey of the role of the FCES from an insider perspective consult Confederação Nacional do Comércio (CNC), Mercado Comun do Sul -Foro Consultivo Econômico-Social (Rio de Janeiro: CNC, 2000).
51. This quote was made with the request to remain anonymous.
52. For example, the interview with Jayme Quintas Perez, Economista, Assessor Empresarial (Seção Brasileira) Foro Consultive Economico-Social, Confederação Nacional do Comércio (CNC) and Délio Urpia de Seixas, Economista, Confederação Nacional do Comércio (CNC), 4 September 2002.

4   The Relationship between Domestic and Regional Organized Business Interests in the Mercosur: Conflict and Convergence

1. Peter Nunnenkamp, 'European FDI Strategies in Mercosur Countries' Kiel Working Paper No. 1047 (Kiel: Kiel Institute of World Economics, 2001), 12–14.

2. Bernardo Kosacoff, 'The Development of Argentine Industry', in Bernardo Kosacoff, ed., *Corporate Strategies under Structural Adjustment in Argentina* (Houndmills, Basingstoke and London: Macmillan Press Ltd., 2000), 44–45.
3. Kosacoff, 'The Development of Argentine Industry', 46–47.
4. Email correspondence with Andrés López, 3 April 2003.
5. Email correspondence with Andrés López, 9 January 2003.
6. For the two paragraphs see Klein, *El Mercosur – Empresarios y Sindicatos frente a los Desafíós del Proceso de Integración*, 87.
7. Edwin Williamson, *The Penguin History of Latin America* (London: Penguin Books, 1992), 480–81.
8. Email correspondence with Andrés López, 3 April 2003.
9. Klein, *El Mercosur – Empresarios y Sindicatos frente a los Desafíós del Proceso de Integración*, 81; see also Daniel R. García Delgado, Estado & Sociedad – la nueva relación a partir del cambio estructural (Buenos Aires: Grupo Editorial Norma SA, 1994), 142.
10. Carlos H. Acuña, 'Political Struggle and Business Peak Associations: Theoretical Reflections on the Argentine Case', in Francisco Durand and Eduardo Silva, eds, *Organised Business, Economic Change, Democracy in Latin America* (Miami: North-South Center Press, 1998), 69–70 [emphasis in the original].
11. Acuña, 'Political Struggle and Business Peak Associations: Theoretical Reflections on the Argentine Case', 62, 63 [for the quote], 64.
12. Acuña, 'Political Struggle and Business Peak Associations: Theoretical Reflections on the Argentine Case', 67.
13. Acuña, 'Political Struggle and Business Peak Associations: Theoretical Reflections on the Argentine Case', 66.
14. Kosacoff, 'The Development of Argentine Industry', 49–50.
15. Email correspondence with Andrés López, 3 April 2003.
16. Roberto Lavagna, 'Comercio Exterior y Política Comercial en Brasil y Argentina. Una Evolución Comparada', in José María Lladós and Samuel Pinheiro Guimarães, eds, *Perspectivas Brasil y Argentina* (Brasilia and Buenos Aires: IPRI-CARI, 1999), 212 (own translation).
17. Lavagna, 'Comercio Exterior y Política Comercial en Brasil y Argentina. Una Evolución Comparada', 215.
18. For the paragraph see Williamson, *The Penguin History of Latin America*, 433.
19. For the two paragraphs see Mónica Hirst, 'Brasil – Argentina a la sombra del futuro', in José María Lladós and Samuel Pinheiro Guimarães, eds, *Perspectivas Brasil y Argentina* (Brasilia and Buenos Aires: IPRI-CARI, 1999), 388.
20. Jorge Campbell, Ricardo Rozemberg and Gustavo Svarzman, 'Argentina – Brasil en los '80s: Entre la cornisa y la integración', in Jorge Campbell, ed., *Mercosur – Entre la Realidad y la Utopía* (Buenos Aires: Grupo Editor Latinoamericano, 1999), 72–74.
21. Interview with Guilherme Duque Estrada de Moraes, 26 August 2002; see also Claudia Sanchez Bajo, 'Mercosur's Open Regionalism and Regulation: Focusing on the Petrochemicals and Steel Sectors', Paper presented to the

International Studies Association Convention February 1999 (http://www.ciaonet.org/isa/sac01/, 6 January 2003).
22. Hirst, 'Brasil – Argentina a la sombra del futuro', 388.
23. Interview with Guilherme Duque Estrada de Moraes, 26 August 2002.
24. The Peronist party derives its name from Juan Domingo Perón, who first was in power from 1946–55, and then again from 1973–76. At the beginning, the Peronist Party aligned itself with the radical right, whereas in the 1960s and during Perón's second time in power it associated itself closely with both, the radical right and the radical left. Alfonsín, by contrast, was a member of the Radical party, which draws support mainly from the urban middle classes, parts of the working class and some landowners; see email correspondence with Andrés López, 3 April 2003; Williamson, *The Penguin History of Latin America*, 459–76.
25. Aldo Ferrer, *El capitalismo argentino* (México, Argentina, Brasil, Chile, Columbia, España, Estados Unidos de América, Perú and Venezuela: Fondo de Cultura Económica, 2000), 89.
26. Consult for example, Ferrer, *El capitalismo argentino*, 90; Kosacoff, 'The Development of Argentine Industry', 58–60; email correspondence with Andrés López, 3 April 2003; Statistical Yearbook for Latin America and the Caribbean 2003 (Santiago de Chile: CEPAL, 2004), chapter 2/III, table 248 A (www.eclac.cl/badestat/anuario_2003, 5 January 2005).
27. Edmund Amann and Werner Baer, 'Neoliberalism and its Consequences in Brazil' *Journal of Latin American Studies* 34(4) 2002, 947–48.
28. Williamson, *The Penguin History of Latin America*, 434–35.
29. For the data see Foreign Trade 4 (CNI, 2001), 41; Averbug argues that even between 1988 and 1989, average tariff rates fell from 41.2 per cent to 17.8 per cent. See André Averbug, 'Brazilian Trade Liberalisation and Integration in the 1990s' (Rio de Janeiro: BNDES, no publication date), 2.
30. Email correspondence with Sandra Polónia Rios, 10 January 2003.
31. For the paragraph see Klein, *El Mercosur – Empresarios y Sindicatos frente a los Desafiós del Proceso de Integración*, 92–93.
32. For an excellent overview of the emergence and the evolving structures of interest representation in Brazil consult Philippe C. Schmitter, *Interest Conflict and Political Change in Brazil* (Stanford, California: Stanford University Press, 1971).
33. Klein, *El Mercosur – Empresarios y Sindicatos frente a los Desafiós del Proceso de Integración*, 91.
34. For the paragraph see Paul Cammack, 'Brasilien' in Walther E. Bernecker, Raymond T. Buve, John R. Fisher, Horst Pietschmann and Hans Werner Tobler, eds, *Handbuch der Geschichte Lateinamerikas – Band 3* (Stuttgart: Klett-Clotta, 1996), 1092–94; see also www.cni.org.br/f-ent.htm, 29 December 2004.
35. Interview with Ricardo Markwald, Director Geral, Fundação Centro de Estudos do Comércio Exterior (FUNCEX), 3 September 2002; see also Timothy J. Power and Mahrukh Doctor, 'The Resilience of Corporatism: Continuity and Change in Brazilian Corporatist Structures' University

of Oxford Centre for Brazilian Studies Working Paper Series (Oxford: University of Oxford Centre for Brazilian Studies, 2002), 21.
36. Cammack, 'Brasilien', 1093–94.
37. Kurt Weyland, 'The Fragmentation of Business in Brazil', in Francisco Durand and Eduardo Silva, eds, *Organised Business, Economic Change, Democracy in Latin America* (Miami: North-South Center Press, 1998), 79.
38. Mahrukh Doctor, 'The Interplay of States and Markets: The Role of Business-State Relations in Attracting Investment to the Automotive Industry in Brazil' Working Paper CBS-40-2003 (Oxford: University of Oxford Centre for Brazilian Studies, 2003), 8 [emphasis in the original].
39. Klein, *El Mercosur – Empresarios y Sindicatos frente a los Desafiós del Proceso de Integración*, 92.
40. Peter R. Kingstone, 'The Limits of Neoliberalism: Business, the State, and Democratic Consolidation in Brazil', Paper prepared for the 20th International Congress of the Latin American Studies Association, April 1997, Guadalajara, Mexico, 14; see also Ben Schneider, 'Business Politics in Democratic Brazil', in Maria D'Alva Gil Kinzo, ed., *Reforming the State: Business, Unions and Regions in Brazil* (London: Institute of Latin American Studies, University of London, 1997), 12–15.
41. 'Livre para crescer' translates as 'Free to grow' (own translation).
42. Weyland, 'The Fragmentation of Business in Brazil', 84.
43. IEDI – 12 ANOS (São Paulo: IEDI, July 2001), 5.
44. Klein, *El Mercosur – Empresarios y Sindicatos frente a los Desafiós del Proceso de Integración*, 91.
45. Schneider, 'Business Politics in Democratic Brazil', 14.
46. IEDI – 12 ANOS, 27; Schneider, 'Business Politics in Democratic Brazil', 14–15.
47. PNBE, PNBE: Cidania, Desenvolvimento e Justiçia Social (http://www.pnbe.org.br/historico.asp and http://www.pnbe.org.br/realiza.asp, accessed 12 June 2003).
48. Ben Ross Schneider, 'Big Business and the Politics of Economic Reform: Confidence and Concertation in Brazil and Mexico', in Sylvia Maxfield and Ben Ross Schneider, eds, *Business and the State in Developing Countries* (Ithaca, New York and London: Cornell University Press, 1997), 208.
49. Doctor, 'The Interplay of States and Markets: The Role of Business-State Relations in Attracting Investment to the Automotive Industry in Brazil', 8.
50. Ben Ross Schneider, 'Business Politics and Regional Integration: The Advantages of Organisation in NAFTA and Mercosur', in Victor Bulmer-Thomas, ed., *Regional Integration in Latin America and the Caribbean: The Political Economy of Open Regionalism* (London: Institute of Latin American Studies, 2001), 176.
51. José de Souza Martins, 'Clientilism and Corruption in Comntemporary Brazil', in Walter Little and Eduardo Posada-Carbó, eds, *Political Corruption in Europe and Latin America* (Houndmills, Basingstoke and London: Macmillan in association with the Institute of Latin American Studies,

University of London, 1996), 195; Kurt Weyland, 'The Politics of Corruption in Latin America' *Journal of Democracy* 9(2) 1998, 119.

52. De Souza Martins, 'Clientilism and Corruption in Comntemporary Brazil', 195.
53. Statistical Yearbook for Latin America and the Caribbean 2003, chapter 2/V, table 279.
54. La inversión extranjera en America Latina y el Caribe 2001 (Santiago de Chile: CEPAL, 2002), 17.
55. La inversión extranjera en America Latina y el Caribe 2001, 94–95.
56. La inversión extranjera en America Latina y el Caribe 2001, 96–98; email correspondence with Andrés López, 3 April 2003.
57. Email correspondence with Andrés López, 3 April 2003.
58. Bernardo Kosacoff, 'The Responses of Transnational Corporations', in Bernardo Kosacoff, ed., *Corporate Strategies Under Structural Adjustment in Argentina* (Houndmills, Basingstoke and London: Macmillan Press Ltd., 2000), 71.
59. Responsible for the National Privatisation Programme (PND) is the Brazilian Development Bank (BNDES).
60. Source: BNDES; proceeds on the federal level also include money generated through the sale of licenses for the frequency spectrum used by mobile phones (2G, 2.5G etc.).
61. Judith A. Teichman, *The Politics of Freeing Markets in Latin America* (Chapel Hill and London: University of North Carolina Press, 2001), 116–17.
62. This statement by an interviewee was made with the request to remain anonymous.
63. Interview with Christian Lohbauer, 28 August 2002.
64. 'A very big deal' *The Economist* 4 December 1997.
65. Daniel Chudnovsky and Andrés López, *La transnacionalización de la economiá argentina* (Buenos Aires: Eudeba y CENIT, 2001), 41; consult also Armando Castelar Pinheiro, Fabio Giambiagi and Maurício Mesquita Moreira, 'Brazil in the 1990s: A Successful Transition?' *Textos para Discussão 91* (Rio de Janeiro: BNDES 2001), 13–14.
66. Interview with Sandra Polónia Rios, 2 September 2002 and interview with Christian Lohbauer, 28 August 2002; consult also Schneider, 'Business Politics and Regional Integration: The Advantages of Organisation in NAFTA and Mercosur', 175.
67. Email correspondence with Andrés López, 9 January 2003.
68. Email correspondence with Sandra Polónia Rios, 10 January 2003; for an interesting example, the Argentine industrial group Arcor, consult Bernardo Kosacoff, Jorge Forteza, María Inés Barbero, F. Porta and E. Alejandro Stengel, *Going Global from Latin America: The Arcor Case* (Buenos Aires: McGrawHill Interamericana, 2002).
69. Data from the BNDES; Teichman, *The Politics of Freeing Markets in Latin America*, 111.
70. Nunnenkamp, 'European FDI Strategies in Mercosur Countries', 15.
71. Interview with Christian Lohbauer, 28 August 2002.
72. Interview with Sandra Polónia Rios, 2 September 2002.

73. Interview with Sandra Polónia Rios, 2 September 2002; Ian Katz, 'Adios Argentina' Business Week. 17 January 2000.
74. Interview with Antonio Estrany y Gendre, 26 March 2002.
75. Afonso Ferreira and Giuseppe Tullio, 'The Brazilian Exchange Rate Crisis of January 1999' *Journal of Latin American Studies* 34, 2002, 150, 152–55, 159.
76. See Diana Tussie, Ignacio Labaqui and Cintia Quiliconi, 'Disputas comerciales e insuficiencias institucionales: ¿de la experiencia a la esperanza?, in Daniel Chudnovsky and José María Fanelli, ed., *El desafío de integrarse para crecer* (Buenos Aires: Siglo Veintiuno de Argentina Editores, 2001), 208–210; Luiz Felipe de Seixas Corrêa, 'La visión estratégica brasileña del processo de integración', in Jorge Campbell, ed., *Mercosur – Entre la Realidad y la Utopía* (Buenos Aires: Grupo Editor Latinoamericano, 1999), 255.
77. Interview with Rodolfo Rúa Boiero, Presidente, Centro de Estudios de Integracion Economica y Comercio Internacional, an associated entity of the Cámara Argentina de Comercio (CAC), 26 April 2002.
78. It is interesting to note that 'Fundación Invertir' translates as 'Foundation Invest', thus explicitly linking it to neo-liberal reform and attracting FDI.
79. Interview with Antonio Estrany y Gendre, President, 26 March 2002.
80. Email correspondence with Reinhold Meyer, Sub-director, Argentine-German Chamber of Industry and Commerce (CADICAA), 24 April 2002.
81. Interview with Antonio Estrany y Gendre, 26 March 2002.
82. Interview with Antonio Estrany y Gendre, 26 March 2002.
83. Interview with Antonio Estrany y Gendre, 26 March 2002.
84. 'Crece núcleo empresario' Clarín.com (http://old.clarin.com/diario/2003/02/04/e-00902.htm, 7 February 2003); 'En medio de la crisis, crean una poderosa agrupación empresaria' Clarín.com (http://old.clarin.com/diario/2002/05/29/e-01601.htm, 4 November 2002).
85. Interview with Sandra Polónia Rios, 2 September 2002.
86. Doctor, 'The Interplay of States and Markets: The Role of Business-State Relations in Attracting Investment to the Automotive Industry in Brazil', 7.
87. Marukh Doctor and Carlos Pereira, *Workshop Report: Changing Nature of Business-State Relations in Brazil: Strategies of Foreign and Domestic Capital* (Oxford: University of Oxford Centre for Brazilian Studies, 2002), 2; see also Renato Boschi, Eli Diniz and Fabiano Santos, Elites Políticas e Econômicas no Brasil Contamporãneo (São Paulo: Fundação Konrad Adenauer, 2000), 40–41.
88. Interview with Sandra Polónia Rios, 2 September 2002.
89. CNI, *A Indústria e o Brasil: Uma Agenda para o Crescimento* (Brasília: CNI, 2002).
90. IEDI, *Mercosul: Sua Importância E Próximos Passos* (São Paulo: IEDI, 2003).
91. 'New Latin American leaders give trade bloc some clout' *The Wall Street Journal*, 16 June 2003; 'Brazil's Lula, Argentina's Kirchner decide on steps to revive Mercosur' BBC Monitoring Service, 14 June 2003.
92. IEDI, *Mercosul: Sua Importância E Próximos Passos*.

5 Two Case Studies of Interest Representation within Organized Business: The Chemical Industry in the Mercosur and the MEBF

1. The chemical industry consists of a number of different specialisations, for example, petrochemicals, pharmaceuticals, agrochemicals and so on. The business associations of the chemical industry discussed in this chapter represent the chemical sector as a whole. In cases where the chapter refers explicitly to the petrochemical industry, this is done to reflect either individual authors' preferences or use of the term or both. The petrochemical industry is a good indicator for the whole of the chemical sector, as it produces many basic products and intermediate products needed for other parts of the chemical industry, such as pharmaceuticals and plastics.
2. Sanchez Bajo, 'Mercosur's Open Regionalism and Regulation: Focusing on the Petrochemicals and Steel Sectors', 2–3.
3. Interview with José Maria Fumagalli, 12 April 2002.
4. Interview with Guilherme Duque Estrada de Moraes, 26 August 2002.
5. Interview with José Maria Fumagalli, 12 April 2002.
6. Interview with Guilherme Duque Estrada de Moraes, 26 August 2002.
7. For the following paragraphs consult Lia Hasenclever, Andrés López and José Clemente de Oliveira, 'The Impact of Mercosur on the Development of the Petrochemical Sector' *Integration & Trade Journal*, 7–8, January–August 1999, 171–76.
8. Hasenclever et al., 'The Impact of Mercosur on the Development of the Petrochemical Sector', 174.
9. Hasenclever et al., 'The Impact of Mercosur on the Development of the Petrochemical Sector', 175.
10. Werner Baer, *The Brazilian Economy – Growth and Development*, 5th edition. (Westport, Connecticut and London: Praeger, 2001), 237.
11. Own calculations based on data provided by the Brazilian Central Bank. See Banco Central do Brasil, Departemento de Capitais Estrangeiros e Câmbio, Censo de Capitais Estrangeiros – Periodo-Base 1995 (www.bcb.gov.br/?CENSO1995, 29 December 2004).
12. Own calculations based on data provided by the Brazilian Central Bank. See Banco Central do Brasil, Departemento de Capitais Estrangeiros e Câmbio, Censo de Capitais Estrangeiros – Periodo-Base 2000 (www.bcb.gov.br/?CENSO2000RES, 29 December 2004).
13. Baer, *The Brazilian Economy – Growth and Development*, 238–40.
14. Email correspondence with Guilherme Duque Estrada de Moraes, 11 June 2004.
15. Hasenclever et al., 'The Impact of Mercosur on the Development of the Petrochemical Sector', 174.
16. Hasenclever et al., 'The Impact of Mercosur on the Development of the Petrochemical Sector', 175.
17. Chudnovsky and López, *La transnacionalización de la economía argentina*, 219.

18. Chudnovsky and López, *La transnacionalización de la economía argentina*, 218 (own translation).
19. Daniel Chudnovsky and Andrés López, 'El Caso Argentino', in Daniel Chudnovsky, ed., *El boom de inversion extranjera directa en el Mercosur* (Buenos Aires: Siglo Veintiuno de Argentina Editores and Red de Investigaciones Económicas del Mercosur, 2001), 56–57.
20. Interview with Guilherme Duque Estrada de Moraes, 26 August 2002 and interview with José Maria Fumagalli, 12 April 2002.
21. Perfil de la Cámara de la Industria Química y Petroquímica (Buenos Aires: CIQyP, 2001); Relatório Annual – A Abiquim e a Indústria Química Brasileira em 2001 (São Paulo: ABIQUIM, 2002), 22.
22. Interview with Guilherme Duque Estrada de Moraes, 26 August 2002.
23. Interview with Santiago González Cravino, 9 April 2002.
24. Interview with José Maria Fumagalli, 12 April 2002.
25. Interview with Guilherme Duque Estrada de Moraes, 26 August 2002.
26. Interview with José Maria Fumagalli, 12 April 2002 and interview with Guilherme Duque Estrada de Moraes, 26 August 2002.
27. For the statistical data consult Relatório Annual – A Abiquim e a Indústria Química Brasileira em 2001, 7.
28. Relatório Annual – A Abiquim e a Indústria Química Brasileira em 2001, 7.
29. Hasenclever et al., 'The Impact of Mercosur on the Development of the Petrochemical Sector', 189–90.
30. For the paragraph see: Hasenclever et al., 'The Impact of Mercosur on the Development of the Petrochemical Sector', 177–78; Sanchez Bajo, 'Mercosur's Open Regionalism and Regulation: Focusing on the Petrochemicals and Steel Sectors', 2; Wyn Grant, 'Associational Systems in the Chemical Industry', in Alberto Martinelli, ed., *International Markets and Global Firms – A Comparative Study of Organised Business in the Chemical Industry* (London, Newbury Park and New Delhi: Sage Publications, 1991), 48.
31. Interview with José Maria Fumagalli, 12 April 2002.
32. Relatório Annual – A Abiquim e a Indústria Química Brasileira em 2001, 7; own calculations based on data provided by the same source.
33. Hasenclever et al., 'The Impact of Mercosur on the Development of the Petrochemical Sector', 176.
34. Relatório Annual – A Abiquim e a Indústria Química Brasileira em 2001, 9.
35. Email correspondence with Guilherme Duque Estrada de Moraes, 11 June 2004.
36. Skidmore and Smith, *Modern Latin America*, 175.
37. Baer, *The Brazilian Economy – Growth and Development*, 372.
38. Jon Peter, 'New Generations Face Old Struggles in Brazil' Washingtonpost. com 13 November 2003; 'Brazil: Critics fear Lula's land reform plans will fall short of mark' Correio Braziliense web site [BBC Monitoring Service] 20 November 2003.
39. Hasenclever et al., 'The Impact of Mercosur on the Development of the Petrochemical Sector', 178.
40. Baer, *The Brazilian Economy – Growth and Development*, 290–91.

41. Alberto Martinelli, 'Introduction', in Alberto Martinelli, ed., *International Markets and Global Firms – A Comparative Study of Organised Business in the Chemical Industry* (London, Newbury Park, New Delhi: Sage Publications, 1991), 5.
42. Interview with José Maria Fumagalli, 12 April 2002.
43. Interview with Guilherme Duque Estrada de Moraes, 26 August 2002; Perfil de la Cámara de la Industria Química y Petroquímica; Relatório Annual – A Abiquim e a Indústria Química Brasileira em 2001, 15–22.
44. Interview with Sandra Polónia Rios, 2 September 2002 and interview with Christian Lohbauer, 28 August 2002.
45. Interview with Guilherme Duque Estrada de Moraes, 26 August 2002; Perfil de la Cámara de la Industria Química y Petroquímica; Annual Report 2002 – Abiquim and the Brazilian Chemical Industry (São Paulo: ABIQUIM, 2003), 2.
46. Interview with Rodolfo Rúa Boiero, 26 April 2002.
47. Fumagalli, 'Interacción pública y privada en el diseño de políticas comerciales', 4–7.
48. Interview with Sandra Polónia Rios, 2 September 2002.
49. Newsletter MEBF, Issue 1, 5/99, 7.
50. Interview with Sandra Polónia Rios, 2 September 2002.
51. Rivka T. van Deijk, 'Hacia una Asociacíon Interregional entre el Mercosur y la Unión Europea' (unpublished dissertation, University of Amsterdam, 2002).
52. Luis Xavier Grisanti, 'Europe and Latin America: The Challenge of a Strategic Partnership' *European Foreign Affairs Review* 5(2000), 5.
53. The Mercosur-EU FTA is officially known as the Interregional Association Agreement.
54. The interviewee requested anonymity for this remark.
55. For a comprehensive survey of the TABD see David Coen and Wyn Grant, 'Corporate Political Strategy and Global Policy: a Case Study of the Transatlantic Business Dialogue' *European Business Journal* 13(1) 2001, 37–44.
56. The interviewee requested anonymity for this remark.
57. The interviewee requested anonymity for this remark.
58. Email correspondence with Guilherme Duque Estrada de Moraes, 11 June 2004.
59. 'Mercosur/European Union Brasilia Declaration' MEBF (Brasilia: October 2003), in particular 2–6.
60. For more information on the MEBF position papers and related information and documentation see www.mebf.org.
61. Interview with Sandra Polónia Rios, 2 September 2002.
62. Interview with Ricardo Markwald, Director Geral, Fundação Centro de Estudos do Comércio Exterior (FUNCEX), 3 September 2002.
63. The interviewee requested anonymity for this remark.
64. 'Brasilien wird von Stahlfirmen umworben – Arcelor kann Pläne nicht verwirklichen' Mercosur Newsletter November 2003 (Stuttgart: local global GmbH, 2003).

65. Interview with Sandra Polónia Rios, 2 September 2002 and interview with Reinhold Meyer, Sub-director, Argentine-German Chamber of Industry and Commerce (CADICAA), 11 April 2002.
66. Interview with Jorge Enrico, Executive Director Argentina, MEBF, 11 April 2002.
67. See also Sandra Polónia Rios, 'Mercosur Industrial Council will have an active participation in the MEBF' Newsletter MEBF, Issue III, 3/2000, 4.
68. Interview with Alberto Pfeiffer, Director Ejecutivo, Consejo Empresario de America Latina (CEAL), 26 August 2002.
69. Carlos Marian Bittencourt, 'O Sector Privado no Processo de Integração Continental' (CEAL – Capítulo Brasileiro; speech prepared for the VI FEMA, April 2001).
70. Interview with Lars Grabenschröer, 28 August 2002.
71. Interview with Antonio Estrany y Gendre, 26 March 2002.
72. An example for this is Antonio Estrany y Gendre himself, who at one point held the positions of President of the CICYP, President of the BNHI, President VI FEMA, co-Chairman of the MEBF Working Group Investment/Privatisation and Senior Vice-President of the Bridas Corporation simultaneously.
73. Interview with Sandra Polónia Rios, 2 September 2002; Newsletter MEBF, Issue 1, 5/99, 7; BDI translates as Federation of German Industry (own translation).
74. Interview with Lars Grabenschröer, 28 August 2002 and Interview with Reinhold Meyer, 11 April 2002.
75. Interview with Reinhold Meyer, 11 April 2002.

6 The Regionalization of Organized Business Interests in the Mercosur: A Theoretical and Empirical Analysis

1. Email correspondence with Andrés López, 26 February and 5 March 2003.
2. Page, 'The Insider/Ousider Distinction: an Empirical Investigation', 212.
3. Email correspondence with Andrés López, 26 February 2003.
4. Schneider, 'Business Politcs and Regional Integration: The Advantages of Organisation in NAFTA and Mercosur', 175.
5. Andrew Hurrell, 'The Politics of Regional Integration in MERCOSUR', in Victor Bulmer-Thomas, ed., *Regional Integration in Latin America and the Caribbean: The Political Economy of Open Regionalism* (London: Institute of Latin American Studies, 2001), 197; Schneider, 'Business Politcs and Regional Integration: The Advantages of Organisation in NAFTA and Mercosur', 180.
6. Email correspondence with Andrés López, 26 February 2003.
7. Grant, Pressure Groups and British Politcs, 20; Richardson, 'Government, Interest Groups and Policy Change', 1010; Hurrell, 'The Politics of Regional Integration in MERCOSUR', 198–99.

8. Charles E. Lindblom, *Politics and Markets – The World's Political-Economic Systems* (New York: Basic Books, 1977), 170–188.
9. Stephan Haggard, Sylvia Maxfield and Ben Ross Schneider, 'Theories of Business and Business-State Relations', in Sylvia Maxfield and Ben Ross Schneider, eds, *Business and the State in Developing Countries* (Ithaca, New York and London: Cornell University Press, 1997), 41.
10. Gill and Law, 'Global Hegemony and the Structural Power of Capital', 98 [emphasis in the original].
11. For an excellent discussion of private-interest government consult Wolfgang Streeck and Philippe C. Schmitter, eds, *Private Interest Government – Beyond Market and State* (London, Beverly Hills, New Delhi: Sage Publications, 1985), in particular 1–29.
12. Gill and Law, 'Global Hegemony and the Structural Power of Capital', 98.
13. For a good discussion of the overall importance of trust and reliability in the state for business confidence refer also to Schneider, 'Big Business and the Politics of Economic Reform: Confidence and Concertation in Brazil and Mexico', 196–200.
14. William Coleman and Wyn Grant, 'The Organisational Cohesion and Political Access of Business' *European Journal of Political Research* 16(5) 1988, 467–87.
15. Peter Evans, 'State Structures, Government-Business Relations, and Economic Transformation', in Sylvia Maxfield and Ben Ross Schneider, eds, *Business and the State in Developing Countries* (Ithaca, New York and London: Cornell University Press, 1997), 65.
16. Grant, *Pressure Groups and British Politics*, 20.
17. Weyland, 'The Fragmentation of Business in Brazil', 90.
18. Schneider, 'Big Business and the Politics of Economic Reform: Confidence and Concertation in Brazil and Mexico', 213.
19. Evans, 'State Structures, Government-Business Relations, and Economic Transformation', 65.
20. Email correspondence with Andrés López, 3 April 2003.
21. On the post-Washington consensus debate in relation to regionalism in the Southern Cone consult Phillips, 'Governance after Financial Crisis: South American Perspectives on the Reformulation of Regionalism', 383–98.
22. Helen V. Milner and Robert O. Keohane, 'Internationalisation and Domestic Politics: An Introduction', in Robert O. Keohane and Helen V. Milner, eds, *Internationalisation and Domestic Politics* (Cambridge: Cambridge University Press, 1996), 3.
23. Geoffrey R.D. Underhill, 'From Ships Passing in the Night to a Dialogue of the Deaf: the Contribution of International Relations Theory to Understanding Organised Business', in Justin Greenwood and Henry Jacek, eds, *Organised Business and the New Global Order* (Houndmills, Basingstoke and New York: Palgrave Macmillan, 2000), 37–38.
24. Strange, *States and Markets*, 18.
25. Strange, *States and Markets*, 25.
26. Helen V. Milner, *Interests, Institutions, and Information – Doemstic Politics and International Relations* (Princeton, New Jersey: Princeton University, 1997), 16 [emphasis in the original].

27. For a very useful and critical discussion of attempts to advocate the 'merging' of CPE and IPE consult G.P.E. Walzenbach, 'The Doubtful Handshake: From International to Comparative Political Economy?', in Thomas C. Lawton, James N. Rosenau and Amy C. Verdun, eds, *Strange Power – Shaping the Parameters of International Relations and International Political Economy* (Aldershot, Burlington USA, Singapore and Sidney: Ashgate, 2000), 369–89.

28. Justin Greenwood, 'Conclusion', in Justin Greenwood and Henry Jacek, eds, *Organised Business and the New Global Order* (Houndmills, Basingstoke and New York: Palgrave Macmillan, 2000), 241.

29. Greenwood, 'Conclusion', 241–42.

30. Henry Jacek, 'Introduction', Justin Greenwood and Henry Jacek, eds, *Organised Business and the New Global Order* (Houndmills, Basingstoke and New York: Palgrave Macmillan, 2000), 3–4.

31. Jan Aart Scholte, *Globalisation – a Critical Introduction* (Houndmills, Basingstoke and New York: Palgrave Macmillan, 2000), 74.

32. Strange, *States and Markets*; James Stopford and Susan Strange, *Rival States, Rival Firms: Competition for World Market Shares* (Cambridge: Cambridge University Press, 1991).

33. Scholte, *Globalisation – a critical introduction*, 74.

34. Hirst and Thompson, *Globalisation in Question*, 18.

35. Email correspondence with Andrés López, 9 January 2003, and with Sandra Polónia Rios, 10 January 2003.

36. For the historical overview see Skidmore and Smith, *Modern Latin America*, 42–51; Cammack, *Brasilien*, 1060–74; Peter Waldmann, Argentinien, in Walther E. Bernecker, Raymond T. Buve, John R. Fisher, Horst Pietschmann and Hans Werner Tobler, *Handbuch der Geschichte Lateinamerikas – Band 3* (Stuttgart: Klett-Clotta, 1996), 889–917.

37. For structuralism and dependency theory in the context of Latin America consult for example, Fernando Enrique Cardoso, *Dependency and Development in Latin America* (expanded and revised edition) (Berkeley, California and London: University of California Press, 1997); André Gunder Frank, *Captialism and Underdevelopment in Latin America* (New York: Monthly Review Press, 1967); Ana Maria Bianchi and Cleofas Salviano Jr, 'Raúl Prébisch and the Beginnings of the Latin American School of Economics: A Rhetorical Perspective' *Journal of Economic Methodology* 6(3) 1999, 423–38.

38. Teichman, *The Politics of Freeing Markets in Latin America*, 1.

39. José María Fanelli, Roberto Frenkel and Guillermo Rozenwurcel, 'Growth and Sturctural Reform in Latin America: Where We Stand'. in William C. Smith, Carlos H. Acuña and Eduardo A. Gamarra, eds, *Latin American Political Economy in the Age of Neoliberal Reform – Theoretical and Comparative Perspectives for the 1990s* (University of Miami: North-South Center Press, 1994), 107.

40. John Gerard Ruggie, 'International Regimes, Transactions, and Change: Embedded Liberalism in the Postwar Economic Order' *International Organization* 36(2) 1982, 195–231; John Gerard Ruggie, 'At Home Abroad, Abroad at Home: International Liberalisation and Domestic Stability in

the New World Economy' *Millennium: Journal of International Studies* 24(3) 1994, 507–26; Eric Helleiner, 'When Finance Was the Servant: International Capital Movements in the Bretton Woods Order', in Philip G. Cerny, ed., *Finance and World Politics – Markets, Regimes and States in the Post-hegemonic Era* (Aldershot, Hampshire and Brookfield, Vermont: Edward Elgar, 1993), 38–39.

41. See also Jessop, 'Reflections on Globalisation and Its (Il)logic(s)', 19.
42. See also Phillips, *The Southern Cone Model – the Political Economy of Regional Capitalist Development in Latin America*, 215–16.
43. 'Trade wind' *The Economist* 28 June 2003, 68–69; 'North, south or both' *The Economist* 24 May 2003, 52; 'Brazil: Minister says Mercosur may negotiate services, investments in FTAA' BBC Monitoring Service 3 July 2003.
44. In 2003, plans to enhance the Mercosur after years of problems and institutional weakness included the creation of a directly elected Mercosur parliament which would take over responsibility for Mercosur-related legislation from national assemblies thus speeding-up acceptance and implementation of Mercosur laws (a significant problem in the past), and the creation of a Mercosur monetary institute with the right to spend US$ 1 billion or 3 per cent of Argentina's and Brazil's foreign currency reserves in foreign currency markets to keep the exchange between Brazil and Argentina stable. As noted earlier, currency instability and continuing devaluations as well as overvaluations lie at the heart of Mercosur's past problems of stabilising and accelerating integration. The monetary institute was also meant to study the feasibility of a common currency for the Mercosur (similar to the European Monetary Institute). By 2004, the Mercosur and its associated members Bolivia and Chile intended to introduce a common index to measure consumer price increases (IPCA). This was essential, as the Mercosur agreed to achieve a maximum of 5 per cent inflation by 2005, a 3 per cent current account deficit by 2004 and a maximum of 40 per cent debt/GDP ratio by 2010. The IPCA is thus necessary to harmonise official statistics across the Mercosur; consult 'Neues Ziel des Mercosur: Ein gemeinsamer Markt ab 2006' Mercosur Newsletter Juni 2003 (Stuttgart: local global GmbH, 2003).
45. Interview with Alberto Pfeiffer, Director Ejecutivo, Consejo Empresario de America Latina (CEAL), 26 August 2002.
46. Intelligence Trade Report, Año VII, No. 72, Enero de 2003, 3.
47. Intelligence Trade Report, Año VII, No. 72, Enero de 2003, 6–9.
48. 'Grupo Brasil fordert Stärkung des Mercosur'Mercosur Newsletter Juli 2003 (Stuttgart: local global GmbH, 2003).
49. Sandholtz and Zysman, '1992: Recasting the European Bargain', 196.
50. Phillips, 'Governance after Financial Crisis: South American Perspectives on the Reformulation of Regionalism', 387.
51. Moravcsik, 'Preferences and Power in the European Community: a Liberal Intergovernmentalist Approach', 297–300; Andrew Moravcsik, 'Negotiating the Single European Act: National Interests and Conventional Statecraft in the European Community', in Brent F. Nelsen and Alexander C.-G. Stubb, eds, *The European Union – Readings on the*

Theory and Practice of European Integration, 2nd edition (Boulder, Colorado and London: Lynne Rienner Publishers, 1998), 223–24.

52. Stefan A. Schirm, *Globalization and the New Regionalism – Global Markets, Domestic Politics and Regional Cooperation* (Cambridge: Polity Press, 2002), 7 [emphases in the original].

53. Email correspondence with Andrés López, 3 April 2003.

54. Schirm, *Globalization and the New Regionalism – Global Markets, domestic politics and regional cooperation*, 15–23.

55. Gamble and Payne, 'Conclusion: The New Regionalism', 258.

7 Organized Business Interests in the Mercosur: Conflict, Convergence and Influence

1. Wyn Grant, 'Introduction' in Wyn Grant, ed., *Business Interests, Organizational Development and Private Interest Government* (Berlin and New York: Walter de Gruyter, 1987), 6.

2. Phillips, *The Southern Cone Model – the Political Economy of Regionalist Capitalist Development in Latin America*, 253–60.

3. Phillips, *The Southern Cone Model – the Political Economy of Regionalist Capitalist Development in Latin America*, 249 [for the quote], 260, 262.

4. Interview with Ricardo Markwald, 3 September 2002, interview with Lars Grabenschröer, 28 August 2002; see also Phillips, *The Southern Cone Model – the Political Economy of Regionalist Capitalist Development in Latin America*, 215.

5. See also Volker Schneider and Jürgen R. Grote, 'Introduction – Business Associations, Associative Order and Internationalisation', in Wolfgang Streeck, Volker Schneider, Jürgen R. Grote and Jelle Visser, *Governing Interests: Business Associations Facing Internationalisation* (Oxford: Routledge, 2006), 1–20.

6. 'The tortoise and the hare' *The Economist* 22 March 2008, 63.

7. 'This time it will be different' *The Economist* 17 January 2008; 'The tortoise and the hare' *The Economist* 22 March 2008, 63.

8. Santiago Mosquera, 'Argentina' Global Insight Monthly Outlook January 2008, 1–2, 5–6; 'The tortoise and the hare' *The Economist* 22 March 2008, 63.

9. Eliana Raszewski, 'Argentine Price Controls Spark Milk, Meat Shortages' bloomberg.com 16 April 2007 (http://www.bloomberg.com/apps/news?pid=20601086&refer=latin_america&sid=aRNeAbzXyETk, 24 March 2008).

10. 'Argentina – Summer Sees Return of Power Cuts' *Latin America Monitor: Southern Cone Monitor* February 2008.

11. Mosquera, 'Argentina', 1–2.

12. 'Same old faces' *The Economist* 19 November 2007.

13. 'The tortoise and the hare' *The Economist* 22 March 2008, 63–4

14. 'US reject 4 + 1 agreement with Mercosur' MercoPress 9 February 2005 (www.bilaterals.org/article/artcile-print.php3?id_article=1268, 14 April 2004).

15. Brazil, US pursue FTAA rapprochement; Mercosur Cosies up to Central America *BRIDGES Weekly Trade Digest* 9(8) 2005 (www.ictsd.org/weekly/05-03-09/story4.htm, 18 March 2005).

16. See Mario E. Carranza, 'Mercosur and the End Game of the Ftaa Negotiations: Challenges and Prospects after the Argentine Crisis' *Third World Quarterly* 25(2) 2004, 319–37.

17. CAFTA is a trade agreement between the US and six Central American countries: Costa Rica, Dominican Republic, El Salvador, Guatemala, Honduras and Nicaragua.

18. 'Commerce between friends and foes' *The Economist* 4 October 2007; Washington Office on Latin America – Overview of CAFTA (http://www.wola.org/index.php?&option=com_content&task=blogsection&id=6&Itemid=&topic=Rights+and+Development&sub=1&content_topic=CAFTA, 17 December 2007).

19. 'A turning point?' *The Economist* 5 July 2007.

20. CAN was founded in 1969 as the Pacto Andino by the Cartagena Agreement and renamed CAN in 1997. Its members are Bolivia, Columbia, Ecuador, Peru and Venezuela.

21. For a recent assessment of the ongoing Mercosur-EU FTA negotiations see Mahrukh Doctor, 'Why Bother with Inter-Regionalism? Negotiations for a European Union Mercosur Agreement' *Journal of Common Market Studies* 45(2) 2007, 218–314; for an overview for the CAN-EU negotiations see, for example, the CAN website: 'Negociaciones CAN-UE para un Acuerdo de Asociación' (http://www.comunidadandina.org/exterior/can_ue.htm, 17 December 2007).

22. 'A turning point?' *The Economist* 5 July 2007.

23. 'India signs free trade deal with South American bloc' (www.bilaterals.org/article.php3?id_article=1479&var_recherche=South+America, 13 March 2005).

24. Ranja Sengupta, 'Free Trade between Mercosur and India: New Bonds, New Boundaries' (http://www.globalpolicy.org/globaliz/econ/2003/0718indiamercosur.htm, 21 April 2005).

25. 'Mercosur-SADC-India trade deal in the offing' *Business Report* 21 November 2004 (www.tralac.org/scripts/content.php?id=3001) 13 March 2005.

26. 'Mercosur-Israel Free Trade Agreement' Brazilian Embassy in Washington website, published 18 December 2007 (http://www.brasilemb.org/index.php?option=com_content&task=view&id=248&Itemid=125, 24 March 2008).

27. Email correspondence with Andrés López, 3 April 2003.

28. See also Jean Grugel, 'Regionalist governance and transnational collective action in Latin America' *Economy and Society* 35(2) 2006, 209–231.

29. See also Eli Diniz and Renato Boschi, 'The business class and development strategies' Brazilian Review of Social Sciences 1, 2005, 1–24 [English edition].

List of Interviewees

Argentina

Business community

Antonio Estrany y Gendre, President, Consejo Interamericano de Comercio y Producción (CICYP)
Reinhold Meyer, Subdirector, Argentine-German Chamber of Industry and Commerce (CADICAA)

Research community

Bernardo Kosacoff, Director, UN-CEPAL, Buenos Aires
Andrés López, Researcher, Centro de Investigaciones para la Transformación (CENIT)
Felíx Peña, Director, International Trade Institute, Fundación Bank Boston
Rodolfo Rúa Boiero, Presidente, Centro de Estudios de Integracion Economica y Comercio Internacional, an associated entity of the Cámara Argentina de Comercio (CAC)
Cintia Quiliconi, Researcher, FLACSO Argentina

Brazil

Business community

Lars Grabenschröer, Abteilungsleiter Volkswirtschaft, Deutsch-Brasilianische Industrie- und Handelskammer (AHK Brasil)
Christian Lohbauer, Gerente de Relações Internacionais, Federação das Indústrias do Estado de São Paulo (FIESP), Centro das Indústrias do Estado de São Paulo (CIESP)
Jayme Quintas Perez, Economista, Assessor Empresarial (Seção Brasileira) Foro Consultive Economico-Social, Confederação Nacional do Comércio (CNC)
Alberto Pfeiffer, Director Ejecutivo, Consejo Empresario de América Latina (CEAL)
Sandra Polónia Rios, Coordinator, International Integration Unit, National Confederation of Industry (CNI)
Délio Urpia de Seixas, Economista, Confederação Nacional do Comércio (CNC)

Research community

Ricardo Markwald, Director Geral, Fundação Centro de Estudos do Comércio Exterior (FUNCEX)

Uruguay

Business community

Jorge L. Bardier, Presidente, External Trade Commission, Cámara de Industrias del Uruguay
Santiago González Cravino, Director, Mercosur Administrative Secretariat
Sven Heldt, Director Gerente, Uruguayan-German Chamber of Industry and Commerce (AHK Uruguay)

Petrochemical/chemical industry

Guilherme Duque Estrada de Moraes, Executive Vice-President and CEO, Brazilian Chemical Industry Association (ABIQUIM)
Jose Maria Fumagalli, Executive Director, Cámara de la Industria Química y Petroquímica (CIQYP), Secretary of the Mercosur Department of the Union Industrial de Argentina (UIA), Secretary of the Council of the Chemical Industry of the Mercosur (CIQUIM)

MEBF

Jorge Enrico, Executive Director Argentina, Mercosur-EU Business Forum
Interview with a MEBF representative from the European side

Bibliography

Acuña, Carlos H. 'Political Struggle and Business Peak Associations: Theoretical Reflections on the Argentine Case'. In Francisco Durand and Eduardo Silva, eds. *Organised Business, Economic Change: Democracy in Latin America*, Miami: North-South Center Press, 1998, 51–72.

Alimonda, Héctor. 'Brazilian Society and Regional Integration'. *Latin American Perspectives* 27(6) 2000, 27–44.

Allen, Robert L. 'Integration in Less Developed Area'. *Kyklos* 14(3) 1961, 315–36.

Amann, Edmund and Werner Baer. 'Neoliberalism and Its Consequences in Brazil'. *Journal of Latin American Studies* 34(4) 2002, 9945–59.

Amin, Samir. 'The Challenge of Globalisation'. *Review of International Political Economy* 3(2) 1996, 216–59.

Apeldoorn, Bastiaan van. 'The European Round Table of Industrialists: Still a Unique Player?' In Justin Greenwood, ed. *The Effectiveness of EU Business Associations*, Houndmills, Basingstoke and New York: Palgrave Macmillan, 2002, 194–205.

Armstrong, David. 'Globalisation and the Social State'. *Review of International Studies* 24(4) 1998, 461–78.

Averbug, André. 'Brazilian Trade Liberalisation and Integration in the 1990s'. Rio de Janeiro: BNDES, no publication date.

Baer, Werner. *The Brazilian Economy – Growth and Development*. 5th edition. Westport, Connecticut and London: Praeger, 2001.

Balassa, Bela. 'Towards a Theory of Economic Integration'. *Kyklos* 14(1) 1961, 1–17.

Balassa, Bela. *The Theory of Economic Integration*. London: Allen & Unwin Ltd., 1965.

Beeson, Mark and Kanishka Jayasuriya. 'The Political Rationalities of Regionalism: APEC and the EU in Comparative Perspective'. *The Pacific Review* 11(3) 1998, 3311–36.

Betts, Paul. 'The quiet knights of Europe's round table'. *Financial Times* 20 March 2001, 16.

Betts, Paul and Brian Groom. 'Industry urges faster EU reform'. *Financial Times* 20 March 2001, 1.

Bianchi, Ana Maria and Cleofas Salviano Jr. 'Raúl Prébisch and the Beginnings of the Latin American School of Economics: A Rhetorical Perspective'. *Journal of Economic Methodology* 6(3) 1999, 423–38.

Birch, Melissa H. 'Mercosur: The Road to Economic Integration in the Southern Cone'. *International Journal of Public Administration* 23(5–8) 2000, 1387–413.

Birchfield, Vicki. 'Contesting the Hegemony of Market Ideology: Gramsci's "Good Sense" and Polanyi's "Double Movement"'. *Review of International Political Economy* 6(1) 1999, 27–54.

Bisang, Roberto. 'The Responses of National Holding Companies'. In Bernardo Kosacoff, ed. *Corporate Strategies under Structural Adjustment in Argentina*, Houndmills, Basingstoke and London: Macmillan Press Ltd., 2000, 136–69.

Bittencourt, Carlos Mariani. 'O Sector Privado no Processo de Integração Continental'. CEAL – Capítulo Brasileiro; speech prepared for the VI FEMA, April 2001.

Blom-Hansen, Jens. 'Still Corporatism in Scandinavia? A Survey of recent Empirical Findings'. *Scandinavian Political Studies* 23(2) 2000, 157–81.

Blondel, Jean. 'Then and Now: Comparative Politics'. *Political Studies* 47(2) 1999, 152–160.

Boschi, Renato, Eli Diniz and Fabiano Santos. *Elites Políticas e Econômicas no Brasil Contamporãneo*. São Paulo: Fundação Konrad Adenauer, 2000.

Bottoms, Anthony. 'The Relationship between Theory and Research in Criminology'. In Roy D. King and Emma Wincup, eds. *Doing Research on Crime and Justice*, Oxford: Oxford University Press, 2000, 15–59.

Bouzas, Roberto. 'El proceso de integración en el Mercosur'. In Bernardo Kosacoff, Gabriel Yoguel, Carlos Bonvecchi y Adrián Ramos, eds. *El desempeño industrial argentino – Más allá de la sustitución de importaciones*, Buenos Aires: Naciones Unidas – CEPAL, Oficina de Buenos Aires, 2000, 177.

Bowles, Paul. 'Regionalism and Development after (?) the Global Crisis'. *New Political Economy* 5(3) 2000, 433–55.

Breslin, Shaun and Richard Higgott. 'Studying Regions: Learning from the Old, Constructing the New'. *New Political Economy* 5(3) 2000, 333–52.

Brook, Christopher. 'Regionalism and Globalism'. In Anthony McGrew and Christopher Brook, eds. *Asia Pacific in the New World Order*, London: Routledge, published for The Open University, 1998, 230–46.

Burnham, Peter, Karin Gilland, Wyn Grant and Zig Layton-Henry. *Research Methods in Politics*. Houndmills, Basingstoke and New York: Palgrave Macmillan, 2004.

Burt, Tim and Victor Mallett. 'French lessons from "Le Cost-Killer" of Nissan'. *FT.com site* 22 May 2001.

Cammack, Paul. 'Brasilien'. In Walther E. Bernecker, Raymond T. Buve, John R. Fisher, Horst Pietschmann and Hans Werner Tobler, eds. *Handbuch der Geschichte Lateinamerikas – Band 3*, Stuttgart: Klett-Clotta, 1996, 1049–166.

Campbell, Jorge, Ricardo Rozemberg and Gustavo Svarzman. 'Argentina – Brasil en los '80s: Entre la cornisa y la Integración.' In Jorge Campbell, ed. *Mercosur – Entre la Realidad y la Utopía*, Buenos Aires: Grupo Editor Latinoamericano, 1999, 39–121.

Campos Filho, Leonardo. *New Regionalism and Latin America: The Case of Mercosur*. London: University of London, Institute of Latin American Studies Research Papers, 1999.

Caporaso, James A. 'Across the Great Divide: Integrating Comparative and International Politics'. *International Studies Quarterly* 41, 1997, 563–92.

Cárdenas, Emilio J. and Guillermo Tempesta. 'Arbitral Awards under Mercosur's Dispute Settlement Mechanism'. *Journal of International Economic Law* 4(2) 2001, 337–66.

Cardoso, Fernando Enrique. *Dependency and Development in Latin America* (expanded and revised edition). Berkeley, California and London: University of California Press, 1997.

Carranza, Mario E. 'Mercosur and the End Game of the FTAA Negotiations: Challenges and Prospects after the Argentine Crisis'. *Third World Quarterly* 25(2) 2004, 319–37.

Cason, Jeffrey. 'On the Road to Southern Cone Economic Integration'. *Journal of Interamerican Studies and World Affairs* 42(1) 2000, 23–42.

Castelar Pinheiro, Armando, Fabio Giambiagi and Maurício Mesquita Moreira. 'Brazil in the 1990s: A Successful Transition?' *Textos para Discussão 91* Rio de Janeiro: BNDES, 2001.

Cerny, Philip G. 'Globalising the Political and Politicising the Global: Concluding Reflections on International Political Economy as a Vocation'. *New Political Economy* 4(1) 1999, 147–62.

Chow, Peter C. 'Asia Pacific Economic Integration in Global Perspective'. In James C. Hsiung, ed. *Asia Pacific in the New World Politics* Boulder, Colorado and London: Lynne Rienner Publishers, 1993, 195–211.

Chudnovsky, Daniel and Andrés López. 'El Caso Argentino'. In Daniel Chudnovsky, ed. *El boom de inversion extranjera directa en el Mercosur* Buenos Aires: Siglo Veintiuno de Argentina Editores and Red de Investigaciones Económicas del Mercosur, 2001, 51–122.

Chudnovsky, Daniel and Andrés López. 'La inversión extranjera directa en el Mercosur: un análisis comparativo'. In Daniel Chudnovsky, Andrés López, Mariano Laplane, Gustavo Bittencourt, Fernando Massi, Rosario Domingo, Fernando Sarti, Célio Hiratuka and Rodrigo Sabbatini eds. *El boom de inversión directa en el Mercosur*, Madrid: Siglo Veintiuno and Red de Investigaciones Económicas del Mercosur, 2001, 1–50.

Chudnovsky, Daniel and Andrés López. *La transnacionalización de la economiá argentina*. Buenos Aires: Eudeba y CENIT, 2001.

Coates, David. *Models of Capitalism – Growth and Stagnation in the Modern Era*. Cambridge: Polity Press, 2000.

Coen, David. 'The European Business Lobby'. *Business Strategy Review* 8(4) 1997, 17–25.

Coen, David and Wyn Grant. 'Corporate Political Strategy and Global Policy: A Case Study of the Transatlantic Business Dialogue'. *European Business Journal* 13(1) 2001, 37–44.

Coleman, William and Wyn Grant. 'The Organisational Cohesion and Political Access of Business'. *European Journal of Political Research* 16(5) 1988, 467–87.

Colitt, Raymond. 'EU extends proposal to infighting Mercosur'. *FT.com site* 10 July 2001.

Crouch, Colin and Wolfgang Streeck. 'Introduction: The Future of Capitalist Diversity'. In Colin Crouch and Wolfgang Streeck, eds. *Political Economy of Modern Capitalism – Mapping Convergence and Diversity,* London, Thousand Oaks and New Delhi: Sage Publications, 1997, 1–18.

Deijk, Rivka T. van. 'Hacia una Asociacíon Interregional entre el Mercosur y la Unión Europea' Unpublished dissertation, University of Amsterdam, 2002.

Devetak, Richard and Richard Higgott. 'Justice Unbound? Globalisation, States and the Transformation of the Social Bond'. *International Affairs* 75(3) 1999, 483–98.

Dickins, Amanda. 'The Evolution of International Political Economy'. *International Affairs* 82(3) 2006, 479–92.

Dinan, Desmond. *Ever Closer Union?* Houndmills, Basingstoke and London: The Macmillan Press Ltd., 1994.

Diniz, Eli and Renato Boschi. 'The Business Class and Development Strategies'. *Brazilian Review of Social Sciences* 1, 2005, 1–24 [English edition].

Doctor, Mahrukh. 'The Interplay of States and Markets: The Role of Business-State Relations in Attracting Investment to the Automotive Industry in Brazil'. *Working Paper CBS-40-2003* Oxford: University of Oxford Centre for Brazilian Studies, 2003.

Doctor, Mahrukh. 'Why Bother with Inter-Regionalism? Negotiations for a European Union Mercosur Agreement'. *Journal of Common Market Studies* 45(2) 2007, 218–314.

Doctor, Marukh and Carlos Pereira. *Workshop Report: Changing Nature of Business-State Relations in Brazil: Strategies of Foreign and Domestic Capital* Oxford: University of Oxford Centre for Brazilian Studies, 2002.

Druckerman, Pamela. 'Argentina's Plan to Rescue Its Economy Annoys Brazil – Mercosur Members Will Lose Some Prized Privileges under Cavallo's Proposal'. *The Wall Street Journal* 5 April 2001.

Evans, Peter. 'State Structures, Government-Business Relations, and Economic Transformation'. In Sylvia Maxfield and Ben Ross Schneider, eds. *Business and the State in Developing Countries,* Ithaca, New York and London: Cornell University Press, 1997, 63–87.

Falk, Richard. 'State of Siege: Will Globalisation Win Out?' *International Affairs* 73(1) 1997, 123–36.

Fanelli, José María, Roberto Frenkel and Guillermo Rozenwurcel. 'Growth and Sturctural Reform in Latin America: Where We Stand'. In William C. Smith, Carlos H. Acuña and Eduardo A. Gamarra, eds. *Latin American Political Economy in the Age of Neoliberal Reform – Theoretical and Comparative Perspectives for the 1990s,* University of Miami: North-South Center Press, 1994, 101–25.

Ferreira, Afonso Ferreira and Giuseppe Tullio. 'The Brazilian Exchange Rate Crisis of January 1999'. *Journal of Latin American Studies* 34, 2002, 143–64.

Ferrer, Aldo. *El capitalismo argentino.* México, Argentina, Brasil, Chile, Columbia, España, Estados Unidos de América, Perú and Venezuela: Fondo de Cultura Económica, 2000.

Fishman, Nina. 'Reinventing Corporatism'. *The Political Quarterly* 68(1) 1997, 31–40.

Floyd, David. 'Globalisation or Europeanisation of Business Activity? Exploring the Critical Issues'. European Business Review, 13(2) 2001, 109–13.

Fritsch, Winston and Alexandre A. Tombini. 'The Mercosul: An Overview'. In Roberto Bouzas and Jaime Ross, eds. *Economic Integration in the Western Hemisphere*, Notre Dame and London: University of Notre Dame Press, 1994, 81–99.

Fumagalli, José Maria. 'Interacción pública y privada en el diseño de políticas comerciales'. CIQyP, Buenos Aires, July 2002; internal document, not published, 1–26.

Gamble, Andrew and Anthony Payne. 'Conclusion: The New Regionalism'. In Andrew Gamble and Anthony Payne, eds. *Regionalism and World Order*, Houndmills, Basingstoke and London: Macmillan, 1996, 247–64.

García Delgado, Daniel R. *Estado & Sociedad – la nueva relación a partir del cambio estructural* Buenos Aires: Grupo Editorial Norma SA, 1994.

Gill, Stephen. 'Epistemology, Ontology, and the "Italian school"'. In Stephen Gill, ed. *Gramsci, Historical Materialism and International Relations* Cambridge: Cambridge University Press, 1993, 21–48.

Gill, Stephen. 'Globalisation, Market Civilisation, and Disciplinary Neoliberalism'. *Millennium: Journal of International Studies* 24(3) 1995, 399–423.

Gill, Stephen Gill and David Law. 'Global Hegemony and the Structural Power of Capital'. In Stephen Gill, ed. *Gramsci, Historical Materialism and International Relations* Cambridge: Cambridge University Press, 1993, 93–124.

Grant, Wyn. 'Associational Systems in the Chemical Industry'. In Alberto Martinelli, ed. *International Markets and Global Firms – A Comparative Study of Organised Business in the Chemical Industry* London, Newbury Park and New Delhi: Sage Publications, 1991, 47–60.

Grant, Wyn. *Business and Politics in Britain*. 2nd edition. Houndmills, Basingstoke and London: Macmillan, 1993.

Grant, Wyn. 'Introduction'. In Wyn Grant, ed. *Business Interests, Organizational Development and Private Interest Government* Berlin and New York: Walter de Gruyter, 1987, 1–17.

Grant, Wyn. *Pressure Groups and British Politics* Houndmills, Basingstoke: Macmillan Press Ltd., 2001.

Greenwood, Justin. 'Conclusion'. In Justin Greenwood and Henry Jacek, eds. *Organised Business and the New Global Order*, Houndmills, Basingstoke and New York: Palgrave Macmillan, 2000, 241–57.

Greenwood, Justin. ed. *The Effectiveness of EU Business Associations* Houndmills, Basingstoke and New York: Palgrave Macmillan, 2002.

Greenwood, Justin. *Interest Representation in the European Union* Houndmill, Basingstoke and New York: Palgrave Macmillan, 2003.

Grisanti, Luis Xavier. 'Europe and Latin America: The Challenge of a Strategic Partnership'. *European Foreign Affairs Review* 5, 2000, 1–7.

Grugel, Jean. 'Regionalist Governance and Transnational Collective Action in Latin America'. *Economy and Society* 35(2) 2006, 209–31.

Grugel, Jean and Marcelo de Almeida Medeiros. 'Brazil and Mercosur'. In Jean Grugel and Wil Hout, eds. *Regionalism across the North-South Divide – State Strategies and Globalisation*, London and New York: Routledge, 1999, 46–61.

Gunder Frank, André. *Captialism and Underdevelopment in Latin America.* New York: Monthly Review Press, 1967.

Haas, Ernst B. *The Uniting of Europe – Political, Social and Economic Forces 1950–1957.* Stanford, California: Stanford University Press, 1958.

Haas, Ernst B. *The Uniting of Europe – Political, Social and Economic Forces 1950–1957.* 2nd edition. Stanford, California: Stanford University Press, 1968.

Haggard, Stephan, Sylvia Maxfield and Ben Ross Schneider. 'Theories of Business and Business-State Relations'. In Sylvia Maxfield and Ben Ross Schneider, eds. *Business and the State in Developing Countries,* Ithaca, New York and London: Cornell University Press, 1997, 36–60.

Hall, Peter A. and David Soskice. 'An Introduction to Varieties of Capitalism'. In Peter A. Hall and David Soskice, eds. *Varieties of Capitalism – The Institutional Foundations of Comparative Advantage,* Oxford: Oxford University Press, 2001, 1–68.

Hasenclever, Lia, Andrés López and José Clemente de Oliveira. 'The Impact of Mercosur on the Development of the Petrochemical Sector'. *Integration & Trade Journal,* 7–8, January–August 1999, 171–96.

Helleiner, Eric. 'Explaining the Globalisation of Financial Markets: Bringing States Back in'. *Review of International Political Economy* 2(2) 1995, 315–41.

Helleiner, Eric. 'When Finance Was the Servant: International Capital Movements in the Bretton Woods Order'. In Philip G. Cerny, ed. *Finance and World Politics – Markets, Regimes and States in the Post-hegemonic Era* Aldershot, Hampshire and Brookfield, Vermont: Edward Elgar, 1993, 20–48.

Hettne, Björn and Frederik Söderbaum. 'Theorising the Rise of Regionness'. *New Political Economy* 5(3) 2000, 457–72.

Higgott, Richard. 'The Pacific and beyond: APEC, ASEM and Regional Economic Management'. In Grahame Thompson, ed. *Economic Dynamism in the Asia-Pacific* London: Routledge, published for The Open University, 1998, 335–55.

Higgott, Richard. 'The Political Economy of Globalisation in East Asia – the Salience of "Region Building"'. In Kris Olds, Peter Dicken, Philip F. Kelly, Lily Kong and Henry Wai-chung Yeung, eds. *Globalisation and the Asia-Pacific - Contested Territories,* London and New York: Routledge in Association with the Centre for the Study of Globalisation and Regionalisation, University of Warwick, 1999, 91–106.

Hirst, Mónica. 'Brasil – Argentina a la sombra del futuro'. In José María Lladós and Samuel Pinheiro Guimarães, eds. *Perspectivas Brasil y Argentina,* Brasilia and Buenos Aires: IPRI-CARI, 1999, 387–99.

Hirst, Mónica. 'Mercosur and the New Circumstances of Its Integration'. *Cepal Review No. 46,* 1992, 139–49.

Hirst, Mónica. 'Mercosur's Complex Political Agenda'. In Riordan Roett, ed. *Mercosur – Regional Integration, World Markets* Boulder, Colorado and London: Lynne Rienner Publishers, 1999, 35–47.

Hirst, Paul and Grahame Thompson. *Globalisation in Question*. Cambridge: Polity Press, 1996.

Hix, Simon. 'The Study of the European Union Ii: The "New Governance" Agenda and Its Rival'. *Journal of European Public Policy* 5(1) 1998, 38–65.

Hoffmann, Stanley. 'Obstinate or Obsolete? The Fate of the Nation-State and the Case of Western Europe'. In Brent F. Nelsen and Alexander C.-G. Stubb, eds. *The European Union – Readings on the Theory and Practice of European Integration* 2nd edition. Boulder, Colorado and London: Lynne Rienner Publishers, 1998, 157–71.

Holland, Tom. 'ASEAN: Latin Lesson'. *Far Eastern Economic Review* 28 December 2000, 109.

Hout, Wil. 'Theories of International Relations and the New Regionalism'. In Jean Grugel and Wil Hout, eds. *Regionalism across the North-South Divide – State Strategies and Globalisation,* London and New York: Routledge, 1999, 14–28.

Hurrell, Andrew. 'Explaining the Resurgence of Regionalism in World Politics'. *Review of International Studies* 21(4) 1995, 331–58.

Hurrell, Andrew. 'The Politics of Regional Integration in MERCOSUR'. In Victor Bulmer-Thomas, ed. *Regional Integration in Latin America and the Caribbean: The Political Economy of Open Regionalism* London: Institute of Latin American Studies, 2001, 194–211.

Hurrell, Andrew and Anand Menon. 'Politics Like Any Other? Comparative Politics, International Relations and the Study of the EU'. *West European Politics* 19(2) 1996, 386–402.

Jacek, Henry. 'Introduction'. In Justin Greenwood and Henry Jacek, eds. *Organised Business and the New Global Order,* Houndmills, Basingstoke and New York: Palgrave Macmillan, 2000, 1–19.

Jachtenfuchs, Michael. 'Theoretical Perspectives on European Governance'. *European Law Journal* 1(2) 1995, 115–33.

Jelin, Elizabeth. 'Dialogues, Understandings and Misunderstandings: Social Movements in Mercosur'. *International Social Science Journal* 51(159) 1999, 37–48.

Jessop, Bob. 'Reflections on Globalisation and Its (Il)Logic(s)'. In Kris Olds, Peter Dicken, Philip F. Kelly, Lily Kong and Henry Wai-chung Yeung, eds. *Globalisation and the Asia-Pacific – Contested Territories,* London and New York: Routledge in Association with the Centre for the Study of Globalisation and Regionalisation, University of Warwick, 1999, 19–38.

Jørgense, Knud Erik and Ben Rosamond. 'Europe: Regional Laboratory or a Global Polity?' *CSGR Working Paper No. 71/01.*

Kaltenthaler, Karl and Frank O. Mora. 'Explaining Latin American Economic Integration: The Case of the Mercosur'. *Review of International Political Economy* 9(1) 2002, 72–97.

Katz, Ian. 'Adios, Argentina'. *Business Week* 17 January 2000.

Katzenstein, Peter J. 'Introduction: Domestic and International Forces and Strategies of Foreign Economic Policy'. In Peter J. Katzenstein, ed. *Between Power and Plenty – Foreign Economic Policies of Advanced Industrial States*

Madison, Wisconsin and London: The University of Wisconsin Press, 1978, 3–22.

Katzenstein, Peter J. '*Small States* and Small States Revisited'. *New Political Economy* 8(1) 2003, 9–30.

Katzenstein, Peter J. *Small States in World Markets – Industrial Policy in Europe.* Ithaca, New York: Cornell University Press, 1985.

Keohane, Robert O. and Stanley Hoffmann. 'Conclusions: Community Politics and Institutional Change'. In William Wallace, ed. *The Dynamics of European Integration* London: The Royal Institute of International Affairs, 1992, 276–300.

Kingstone, Peter R. 'The Limits of Neoliberalism: Business, the State, and Democratic Consolidation in Brazil'. Paper prepared for the 20th International Congress of the Latin American Studies Association, April 1997, Guadalajara, Mexico.

Klein, Wolfram F. *El Mercosur – Empresarios y Sindicatos frente a los Desafiós del Proceso de Integración* Caracas: Editorial Nueva Sociedad, 2000.

Kosacoff, Bernardo. 'The Development of Argentine Industry'. In Bernardo Kosacoff, ed. *Corporate Strategies under Structural Adjustment in Argentina* Houndmills, Basingstoke and London: Macmillan Press Ltd., 2000, 36–64.

Kosacoff, Bernardo. 'The Responses of Transnational Corporations'. In Bernardo Kosacoff, ed. *Corporate Strategies under Structural Adjustment in Argentina* Houndmills, Basingstoke and London: Macmillan Press Ltd., 2000, 65–99.

Kosacoff, Bernardo, Jorge Forteza, María Inés Barbero, F. Porta and E. Alejandro Stengel. *Going Global from Latin America: The Arcor Case* (Buenos Aires: McGrawHill Interamericana, 2002).

Lane, Jan Erik and Svante Ersson. *Comparative Political Economy – A Developmental Approach* 2nd edition. London and Washington: Pinter, 1997.

Lavagna, Roberto. 'Comercio Exterior y Política Comercial en Brasil y Argentina. Una Evolución Comparada'. In José María Lladós and Samuel Pinheiro Guimarães, eds. *Perspectivas Brasil y Argentina,* Brasilia and Buenos Aires: IPRI-CARI, 1999, 205–26.

Leipziger, Danny M., Claudio Frischtak, Homi J. Kharas and John F. Normand. 'Mercosur: Integration and Industrial Policy'. *The World Economy* 20(5) 1997, 585–603.

Lindberg, Leon N. 'Political Integration: Definitions and Hypotheses'. In Brent F. Nelsen and Alexander C.-G. Stubb, eds. *The European Union – Readings on the Theory and Practice of European Integration* 2nd edition, Boulder, Colorado and London: Lynne Rienner Publishers, 1998, 145–56.

Lindblom, Charles E. *Politics and Markets – The World's Political-Economic Systems.* New York: Basic Books, 1977.

Lucas, John. 'The Politics of Business Associations in the Developing World'. *The Journal of Developing Areas* 32(Fall 1997), 71–96.

Luchi, Roberto and Marcelo Paladino. 'Improving Competitiveness in a Manufacturing Value Chain: Issues Dealing with the Automobile Sector in Argentina and Mercosur'. *Industrial Management and Data Systems* 100(8) 2000, 349–58.

Magri, Julio. 'La Asociación Empresaria para estatizar la deuda externa'. http://www.po.org.ar/po//po757/la.htm, 4 November 2002.

Marchand, Marianne H., Morten Bøås and Timothy M. Shaw. 'The Political Economy of New Regionalism'. *Third World Quarterly* 20(5) 1999, 897–910.

Marks, Gary. 'Structural Policy and Multilevel Governance in the EC'. In Alan W. Cafruny and Glenda G. Rosenthal, eds. *The State of the European Community (Vol. 2) – The Maastricht Debates and Beyond,* Boulder, Colorado: Lynne Rienner Publishers, Inc. and Harlow, Essex: Longman Group UK Ltd., 1993, 391–410.

Martinelli, Alberto. 'Introduction'. In Alberto Martinelli, ed. *International Markets and Global Firms – A Comparative Study of Organised Business in the Chemical Industry* London, Newbury Park and New Delhi: Sage Publications, 1991, 1–17.

Mason, Jennifer. *Qualitative Researching.* London, Thousand Oaks and New Delhi: Sage Publications, 1996.

Mattli, Walter. 'Explaining Regional Integration Outcomes'. *Journal of European Public Policy* 6(1) 1999, 1–27.

Mazey, Sonia and Jeremy Richardson. 'Agenda Setting, Lobbying and the 1996 IGC'. In Geoffrey Edwards and Alfred Pijpers, eds. *The Politics of European Treaty Reform,* London and Washington: Pinter, 1997, 226–48.

McLeod, Iain. ed. *Oxford Concise Dictionary of Politics.* Oxford and New York: Oxford University Press, 1996.

Milner, Helen V. *Interests, Institutions, and Information – Domestic Politics and International Relations.* Princeton, New Jersey: Princeton University, 1997.

Milner, Helen V. and Robert O. Keohane. 'Internationalisation and Domestic Politics: An Introduction'. In Robert O. Keohane and Helen V. Milner, eds. *Internationalisation and Domestic Politics,* Cambridge: Cambridge University Press, 1996, 3–24.

Milner, Mark. 'Peugeot questions Nissan aid decision'. *The Guardian* 2 February 2001, 26.

Mitrany, David. 'A Working Peace System'. In Brent F. Nelsen and Alexander C.-G. Stubb, eds. *The European Union – Readings on the Theory and Practice of European Integration* 2nd edition, Boulder, Colorado and London: Lynne Rienner Publishers, 1998, 93–113.

Mittelman, James M. 'The Globalisation Challenge: Surviving at the Margins'. *Third World Quarterly* 15(3) 1994, 427–43.

Moravcsik, Andrew. *The Choice For Europe – Social Purpose & State Power from Messina to Maastricht.* London: University College London Press, 1998.

Moravcsik, Andrew. 'Negotiating the Single European Act: National Interests and Conventional Statecraft in the European Community'. In Brent F. Nelsen and Alexander C.-G. Stubb, eds. *The European Union – Readings on the Theory and Practice of European Integration* 2nd edition, Boulder, Colorado and London: Lynne Rienner Publishers, 1998, 217–40.

Moravcsik, Andrew. 'Preferences and Power in the European Community: a Liberal Intergovernmentalist Approach'. In Michael O'Neill, ed. *The Politics of European Integration – A Reader* London and New York: Routledge, 1996, 297–300.

Mosquera, Santiago. 'Argentina'. *Global Insight Monthly Outlook January 2008*, 1–10.

Munk Chrstiansen, Peter and Hilmar Rommetvedt. 'From Corporatism to Lobbyism? Parliaments, Executives, and Organised Interests in Denmark and Norway'. *Scandinavian Political Studies* 22(3) 1999, 195–220.

Nunnenkamp, Peter. 'European FDI Strategies in Mercosur Countries'. *Kiel Working Paper No. 1047* Kiel: Kiel Institute of World Economics, 2001.

Ohmae, Kenichi. *The End of the Nation State – The Rise of Regional Economies* London: Harper Collins Publishers, 1996.

Olson, Mancur. *The Logic of Collective Action*. Cambridge, Massachusetts: Harvard University Press, 1965.

Page, Edward C. 'The Insider/Outsider Distinction: An Empirical Investigation'. *British Journal of Politics and International Relations* 1(2) 1999, 205–14.

Pearce, Robert and Ana Teresa Tavares. 'Emerging Trading Blocs and their impact on The Strategic Evolution of Multinationals'. *Managerial Finance* 26(1) 2000, 26–40.

Perraton, Jonathan, David Goldblatt, David Held and Anthony McGrew. 'The Globalisation of Economic Activity'. *New Political Economy* 2(2) 1997, 257–77.

Peter, Jon. 'New Generations Face Old Struggles in Brazil'. *Washingtonpost. com* 13 November 2003.

Phillips, Nicola. 'Global and Regional Linkages'. In Julia Buxton and Nicola Phillips, eds. *Developments in Latin American Political Economy: States, Markets and Actors,* Manchester: Manchester University Press, 1999, 72–90.

Phillips, Nicola, ed. *Globalising International Political Economy*. (Houndmills, Basingstoke: Palgrave Macmillan, 2005).

Phillips, Nicola. 'Governance after Financial Crisis: South American Perspectives on the Reformulation of Regionalism'. *New Political Economy* 5(3) 2000, 383–98.

Phillips, Nicola. *The Southern Cone Model – The Political Economy of Regional Capitalist Development in Latin America*. London and New York: Routledge, 2004.

Phillips, Nicola. 'Special Section: The State Debate in Political Economy: Bridging the Comparative/International Divide in the Study of States'. *New Political Economy* 10(3) 2005, 335–43.

Power, Timothy J. and Mahrukh Doctor. 'The Resilience of Corporatism: Continuity and Change in Brazilian Corporatist Structures'. *University of Oxford Centre for Brazilian Studies Working Paper Series* Oxford: University of Oxford Centre for Brazilian Studies, 2002.

Raszewski, Eliana. 'Argentine price controls spark milk, meat shortages'. *bloomberg.com* 16 April 2007 http://www.bloomberg.com/apps/news?pid= 20601086&refer=latin_america&sid=aRNeAbzXyETk, accessed 24 March 2008.

Richards, Donald G. 'Dependent Development and Regional Integration – A Critical Examination of the Southern Cone Common Market'. *Latin American Perspectives* 24(6) 1997.

Richardson, Jeremy. 'Government, Interest Groups and Policy Change'. *Political Studies* 48(5) 2000, 1006–25.

Rios, Sandra Polónia. 'Mercosur Industrial Council will have an active participation in the MEBF'. *Newsletter MEBF* Issue III, 3/2000, 4.

Ross, George. 'European Integration and Globalisation'. In Roland Axmann, ed. *Globalisation and Europe – Theoretical and Empirical Investigations* London and Washington: Pinter, 1998, 164–83.

Ruggie, John Gerard. 'At Home Abroad, Abroad at Home: International Liberalisation and Domestic Stability in the New World Economy'. *Millennium: Journal of International Studies* 24(3) 1994, 507–26.

Ruggie, John Gerard. 'International Regimes, Transactions, and Change: Embedded Liberalism in the Postwar Economic Order'. *International Organization* 36(2) 1982, 195–231.

Sanchez, Bajo, Claudia. 'Mercosur's Open Regionalism and Regulation: Focusing on the Petrochemicals and Steel Sectors'. Paper presented to the International Studies Association Convention February 1999. http://www.ciaonet.org/isa/sac01/, 6 January 2003.

Sandholtz, Wayne. 'Membership Matters: Limits of the Functional Approach to European Institutions'. *Journal of Common Market Studies* 34(3) 1996, 401–29.

Sandholtz, Wayne and John Zysman. '1992: Recasting the European Bargain'. In Brent F. Nelsen and Alexander C.-G. Stubb, eds. *The European Union – Readings on the Theory and Practice of European Integration* 2nd edition, Boulder, Colorado and London: Lynne Rienner Publishers, 1998, 195–216.

Sangmeister, Hartmut. 'Im Labyrinth der Modernisierung – Lateinamerika zwischen Globalisierung und Regionalisierung'. *Internationale Politik* 54(5) 1999, 15–24.

Schamis, Hector E. 'Distributional Coalitions and the Politics of Economic Reform in Latin America'. *World Politics* 51(2) 1999, 236–68.

Schirm, Stefan A. *Globalization and the New Regionalism – Global Markets, Domestic Politics and Regional Cooperation.* Cambridge: Polity Press, 2002.

Schmitter, Philippe C. *Interest Conflict and Political Change in Brazil.* Stanford, California: Stanford University Press, 1971.

Schmitter, Philippe C. 'Still the Century of Corporatism?' *The Review of Politics* 36(1) 1974, 85–131.

Schneider, Ben Ross. 'Big Business and the Politics of Economic Reform: Confidence and Concertation in Brazil and Mexico'. In Sylvia Maxfield and Ben Ross Schneider, eds. *Business and the State in Developing Countries,* Ithaca, New York and London: Cornell University Press, 1997, 191–215.

Schneider, Ben Ross. 'Business Politics and Regional Integration: The Advantages of Organisation in NAFTA and Mercosur'. In Victor Bulmer-Thomas, ed. *Regional Integration in Latin America and the Caribbean: The Political Economy of Open Regionalism* London: Institute of Latin American Studies, 2001, 67–93.

Schneider, Ben Ross. 'Business Politics in Democratic Brazil'. In Maria D'Alva Gil Kinzo, ed. *Reforming the State: Business, Unions and Regions in Brazil* London: Institute of Latin American Studies, University of London, 1997, 3–23.

Schneider, Volker and Jürgen R. Grote. 'Introduction – Business associations, Associative Order and Internationalisation'. In Wolfgang Streeck, Volker Schneider, Jürgen R. Grote and Jelle Visser, eds. *Governing Interests: Business Associations Facing Internationalisation,* Oxford: Routledge, 2006, 1–20.

Scholte, Jan Aart. *Globalisation – A Critical Introduction* Houndmills, Basingstoke and New York: Palgrave Macmillan, 2000.

Seixas Corrêa, Luiz Felipe de. 'La visión estratégica brasileña del processo de Integración'. In Jorge Campbell, ed. *Mercosur – Entre la Realidad y la Utopía* Buenos Aires: Grupo Editor Latinoamericano, 1999, 229–72.

Sengupta, Ranja. 'Free Trade Between Mercosur and India: New Bonds, New Boundaries'. http://www.globalpolicy.org/globaliz/econ/2003/0718 indiamercosur.htm, 21 April 2005.

Silva, Eduardo and Francisco Durand. 'Organised Business and Politics in Latin America'. In Francisco Durand and Eduardo Silva, eds. *Organized Business, Economic Change, Democracy in Latin America,* University of Miami: North-South Center Press, 1998, 1–50.

Skidmore, Thomas E. and Peter H. Smith. *Modern Latin America* 5th edition. New York and Oxford: Oxford University Press, 2001.

Söderbaum, Frederik. *The Political Economy of Regionalism: The case of Southern Africa.* Houndmills, Basingstoke: Palgrave Macmillan, 2004.

Souza Martins, José de. 'Clientilism and Corruption in Comntemporary Brazil'. In Walter Little and Eduardo Posada-Carbó, eds. *Political Corruption in Europe and Latin America,* Houndmills, Basingstoke and London: Macmillan in association with the Institute of Latin American Studies, University of London, 1996, 195–218.

Stone Sweet, Alec and Wayne Sandholtz. 'European Integration and Supranational Governance'. *Journal of European Public Policy* 4(3) 1997, 297–317.

Stopford, James and Susan Strange. *Rival States, Rival Firms: Competition for World Market Shares.* Cambridge: Cambridge University Press, 1991.

Strange, Susan. 'The Future of Global Capitalism; Or Will Divergence Persist Forever?' In Colin Crouch and Wolfgang Streeck, eds. *Political Economy of Modern Capitalism – Mapping Convergence and Diversity,* London, Thousand Oaks and New Delhi: Sage Publications, 1997, 182–91.

Strange, Susan. 'Globaloney?' *Review of International Political Economy* 5(4) 1998, 704–20.

Strange, Susan. *The Retreat of the State – The Diffusion of Power in the World Economy.* Cambridge: Cambridge University Press, 1996.

Strange, Susan. *States and Markets* 2nd edition. London and Washington: Pinter, 1994.

Streeck, Wolfgang and Philippe C. Schmitter. 'From National Corporatism to Transnational Pluralism: Organised Interests in the Single European Market'. *Politics and Society* 19(2) 1991, 134–64.

Streeck, Wolfgang and Philippe C. Schmitter, eds. *Private Interest Government – Beyond Market and State.* London, Beverly Hills and New Delhi: Sage Publications, 1985.

Teichman, Judith A. *The Politics of Freeing Markets in Latin America*. Chapel Hill and London: University of North Carolina Press, 2001.

Thurston, Charles. 'BASF Bolsters Latin American Investments and E-Commerce'. *Chemical Market Reporter* 15 May 2000.

Tussie, Diana, Ignacio Labaqui and Cintia Quiliconi. 'Disputas comerciales e insuficiencias institucionales: ¿de la experiencia a la esperanza?' In Daniel Chudnovsky and José María Fanelli, ed. *El desafío de integrarse para crecer* Buenos Aires: Siglo Veintiuno de Argentina Editores, 2001, 205–23.

Underhill, Geoffrey R. D. 'Conceptualising the Changing Global Order'. In Richard Stubbs and Geoffrey R. D. Underhill, eds. *Political Economy and the Changing Global Order,* Don Mills, Ontario: Oxford University Press, 2000, 3–24.

Underhill, Geoffrey R.D. 'From Ships Passing in the Night to a Dialogue of the Deaf: The Contribution of International Relations Theory to Understanding Organised Business'. In Justin Greenwood and Henry Jacek, eds. *Organised Business and the New Global Order,* Houndmills, Basingstoke and New York: Palgrave Macmillan, 2000, 20–38.

Underhill, Geoffrey R. D. 'State, Market and Global Political Economy: Genealogy of an (Inter?) Discipline'. *International Affairs* 76(4) 2000, 805–24.

Vas Pereira, Lia. 'Toward the Common Market of the South: Mercosur's Origins, Evolution, and Challenges'. In Riordan Roett, ed. *Mercosur – Regional Integration, World Markets* Boulder, Colorado and London: Lynne Rienner Publishers, 1999, 7–23.

Ventura, Deisy. 'First Arbitration Award in Mercosur – A Community Law in Evolution'. *Leiden Journal of International Law* 13, 2000, 447–58.

Waldmann, Pete. *'Argentinien'*. In Walther E. Bernecker, Raymond T. Buve, John R. Fisher, Horst Pietschmann and Hans Werner Tobler, eds. *Handbuch der Geschichte Lateinamerikas – Band 3,* Stuttgart: Klett-Clotta, 1996, 889–972.

Wallace, Helen. 'Politics and Policy in the EU: The Challenge of Governance'. In Helen Wallace and William Wallace, eds. *Policy-Making in the European Union* 3rd edition, Oxford: Oxford University Press, 1996, 3–36.

Walzenbach, G.P.E. 'The Doubtful Handshake: From International to Comparative Political Economy?' In Thomas C. Lawton, James N. Rosenau and Amy C. Verdun, eds. *Strange Power – Shaping the Parameters of International Relations and International Political Economy,* Aldershot, Burlington USA, Singapore and Sidney: Ashgate, 2000, 369–89.

Weiss, Linda. 'Globalisation and the Myth of the Powerless State'. *New Left Review* 225, 1997, 3–27.

Weiss, Linda. *The Myth of the Powerless State – Governing the Economy in a Global Era*. Cambridge: Polity Press, 1998.

Weiss, Linda, ed. *States in the Global Economy – Bringing Domestic Institutions Back In*. Cambridge: Cambridge University Press, 2003.

Weyland, Kurt. 'The Fragmentation of Business in Brazil'. In Francisco Durand and Eduardo Silva, eds. *Organised Business, Economic Change, Democracy in Latin America,* Miami: North-South Center Press, 1998, 73–97.

Weyland, Kurt. 'The Politics of Corruption in Latin America'. *Journal of Democracy* 9(2) 1998, 108–21.

Williamson, Edwin. *The Penguin History of Latin America* London: Penguin Books, 1992.

Zysman, John. 'The Myth of a "Global" Economy: Enduring National Foundations and Emerging Regional Realities'. *New Political Economy* 1(2) 1996, 157–84.

Newspaper and magazine articles with unattributed authors

'Paraguay to remain in Mercosur despite corporate sector pressure to leave'. *AFX Europe* 20 June 2001.

'Brazilian business association says 2bn US$ investments in Argentina at risk'. *AFX Europe* 9 July 2001.

'US Trade Representative invites Mercosur to discuss FTAA with USA'. *BBC Monitoring Service* 24 August 2001.

'Argentine foreign minister sees trade talks with USA as "fundamental landmark" '. *BBC Monitoring Service* 3 September 2001.

'Brazil's Lula, Argentina's Kirchner decide on steps to revive Mercosur'. *BBC Monitoring Service* 14 June 2003.

'Brazil: Minister says Mercosur may negotiate services, investments in FTAA'. *BBC Monitoring Service* 3 July 2003.

'EU presents trade liberalisation proposal to Mercosur'. *BBC Monitoring Service*, 7 July 2001.

'En medio de la crisis, crean una poderosa agrupación empresaria'. *Clarín.com* http://old.clarin.com/diario/2002/05/29/e-01601.htm 4 November 2002.

'Crece núcleo empresario'. *Clarín.com* http://old.clarin.com/diario/2003/02/04/e-00902.htm 7 February 2003.

'Brazil: Critics fear Lula's land reform plans will fall short of mark'. *Correio Braziliense web site* [BBC Monitoring Service] 20 November 2003.

'A very big deal'. *The Economist* 4 December 1997.

'Buy, buy, buy'. *The Economist* 4 December 1997.

'Trouble in Eldorado'. *The Economist* 11 December 1997.

'Double parked'. *The Economist* 7 January 1999.

'Mercosur's trial by adversity'. *The Economist* 27 May 2000, 69.

'Some realism for Mercosur'. *The Economist* 31 March 2001, 15–16.

'Another blow to Mercosur'. *The Economist* 31 March 2001, 67–68.

'North, south or both'. *The Economist* 24 May 2003, 52.

'Trade wind'. *The Economist* 28 June 2003, 68–69.

'A turning point?' *The Economist* 5 July 2007 [online].

'Commerce between friends and foes'. *The Economist* 4 October 2007 [online].

'Same old faces'. *The Economist* 19 November 2007 [online].

'This time it will be different'. *The Economist* 17 January 2008 [online].

'The tortoise and the hare'. *The Economist* 22 March 2008, 63–64.

'Latin trade'. *Financial Times* 15 December 2000, 16.
'Mercosur threat'. *Financial Times* 4 April 2001, 22.
'Argentina – summer sees return of power cuts'. *Latin America Monitor: Southern Cone Monitor February 2008.*
'Neues Ziel des Mercosur: Ein gemeinsamer Markt ab 2006'. *Mercosur Newsletter Juni 2003* Stuttgart: local global GmbH, 2003.
'Grupo Brasil fordert Stärkung des Mercosur'. *Mercosur Newsletter Juli 2003* Stuttgart: local global GmbH, 2003.
'Brasilien wird von Stahlfirmen umworben – Arcelor kann Pläne nicht verwirklichen'. *Mercosur Newsletter November 2003* Stuttgart: local global GmbH, 2003.
'New Latin American leaders give trade bloc some clout'. *The Wall Street Journal* 16 June 2003.

Other documents and sources referenced in the book

Annual Report 2002 – ABIQUIM and the Brazilian Chemical Industry. São Paulo: ABIQUIM, 2003.
Anuario 1998. Buenos Aires: ADEFA, 1999. www.adefa.com.ar, 29 December 2004.
Banco Central do Brasil, Departemento de Capitais Estrangeiros e Câmbio. *Censo de Capitais Estrangeiros – Periodo-Base 1995.* www.bcb.gov.br/?CENSO1995, 29 December 2004.
Banco Central do Brasil, Departemento de Capitais Estrangeiros e Câmbio. *Censo de Capitais Estrangeiros – Periodo-Base 2000.* www.bcb.gov.br/? CENSO2000RES, 29 December 2004.
Bilaterals.org. 'India signs free trade deal with South American bloc'. www. bilaterals.org/article.php3?id_article=1479&var_recherche=South+America, 13 March 2005.
'Mercosur-Israel Free Trade Agreement'. *Brazilian Embassy in Washington* website, published 18 December 2007. http://www.brasilemb.org/index.php? option=com_content&task=view&id=248&Itemid=125, 24 March 2008.
Business Organisation for Participation in International Negotiations. Brazilian Business Coalition, November 2000.
'Mercosur-SADC-India trade deal in the offing'. *Business Report* 21 November 2004. www.tralac.org/scripts/content.php?id=3001, 13 March 2005.
CAN. 'Negociaciones CAN-UE para un Acuerdo de Asociación'. http://www. comunidadandina.org/exterior/can_ue.htm, 17 December 2007.
CNI. *A Indústria e o Brasil: Uma Agenda para o Crescimento* Brasília: CNI, 2002.
Confederação Nacional do Comércio. *Mercado Comun do Sul -Foro Consultivo Econômico-Social* Rio de Janeiro: CNC, 2000.
Economic Survey of Latin America and the Caribbean 2001–2002 – Current Conditions and Outlook August 2002. Santiago de Chile: CEPAL, 2002.
'The Business Sector vis à vis the FTAA negotiations'. VI Foro Empresarial de las Americas. http://www.vi-fema-abf.org.ar/pressrelease.html, 9 September 2001.

IEDI – 12 ANOS. São Paulo: IEDI, July 2001.

IEDI. *Mercosul: Sua Importância E Próximos Passos* São Paulo: IEDI, 2003.

Indicadores Macroeconómicos del Mercosur. Julio 2002, No. 906, Montevideo: Secretaría Administrativa del Mercosur.

Intelligence Trade Report. Año VII, No. 72, Enero de 2003.

'Just through Mercosur, Argentina will get strengthened in the FTAA'. Interview with Alfredo Neme Scheij, President of the Mercosur Committee at the Argentinean House of Representatives, 23 April 2001. http://www. mercosur.com/info/articuloimp.jsp?noticia=7646, 27 May 2001.

La inversión extranjera en America Latina y el Caribe 2001. Santiago de Chile: CEPAL, 2002.

'Mercosur/European Union Brasilia Declaration'. MEBF Brasilia: October 2003.

Newsletter MEBF. Issue 1, 5/99.

'US reject 4 + 1 agreement with Mercosur'. *MercoPress,* 9 February 2005. www. bilaterals.org/article/artcile-print.php3?id_article=1268, 14 April 2004.

Statistical Yearbook for Latin America and the Caribbean 2003 Santiago de Chile: CEPAL, 2004. www.eclac.cl/badestat/anuario_2003, 5 January 2005.

The Oxford English Dictionary 2nd edition. Oxford: Oxford University Press, 1989, Vol. XIII.

Perfil de la Cámara de la Industria Química y Petroquímica. Buenos Aires: CIQyP, 2001.

PNBE. *PNBE: Cidania, Desenvolvimento e Justiçia Social* http://www.pnbe.org. br/historico.asp and http://www.pnbe.org.br/realiza.asp, 12 June 2003.

Relatório Annual – A Abiquim e a Indústria Química Brasileira em 2001. São Paulo: ABIQUIM, 2002.

Washington Office on Latin America – Overview of CAFTA http://www. wola.org/index.php?&option=com_content&task=blogsection&id=6&Ite mid=&topic=Rights+and+Development&sub=1&content_topic=CAFTA, 17 December 2007.

Selected email correspondence referenced in the book

Guilherme Duque Estrada de Moraes, Executive Vice-President and CEO, Brazilian Chemical Industry Association (ABIQUIM), 11 June 2004.

Andrés López, Researcher, Centro de Investigaciones para la Transformación (CENIT), 9 January 2003.

Andrés López, 26 February 2003.

Andrés López, 5 March 2003.

Andrés López, 3 April 2003.

Reinhold Meyer, Subdirector, Argentine-German Chamber of Industry and Commerce (CADICAA), 24 April 2002.

Sandra Polónia Rios, the Coordinator of the International Integration Unit of the CNI, 10 January 2003.

Index